D0695654

APGRO

Thoughts
for the Journey Home

MARCUS C. GRODI

CHResources
Zanesville, Ohio

CHResources
P.O. Box 83290
Zanesville, OH 43702
740-450-1175
CHResources is a registered trademark of
The Coming Home Network, International

Copyright © 2010 by Marcus Grodi
All rights reserved
Printed in the United States of America
ISBN: 9780980006698

Library of Congress Cataloging-in-Publication Data
Grodi, Marcus.
Thoughts for the journey home / Marcus Grodi.
p. cm.
ISBN 978-0-9800066-9-8 (alk. paper)
1. Catholic converts. 2. Conversion--Catholic Church. I. Title.

BX4668.A1G76 2010
248.2'42--dc22

2010035026

This book or parts thereof may not be reproduced in any form without
prior written permission of the publisher.

Unless otherwise noted, all Scripture quotations are from the Second
Catholic Edition of the Revised Standard Version of the Bible, copyright
1965, 1966, 2006 by the Division of Christian Education of the National
Council of the Churches of Christ in the United States of America. Used by
permission. All rights reserved.

Cover design & page layout by Jennifer Bitler www.doxologydesign.com

DEDICATION & ACKNOWLEDGEMENT

The mere effort to pen a dedicatory page ensures that I will leave someone out — someone who, by God's grace, has made all the difference in my life. So let me thank all of you now for your friendship and grace. Even so, there are two whom I particularly want to mention.

First, I dedicate this book to my wife, Marilyn. She's the love of my life and has walked beside me, step by step, through everything that I mention in this book, for by God's grace, we are walking this journey together. I love you, Marilyn.

Second, I want to acknowledge Paul Thigpen, the new Director of CHResources here at the Coming Home Network International. If these articles are readable, if there is any overall sense to their arrangement, it is all because of Paul's unique editing and writing gifts. He truly can make a silk purse out of this old sow's ear. Thanks, Paul.

CONTENTS

PART TWO: The Difficulties of the Journey Home

PART THREE: The Journey Onward

PART FOUR: The Coming Home Network International

FOREWORD

by Paul Thigpen

The celebrated English convert G. K. Chesterton once observed that "the Church is a house with a hundred gates; and no two men enter at exactly the same angle." As the founding president of the Coming Home Network International, Marcus Grodi can readily affirm the truth of that observation. A convert himself, he has walked alongside hundreds of seekers on their way home to the Catholic Church, each with a unique starting point, each with a distinctive "angle" of entry.

Yet despite the variety of the roads to Rome, they also demonstrate certain parallels. Marcus realizes, as Chesterton did, that it's useful to identify these common patterns in conversion, because recognition of them can help potential converts find their way. It can also assist those who have already arrived home to make sense of their journey, while revealing more clearly to those raised in the Church the treasures that have been theirs all along.

Thoughts for the Journey Home provides insight in all these ways, and much more as well. He brings together here a number of his essays, published over the years, that examine the common joys and satisfactions, burdens and barriers, questions and doubts and fears, that lie along the way. His reflections, both practical and profound, illumine the path for converts, potential converts, and cradle Catholics alike.

The ministry of the Coming Home Network International is focused primarily on a particular kind of convert: non-Catholic clergy on their way to the Catholic Church. In addition to the typical dislocations resulting from conversion, these men and women face special challenges.

They must give up their ordination, their livelihood, and their established self-identity as pastors or other professional ministers. Only a few are able to become Catholic priests. The rest, then, must launch out into unfamiliar vocational territory, many with no training to prepare them. Meanwhile, they usually have families to support — spouses and children who, in the midst of anxiety and confusion about the convert's decision, may strongly oppose it.

Those who find themselves in this difficult, demanding situation will find special sympathy and encouragement in this book. Marcus, himself a former Protestant pastor, has been there, done that, and lived to tell the story. It's a story full of hope, told with humility, honesty, and grace.

My prayer is that this book will find its way, not only to these seekers, but also to all sorts of other readers who are connected, in various ways, to this journey of faith. The wisdom here is for those who are thinking about starting out, and those who are beckoning them; those who are already on the way, and those who walk beside them; those who have arrived, and those who should be welcoming them home.

INTRODUCTION

On the Way Home

I was on a flight to Birmingham, Alabama, to host *The Journey Home*, my live program on EWTN, the Eternal Word Television Network. Seated next to me was a dressed-to-the-hilt businessman. After his second Scotch on the rocks, he turned to me and asked, "So, what do you do for a living?"

"I help Protestant ministers become Catholic."

After a blank stare, he pressed the button for the flight attendant. I wondered if he would ask to be moved to another seat, but instead he merely asked for another drink, a double, and our conversation ceased.

To many people, the conversion of anyone to the Catholic Church, much less a clergyman, is an unfathomable absurdity. Yet during the past fifty-plus years a growing wave of Protestant ministers and laity have been "coming home" to the Catholic Church.

So why would anyone want to do that?

This was my question before I began my own "journey home." For the first forty years of my life, I had never heard of a Protestant minister becoming Catholic. But they are indeed coming home.

In 1993 we founded the Coming Home Network International (CHNetwork for short), an organization whose mission is to help non-Catholic clergy enter the Catholic Church. Since that time, more than eighteen hundred ministers, missionaries, educators, and seminarians from more than a hundred various non-Catholic traditions have contacted us. All these expressed interest in becoming Catholic, and so far more than nine hundred of them have "come home." More than eight hundred are still somewhere along the journey, struggling with a variety of obstacles and pondering the implications for themselves and their families if they convert.

Why, you might ask, are these men and women turning from the familiar traditions, not to mention their ordained ministries and livelihoods, to become Catholic? The following collection of essays addresses this and related questions, arranged into what might be called the stages of the journey: the beginning; the difficulties along the way; and the journey onward. A final section describes specifically the work of the CHNetwork, dedicated to standing beside those on the journey.

Regardless of where you might be on the journey — whether a non-Catholic just beginning your exploration of the Catholic Church's validity, or somewhere along the way encountering new questions or second thoughts, or already home and in need of encouragement, or even a life-long Catholic with friends you'd like to help "come home" — I pray that this collection of essays will serve as an encouragement on your journey of faith.

—*Marcus Grodi*

PART ONE

The Journey Begins

CHAPTER 1

"I Don't Have Time for That!"

My background and spiritual formation were exclusively Protestant. I was baptized, catechized, and confirmed Lutheran. Later, after a few years wandering in the dregs of agnostic scientific materialism, I was "born again" as a charismatic evangelical Congregationalist. Then I completed Protestant seminary and was ordained to the Protestant ministry.

Several years ago, I visited my seminary alma mater. I wasn't certain whether anyone there was aware of my conversion to the Catholic faith, but I knew that if they were, they would hardly appreciate it. So I cautiously strolled down the hallowed halls, waiting for that familiar face to pose that confrontational question. But it never came. I was merely a long-forgotten alumnus.

I was amazed to realize how differently so many things appeared now that I viewed them through Catholic eyes. The newly constructed chapel, with everything arranged to revolve around a central pulpit, was starkly bare.

The old chapel had been a Catholic chapel, since the buildings of this now evangelical Protestant seminary had once been a Carmelite seminary. When I attended, the religious images had all been removed, but the large stone altar and the confessionals were still in place. The old chapel stood practically vacant. The altar area, covered with ping-pong tables, and the confessionals, crammed with folding chairs, were vivid reminders of the disdain still held in this place for its Catholic past.

Later in the morning, I attended an installation service for a prominent Old Testament theologian, now the new president of the seminary. Many of the professors seated around the front of the pulpit area were old acquaintances who should have recognized me, but as I looked around, none gave any sign of recognition.

Suddenly the speaker riveted my attention with a comment that stunned me. During this celebrated theologian's reception sermon, he mentioned in an aside that of course we all know that the Catholic Church still teaches that we are "saved by our works." He then reinforced this claim with several quotes from contemporary Catholic theologians, all of which were taken out of context and without any explanation of Catholic terminology.

I was saddened — not just because, once again, falsehood was being passed along unexamined, but because this prominent theologian apparently thought it unnecessary to double-check his misinformation before he disseminated it.

My visit was capped off by a two-hour, sometimes heated discussion with another Old Testament professor over the authority of Scripture vs. Tradition. He brashly charged, "You Catholics merely change at will anything you call 'Tradition' with a capital 'T' to 'tradition' with a small 't.'"

I asked this learned and lettered scholar whether he had ever taken the time to read the teachings of the Catholic Church in books written by Catholic authors. In particular, had he ever read the documents of the Second Vatican Council, in particular *Lumen Gentium*, the "Dogmatic Constitution on the Church"? That document directly addressed this issue.

He responded matter-of-factly, "Of course not! I don't have time for that!"

This encounter reminded me of how ignorant I myself once had been of what the Catholic Church really teaches. I too had blindly accepted and spread myths about the Church. As a result, I had misinformed hundreds of people. Today I am thankful that I acted in ignorance and not with malice.

You might say that this collection of essays is a small attempt to correct this misinformation. Some of you reading this book may say that you don't "have the time" for an extensive study of genuine Catholic teaching. If so, I ask that you would at least consider reading these essays before you pass along "facts" about the Catholic Church that may not be true. I don't pretend that these essays cover every important issue in apologetics. Nor do they approach systematically the issues addressed. Rather, they take a look at some of the key concerns I considered as I weeded through the myths I had blindly accepted until I found the truth about the Catholic faith.

Chapter 2

Too Busy

Tradition has it that about two thousand years ago, along the shore of the Sea of Galilee, there lived a man named Jethro ben Tubizzi. He made a living repairing kitchen appliances such as oil lamps, grinding wheels, and spatulas. One Saturday afternoon, his usual day off, his neighbor, the blind Methuselah ben Hoepin, came feeling his way along the street wall to Jethro's front door.

"Jethro, you there?"

"Where else?"

"Did you hear? Remember that preacher man from Nazareth I told you about?"

"How could I not hear? Every time I go to a home to fix something, that's all they talk about. Just in the last week, I've repaired fourteen spatulas that fanatical wives had broken over their husbands' heads, arguing about that preacher."

"But he's coming here! In fact, Samuel ben Samuel ben Samuel ben Humble told me he's on his way, right now, in this direction, coming down our street. Can't you hear the noise?"

"Sure I heard the noise. What do you think I am, deaf? Sorry, Meth. But you won't catch me running out after every self-proclaimed messiah.

"Remember my uncle Izzi? How he got caught up in the hubbub over that zealot from Bethsaida, the one who claimed miraculous catches of fish by spitting on his nets? The scribes and Pharisees went out to investigate and caught that charlatan's disciples in the very act of delusion.

"The scribes noticed strange reeds sticking up out of the water around where the nets had been, cast way out in the deep water. One wise scribe decided to test the power of his own spit by drooling it down one of the reeds. Out of the deep burst a coughing disciple, who apparently had been putting fish in the nets. Uncle Izzi barely escaped with his life."

Methuselah shook his head as he stood in the doorway. "But I've been told this Yeshua is not like that at all. No one, including the scribes and Pharisees, has any explanation for His miracles. It's said that He turned water into wine, that He healed lepers and the lame, the deaf, and even the blind!"

"Meth, my old friend, you know I wish you well, but I warn you: Don't get your hopes up, trusting in some miracle worker."

These last words were lost in the rising noise from the street. Methuselah disappeared into the crowd that now had formed outside Jethro's door. All he could hear was the bedlam of almost everyone in town gathering to catch a glimpse of the passing preacher.

Jethro started to rise from his workbench, wiping his hands on a rag, but then stopped.

"Why waste my time? And why should I even let my neighbors see me come to the window, as if I had any interest at all in this charlatan?"

Throwing the rag across the room, Jethro returned to his work. In time the street noise grew so loud that he could no longer concentrate. He wanted to rush to the door and shout for them all to be quiet: "Have you no respect? Can't you see I have work to do?"

But instead of working, he rose from his workbench and left his small house by the back door. It was time for a long walk out in the country away from the crazy, misguided mayhem of his neighbors.

When Jethro returned several hours later, the crowds had dispersed, except for pockets of neighbors gathered in small hushed groups. Avoiding them, he entered his house by the back door and returned to his work.

"Jethro!" came a voice from his front door, familiar, yet with a boldness he had never heard.

He turned, expecting to see the usual slumped body of his blind old friend Methuselah. Instead, before him stood a new Meth, fully erect, his arms extended in a welcoming greeting, his face beaming with joy, his smile struggling to be contained within his wrinkled face. But the most startling thing about him was his eyes, wide open and shining with their own light.

"Methuselah, what's happened?" Jethro said, rising slowly. He dropped his tools as he realized what his friend must have gained — and what he sadly had lost.

I think of that story when I recall one particular day in October 1979. I was living in a studio apartment on Beacon Street in Boston. Three doors down was the Bull and Finch Pub, later to become famous as the setting for *Cheers*, where I ate three nights a week. (They may have based the character of the mailman on me!)

Directly across the street was the beautiful and extensive Public Garden. I was taking a year off from seminary, working as an engineer while discerning whether or not God was calling me back to seminary.

I was off work and looking forward to a relaxing day, spending part of it in front of the television and the rest on a long jog along the Charles River. In passing I had heard and read that this very day Boston was being granted the great "privilege" of a visit by the new Catholic pope, John Paul II. The *Boston Globe*, in my view, had wasted far too many of its news pages discussing the papal visit — articles which, of course, I had no interest in reading.

As the day progressed, the crowds came. Thousands filled the street and the Garden, but I didn't so much as poke my head out the door. Why should I? Why should I have any more interest in a Catholic pope than if, say, the head of the Unification Church were passing by? And besides, I hate crowds.

So I escaped by the alley door for an afternoon jog along the Charles, "far from the madding crowd."

It wasn't until many years later, especially on that day in 2004 when we mourned the Holy Father's death, that I fully realized what a great privilege I had squandered. I'm not saying that the presence of Pope John Paul II outside my door was equivalent to the presence of Jesus in the story about Methuselah. Yet I have come to understand that in the very presence of the successor of Peter, we have the continuous historical fulfillment of Jesus' promise to build His Church on Peter and his successors; the fulfillment of His promise that the gates of hell will never prevail against it; and His promise that He will be with us always.

For many of us, the opportunity to explore the truth of the Catholic Church comes flitting into our lives only occasionally, much as in the anecdotes above. For me, except for that missed visit of the pope, the first forty years of my life went by without any thought given (that I can remember) to the possible validity of the Catholic Church.

Then, by the mercy of grace, I became reacquainted with an old seminary friend who, as a result of his own conversion to the Catholic faith, passed along to me what he had discovered.

Is this possibly the moment, maybe for the first time, that the Lord is inviting you to consider the truth of the Catholic Church? A Church that claims a direct historical connection — an apostolic succession — with the very Church established by Jesus in His hand-chosen Apostles, centered on the leadership of the Apostle Peter? If so, my encouragement to you is this: Don't let this moment pass you by.

CHAPTER 3

Who Has the Authority?

Whenever Christians of different traditions gather over a cup of coffee to discuss differences in theology or doctrine, the result can be either brotherly love or flying fur. Since the latter has too often been the case, the politically correct thing for most contemporary Christians to do is avoid these confrontations.

As a result, all across America, Christian neighbors of one tradition are able to live somewhat peaceably across the street or next door to Christian neighbors of other traditions by not talking about religion. In other parts of the world, however, this strategy hasn't proven so successful.

Let me pose a question: Is this situation what Jesus intended in His great priestly prayer when He prayed these words?

> Holy Father, keep them in your name, which you have given me, *that they may be one, even as we are one.* ... I do not pray for these only, but also for those who believe in me through their word, *that they may all be one;* even as you, Father, are in me, and I in you, that they also may be

in us, so that the world may believe that you have sent me.
The glory which you have given me I have given to them,
that they may be one even as we are one, I in them and you
in me, that *they may become perfectly one,* so that the world
may know that you have sent me and have loved them even
as you have loved me. (Jn 17:11b, 20–23; emphasis added)

Four times Jesus prayed that His followers would always
remain one so that their united witness would convince the
world of who He is and how much our heavenly Father loves
us. Now, nearly two thousand years later, our world is still
pretty much unconvinced, or at least terribly complacent.

Whenever Christians of different traditions do get together
to discuss or debate, the discussion rarely gets down to the
issue at the core of our divisions. Arguments over whether salvation can be lost or who can be baptized or which form of
church government is most biblical or whether women can
be ordained all skirt the true, underlying issue: How will we
finally determine which opinion is true?

Will it be determined by the greatest number of votes? the
greatest number of supporting Bible verses? the longest-stand-
ing tradition? the loudest and fiercest voice?

No. The key issue behind all our divisions is the issue of
authority. Who has the authority to speak for God to declare
what is true?

With thoughts on the overwhelming implications of this
theme — how the abandonment of authority has brought
intellectual and moral chaos into our modern world — I recently had an unanticipated experience that drove this point
disconcertingly home. One morning as I was driving to the
airport, I decided to check out the library at a local university
in a small central Ohio town that I normally pass quickly by.

As I entered the front gate, the marquee described this
155-year-old academic institution as a "Christian College of

Liberal Arts." Driving around the campus looking for the library, I noticed that there were no signs or symbols that gave a clue to this school's religious affiliation. The large chapel, New-England style, had no specifically Christian artwork, and the billboard listed only a chapel service on Thursday evenings and a Catholic Mass on Sunday afternoons.

In the library, I browsed through the religion section and was appalled that the overwhelming majority of the selections were by liberal Protestant, Asian, pagan, or New Age writers. When I found the bookstore and glanced through the lists for upcoming classes, again the books and topics reflected the same theological electicism found in the library. My first thought was for the poor, naïve parents who thought they were safely sending their children to a nurturing Christian environment.

I then wondered how any student at that school who might be searching spiritually could possibly discover the truth of the Christian faith. Then this question crossed my mind: In the nearly two thousand years of Christian history, when had it become possible for schools like this to exist, to proclaim themselves unashamedly "Christian" without any identifiable connection to any specific Christian tradition? I presume that it became possible only in the last two centuries.

But maybe the more relevant question is this: How will the students of that small "Christian" college determine what is true? The stacks upon stacks of books at that liberal arts library reek of relativism and do nothing but encourage these young minds to believe that the only authority they need emanates from their own selves. Is it possible that what they find there at this once-Christian college is in essence the unavoidable trajectory of the idea that all we need to determine truth on our own is the Bible and the Holy Spirit?

I love Jesus Christ. The principal motive that led me from my Protestant tradition into the Catholic Church was my conviction that God's truth is not relative. My primary goal in writing about these matters is not to argue or proselytize, but to clear away confusion and ignorance so that others might discover the joyful, trustworthy, and Spirit-led authority that still exists in the Catholic Church in union with St. Peter.

Those of us who are converts from the Protestant tradition are anything but anti-Protestant. We are thankful for the faithful witness of our families, friends, congregations, and pastors who led us to Jesus Christ and nurtured us in the Christian faith. It is now our desire to help others discover the fullness and power of the faith, as taught by the early Church Fathers and throughout history in Sacred Tradition.

We pray that God will strengthen your faith in Jesus Christ and kindle in your heart a desire to know more about the Church that has weathered all the storms of the last two thousand years. This Church is not without members and even leaders who have committed great sins and blunders. But by God's grace, it still seeks to protect and proclaim the gospel message faithfully.

CHAPTER 4

Does the Bible Teach the Necessity of the Church?

Where does the Bible teach the necessity of the Church? When non-Catholics ask this question, they usually aren't asking specifically about the necessity of the *Catholic* Church. Instead, they want to know whether Jesus intended there to be a Church of any kind through which believers receive the graces and the truth necessary to be saved.

This is a good question and deserves a much longer, more thorough answer than I can give here. But I can briefly outline how, in my own journey from Protestant faith to Catholic faith, I became convinced that Jesus not only intended there to be a Church, but that apart from this Church we cannot be certain of what is true, much less what is necessary for salvation.

I need to begin, though, by explaining my perspective as a Protestant minister. Originally ordained a Congregationalist, I believed that the Scripture that most defined "church" was Matthew 18:20: "For where two or three are gathered in my name, there I am in the midst of them." Like many Protestants, I believed, based on this text, that any local gathering of believers was, therefore, an *ecclesia*, a "church," and could freely discern what is true, guided by the Holy Spirit dwelling within each believer.

I took this text to refer, not just to the local congregation, but also to any gathering of two or more Christians. Any gathering, no matter how small — any home Bible study — was therefore a "church," and as such, a Spirit-led encounter with Jesus.

I operated under this assumption for years, before and during seminary, and on into my first year as an ordained pastor. Then, however, I began to experience the crazy consequences of this assumption.

As a pastor, I found myself fighting the confusion and divisions that this misrepresentation of Scripture generates. I discovered that this institutionalized notion of autonomy reaps nothing but chaos and never results in any form of authentic Christian unity.

There is, in fact, no "least common denominator" upon which all independent evangelical Protestant Christians agree. They are not all Trinitarian; they do not all agree in their theologies of Jesus; they do not all agree upon what is necessary for salvation. They do not agree even upon whether sinners need to be saved.

Maybe the one thing they can agree upon is the necessity of love. Yet they can't agree upon what "love" means or requires. Is this confusion what Jesus promised His followers when He said, "If you continue in my word, you are truly my disciples, and you will know the truth, and the truth will make you free" (Jn 8:31–32)?

Another biblical verse clarified for me why this under-standing of "church" is absurd. St. Paul wrote to his son in the faith, St. Timothy:

> I hope to come to you soon, but I am writing these instruc-tions to you so that, if I am delayed, you may know how one ought to behave in the household of God, which is the church of the living God, the pillar and bulwark of the truth. (1 Tm 3:14–15)

The thousands of autonomous, self-initiated gatherings, and the associations and denominations composed of these in-dependent congregations — not to mention the other denom-inations stemming from the Reformation — cannot identify even one point of theology upon which they all agree. So how can they be considered the "pillar and bulwark of truth"? Could I, as a pastor, claim that my independent Congregational church — or, after I received ordination in a different tradi-tion, that my particular Presbyterian denomination — apart from all other Christian churches, was *the* "pillar and bulwark of truth"?

As I struggled with this dilemma, I was confronted by yet another couple of verses, from within the same passage in Matthew:

> If your brother sins against you, go and tell him his fault, between you and him alone. If he listens to you, you have gained your brother. But if he does not listen, take one or two others along with you, that every word may be confirmed by the evidence of two or three witnesses. If he refuses to listen to them, tell it to the Church; and if he refuses to listen even to the Church, let him be to you as a Gentile and a tax collector. (Mt 18:15–17)

Could Jesus have meant that merely any gathering of two or three believers has the authority to decide the outcome of conflicts between individuals?

If this were true, then essentially the problem would have been solved in the second step, when two or three (and, therefore, a "church") had come together to confront the sinful brother. But Jesus indicated that when this wasn't successful, they were to "tell it to the Church."

This "Church," therefore, must be something different from any merely self-initiated group of believers, no matter how small or large. In fact, how could the existence of thousands of individual independent "churches" or separated denominations carry any kind of authority to make these kinds of decisions — the authority to separate a sinful brother from their gathering, to "let him be ... as a Gentile and a tax collector"? All that any two or three who had been kicked out had to do was declare that *they* were now the true church — and, of course, that happens all the time!

My discovery of the necessity of the Church was confirmed even more solidly when I reread a familiar verse: "You are Peter, and on this rock I will build my Church, and the gates of Hades will not prevail against it" (Mt 16:18).

Setting aside for now the issue of Simon Peter, I recognized that Jesus intended to build His Church: not "churches," nor some "hidden" group of believers visible only to God, nor some kind of later development or dispensation. No, Jesus would build His Church, against which the powers of the evil one would never prevail.

But how and when would Jesus build this Church? In Matthew 16:18 He stated that He would build this Church upon Simon Peter. More specifically, in the context of the entire New Testament, He would build His Church upon His hand-chosen apostles under the leadership of Simon Peter.

To ensure that this Church would have the trustworthy authority to determine what is true, Jesus promised His apostles the Holy Spirit. We read of this in John chapters 14–16. Like the majority of evangelical Protestants, I interpreted the promises of these verses to refer to every Christian in general, and I used this notion to support my understanding of private interpretation of Scripture. Once examined, however, this notion breaks down. Jesus promised to His apostles on the night before He was crucified:

> If you love me, you will keep my commandments. And I will ask the Father, and he will give you another Counselor, to be with you for ever, even the Spirit of truth, whom the world cannot receive, because it neither sees him nor knows him; you know him, for he dwells with you, and will be in you. (Jn 14:15–16)

On the surface so far, this passage seems to support the idea I once held: that all believers know the Holy Spirit because "he dwells with you and will be with you," and we Catholics *do* believe this to be true for all baptized believers. However, some statements following this promise don't make sense when applied *in general* to all believers:

> But the Counselor, the Holy Spirit, whom the Father will send in my name, he will teach you all things, and bring to your remembrance all that I have said to you. (Jn 14:26)

> When the Spirit of truth comes, he will guide you into all the truth; for he will not speak on his own authority, but whatever he hears he will speak, and he will declare to you the things that are to come. (Jn 16:13)

Either the Holy Spirit has been terribly "mixed up" over what is true, leading to such irreconcilable divisions and confusion among Christians, or Christians just don't *hear* very well.

If the latter is true, however, then how can anyone be certain that they *are* hearing the Holy Spirit and following correctly?

It makes more sense, at least to me, that in these verses, Jesus was speaking primarily to His hand-chosen apostles, promising that they would receive the Holy Spirit, who would then help them remember and know the fullness of the deposit of faith.

Much more can obviously be said about this matter. But in my journey, these and other verses helped me to see that the Church established by Jesus Christ in His apostles, and united with the office of Peter, demands our attention and our loyalty. For it is the one trustworthy "pillar and bulwark of truth," guided by the Holy Spirit.

CHAPTER 5

Attack Number Two Bazillion and Five

In the last few years, the traditional beliefs of Catholics, as well as Christians in general, have been challenged by the bold and sometime bawdy claims of a spate of novels and films. Two titles that come to mind because of their popularity, both as books and as movies, are *The Da Vinci Code* and the *Left Behind* series. The latter challenges a number of Catholic teachings, while *The Da Vinci Code* attempts to undermine the belief of all Christians in a resurrected and holy Christ.

These are certainly not the first fictional works to attack the integrity of our faith, nor will they be the last. Others I recall include *Mass Appeal, The Last Temptation of Christ, The Life of Brian, The Name of the Rose,* and *Jesus Christ Superstar.* Some of these works I have read or viewed; others I've simply heard about in ways that have made me pause. Since it's only by God's merciful grace that any of us believe at all, we should always pray for His protection, for ourselves and our families, from this continuous onslaught of misinformation packaged as entertainment.

Many Catholic authors have adequately addressed and countered the false claims of these books, so I won't attempt to duplicate their efforts here. Instead, I'd like to suggest that all these contemporary attacks on the Catholic faith — whether serious or frivolous — stem in some way from the Protestant rejection of the trustworthiness of the Church and Sacred Tradition, and the Protestant over-reliance on *sola scriptura* and private interpretation.

As I make this claim, I'm sensing that I may be provoking the incredulous ire of some readers. But consider what Scripture teaches us about what Jesus our Lord intended.

He chose, from out of the many disciples who followed Him, twelve men to be the foundation of His Church. Of these twelve, Sacred Tradition, in line with the events reported in Matthew chapter 16, has always held that He chose one, Simon Peter, upon whom He would build His Church and to whom He would give the keys of authority and leadership. Jesus then promised, as reported in John chapters 14–16, that He would send the Holy Spirit to guide them into all truth, and this happened first in the Upper Room (see Jn 20) and then in fullness at Pentecost (see Acts 2).

Our Lord also prayed (see Jn 17) that His followers would be one as He and the Father are one: not thousands of independent and sometimes warring groups but, as the Church Fathers would later define her, one holy, Catholic, and apostolic Church. He then sent His apostles forth to make disciples, preaching, teaching, and baptizing. Their oral and written witness (see 2 Thes 2:15) carried the gospel to the then-known regions of the world.

From the beginning, however, false gospels arose from both inside and outside the Church, challenging all aspects of the Christian faith (see Gal 1:6-9). By the fourth century, hundreds of such writings were vying for attention and acceptance. Their promoters sought to have them read in the Church's liturgy as a trustworthy part of the memoirs of the Apostles.

Various lists of accepted books were drawn up, by Church leaders as well as declared heretics. But the issue was finally settled by three separate regional councils of Catholic bishops under the authority of the Church and in union with the Bishop of Rome — the Councils of Rome (382), Hippo (393), and Carthage (397). These councils all declared the same list of books to be included in the inspired canon of Scripture, and this canon remained the accepted foundation of the Christian faith, as a part of Sacred Tradition, until the Reformation in the sixteenth century.

Up until that time, Christians learned what they were to believe based on five sources of truth and in the following order:

The Church. They learned their faith from priests and bishops loyal to the Bishop of Rome (the Pope), whose authority they trusted. They believed that the Holy Spirit, given to the Apostles by Jesus Christ, insured that the Church was guarding and passing on what was true (see Jn 16:13).

Sacred Tradition. This faith was crystallized in the creeds they memorized and the devotions they prayed.

Sacred Scripture. Though few could read or possess books, they heard Scripture read at Mass and proclaimed by street preachers.

Personal inspiration. Christians have always believed, based on so many biblical and historical examples, that God continues to speak and guide His faithful followers. They were quite suspicious, however, when someone claimed that the "Holy

Spirit" was leading them to believe something that contradict-
ed what they had learned from the three sources of truth just
noted. Would the Spirit contradict Himself?

Conscience. Christians knew they were responsible for acting according to the dictates of their conscience. But they also
knew that their conscience had to be formed by the other four
sources of truth.

Nevertheless, the sixteenth-century Protestant Reformation attempted to truncate drastically this array of the sources of truth. The authority and trustworthiness of both the
Church and Sacred Tradition were rejected. Sacred Scripture
alone was declared to be the primary source of truth. It had to
be interpreted by each person, according to his private conscience and understanding, under the assumed inspiration of
the Holy Spirit.

Once the authority of Sacred Tradition and the Church
were dismissed, however, it was inevitable that the remaining
sources of truth would receive the same treatment. In time,
radical theologians, biblical scholars, and philosophers came
to challenge and ridicule Scripture itself. With Church, Scripture, and Tradition all rejected, the reliability of the individual
conscience and the leading of the Holy Spirit were dismissed as
utterly subjective. Modern Christians were left with a hodge-
podge of conflicting opinions and fleeting loyalties.

We shouldn't be surprised, then, when bookstores and the
mass media produce tract after book after play after movie after DVD, all claiming a novel angle to undercut the gospel and
the Church Jesus established as the primary means of grace
for salvation.

How should we respond to these challenges? It's essential,
of course, to increase our knowledge so we can answer every
challenge we may encounter to our faith (see 1 Pt 3:15). But

we must never forget that the bedrock of our faith is not our intellectual ability to answer all comers.

Rather, we must accept the witness of Scripture and the Church that Jesus did not leave us stranded without a trust-worthy authority, a "pillar and bulwark" for our faith (see 1 Tm 3:15). By grace He has given us a trustworthy Church, and by grace He has called us home to that Church. God grant that He will continue, by grace, to help us trust this Church and to defend her when the ignorant assail her.

CHAPTER 6

Was St. Paul Catholic?

During the year of St. Paul (June 2008–June 2009), the Church lifted up the life and teachings of St. Paul for our spiritual enrichment. This great apostle is often championed within the Protestant tradition as the source of certain distinctively Protestant teachings. Given my Protestant past, then, one important question crossed my mind.

No doubt this question arose in the minds of some of our non-Catholic friends and family when they heard that Catholics were celebrating a Year of St. Paul. I could just hear them ask: "Do you honestly think that St. Paul was *Catholic*?"

Before I considered the Catholic faith, I certainly presumed that the Apostle Paul was *not* a Catholic. Of course, I would not have claimed that he was a Protestant, either, because I recognized that Protestantism was a later historical development. But I believed that such a historical development was a necessary reaction against a Roman Church that had strayed far from Paul's true theology.

My childhood Lutheran roots taught me that the key to understanding all of St. Paul was in a verse from Romans:

> For I am not ashamed of the gospel: it is the power of God
> for salvation to every one who has faith, to the Jew first
> and also to the Greek. For in it the righteousness of God
> is revealed through faith for faith; as it is written, "He who
> through faith is righteous shall live." (Rom 1:16–17)

Trained in this way, I believed that all of Paul's theology was centered on the idea that we are not saved through any righteousness of our own, which we may have acquired through our efforts or works. Rather, we are saved by the righteousness of God that we receive solely by faith as a free gift, which covers our sinful unrighteousness.

With this key, all the rest of Paul's writings — in fact, all the rest of the Bible — could be interpreted. If a particular verse didn't quite fit this theological paradigm, then it needed to be reinterpreted, realigned, according to this key.

Later, after my adult "born again experience" (or reconversion) and subsequent years in seminary, I became an ordained, evangelically-minded, Calvinist minister (first a Congregationalist, and then a Presbyterian). Calvinist convictions built on my Lutheran background to emphasize even more the sovereignty of God and the depravity of man, which placed an even more radical spin on the theology of Paul. I learned, believed, and then taught that especially in the Letter to the Romans we find *two* "plans of salvation": "Plan A" and "Plan B."

"Plan A" described how people were saved before the Cross: through works of the Law. But they were irremediably hindered by the depravity of their wills, so they could not on their own sufficiently live a holy and perfect life. They could not be saved.

For this reason, because of His love, God sent his Son (see Jn 3:16), kicking into gear "Plan B." In this plan, through our faith in Jesus Christ — and this alone apart from any works — we receive as a gift the righteousness of God. We are then saved, but not by anything we have ever done. Rather, upon our death, God is blinded to our impurities by the imputed covering of Christ's righteousness, and He welcomes us into His Kingdom.

This, I believed, was Paul's gospel. So I essentially read this notion into every instance when he used the word "gospel" in Scripture (over seventy-five times). For example (in all the following texts, emphasis is added):

> But I do not account my life of any value nor as precious to myself, if only I may accomplish my course and the ministry which I received from the Lord Jesus, to testify to the *gospel* of the grace of God. (Acts 20:24)

> For I am not ashamed of the *gospel*: it is the power of God for salvation to every one who has faith, to the Jew first and also to the Greek. (Rom 1:16)

> For Christ did not send me to baptize but to preach the *gospel*, and not with eloquent wisdom, lest the cross of Christ be emptied of its power. (1 Cor 1:17)

> Brethren, I would have you know that the *gospel* which was preached by me is not man's *gospel*. (Gal 1:11)

> In him you also, who have heard the word of truth, the *gospel* of your salvation, and have believed in him, were sealed with the promised Holy Spirit. (Eph 1:13)

> Only let your manner of life be worthy of the *gospel* of Christ. (Phil 1:27)

Here was the critical question: Was this "Plan A / Plan B" paradigm the one true expression of what St. Paul called "my gospel" (2 Tm 2:8)? After all, I knew many Bible-believing

Christians who radically disagreed with this particular slant on the gospel.

The issue became even more complicated as I wondered what Paul meant when he said to the Christians at Philippi:

> [I am] thankful for *your partnership in the gospel from the first day until now.* ... And you Philippians yourselves know that *in the beginning of the gospel,* when I left Macedonia, no church entered into partnership with me in giving and receiving except you only. (Phil 1:5; 4:15; emphasis added)

In what way had the Philippians had a *partnership* in the gospel? And how had the gospel *been inaugurated* when Paul left Macedonia?

In time, this confusion of interpretations about what was essential to the gospel helped open my heart to the truth and fullness of the Catholic faith. For St. Paul, the gospel was not merely some carefully circumscribed "Plan B," though it included the truth about the redemptive death and resurrection of Jesus Christ on the cross.

Nor was it merely a precise set of standards, though it included morals, ethics, and the "obedience of faith." It was not a list of rites and devotions, though it involved membership through baptism in the Body of Christ — the Church — which included discipline, structure, and authoritative worship. Nor was it limited to one privileged group of people. Rather — and this was what "began" when he left Macedonia — it was for every single person.

No, St. Paul's gospel included all these and more. But it did not consist merely of these. Rather, St. Paul's gospel was and is a life of surrender, obedience, and even suffering — the kind of life he himself modeled, so that he could say to his fellow Christians, "Be imitators of me" (1 Cor 4:16).

CHAPTER 7

By What Authority Do You Preach?

One Sunday many years ago, I was standing in my pulpit preparing to preach. I had done my homework, spending nearly ten hours in prayer, study, and exegesis, consulting all the best books on my shelf, so that what I would proclaim to my flock, which I had been ordained and hired to shepherd, would be true. My flock trusted me for this truth.

I knew that I was expected both by them and by God to proclaim truth. Jesus' words rang in my ears: "Whoever causes one of these little ones who believe in me to sin, it would be better for him if a great millstone were hung round his neck and he were thrown into the sea" (Mk 9:42). I knew that as their pastor I was eternally responsible for what I preached.

As I stood there in my black academic gown covering my otherwise business attire, and ready to read the Scripture text from the recently approved *Common Lectionary,* a thought struck me: Within a fifteen-mile radius of my pulpit were literally twenty-plus other churches with similar pulpits, filled with similarly ordained men and women, all ready to read the same text. I felt paralyzed.

Why? Because I realized that, though we all believed that the Bible was sufficient for leading us into all truth, and that we were each responsible before God for what we preached, we were each teaching different, even contradictory things.

Which of us was right? Which of us, if any, would one day hear the words, "Well done, good and faithful servant" (Mt 25:21)?

One of the many questions that crossed my mind that morning and in the weeks to follow was this: By what authority did I or the rest of my neighboring preachers stand before our congregations and preach? This is a valid question for all ministers to ponder, for even our Lord was challenged by this question by the rightly ordained religious leaders of His day: "By what authority are you doing these things?" (Mk 11:28).

Can just anyone declare that he has a calling from God to set up a pulpit, start a church, and preach? People do that every day, especially here in America. By what authority do these self-proclaimed preachers preach? And to what extent do they truly represent Christ?

The Apostle Paul gave the Roman Christians a clear description of the preaching office and the authority behind it:

> For, "every one who calls upon the name of the Lord will
> be saved." But how are men to call upon him in whom they
> have not believed? And how are they to believe in him of
> whom they have never heard? And how are they to hear
> without a preacher? And how can men preach unless they
> are sent? (Rom 10:13–15)

Paul emphasized very clearly the necessity of being "sent" as the foundation for the authenticity of any preacher and his preaching. This was a critical warning because, already within the lives of these first-generation Christians, false teachers were spreading half-truths, misleading the faithful. Paul exclaimed:

> I am astonished that you are so quickly deserting him who called you in the grace of Christ and turning to a different gospel — not that there is another gospel, but there are some who trouble you and want to pervert the gospel of Christ. ... If any one is preaching to you a gospel contrary to that which you received, let him be accursed. (Gal 1:6, 7, 9)

Where did Paul receive his authority to preach and to declare that his gospel was the true one?

Later in this epistle, Paul claimed that he had not received the gospel he preached from human beings, but directly by divine revelation (see Gal 1:12). How, though, were he and his followers to know that what he was preaching was true? And how can we know whether individuals preaching today are speaking the truth?

Can just anyone today claim that he has had a revelation from God, that he has finally, after all these centuries, received from the Holy Spirit the truth, so that he can start his own church? Some Christians have done precisely this over and over throughout history, especially in the last five hundred years.

When we read through the Epistle to the Galatians, however, we find that Paul wasn't just making an unsupported claim to divine revelation. Instead, the Apostle confirmed the authority and authenticity of his preaching by pointing to one important fact: He had visited with Cephas (Peter) alone for fifteen days and then later received the right hand of fellowship (spiritual unity) from the rest of the apostles, confirming his call to preach the gospel to the uncircumcised (see Gal 1:18–2:10).

So how can someone know today whether the gospel he is preaching is the true gospel?

I came to realize through personal experience how easy it is for a busy Protestant pastor to become deluded into thinking that he is preaching and teaching the truth. In seminary I was taught a method for preparing sermons. Before I consulted with the commentaries, I was first to do my own exegesis and language studies. Then, once I had determined for myself what I thought the text was teaching, I was to check my conclusions with other commentators.

One day, however, as I was perusing my bookshelf of commentaries, I realized that my collection was very selective, hand-picked by myself. These books consisted of what I considered the best evangelical Christian writers with whom I already agreed. In essence, when I checked my commentaries, I was really only checking my conclusions against my own presuppositions.

Even when I took the time to consult commentators of other persuasions, I generally rejected out-of-hand any comments that differed from the consensus of the authors residing in the majority on my shelves. There was little chance in my busy schedule to discover that my limited North American evangelical Presbyterian presuppositions were in fact only a mere whisper in the great cacophony of opinions that exist in modern Christendom.

Many claim that they preach what the Bible "says," yet they fail to see that what they preach contradicts what others preach right across the street — with the same self-assurance of biblical accuracy. Others know this reality well, but somehow think it doesn't matter.

St. Paul warned of confused days ahead, a warning that sounds much like the day in which we live. Here are his instructions to St. Timothy, his chosen apostle, ordained to carry on the preaching of the gospel:

> I charge you in the presence of God and of Christ Jesus who is to judge the living and the dead, and by his appearing and his kingdom: preach the word, be urgent in season and out of season, convince, rebuke, and exhort, be unfailing in patience and in teaching. For the time is coming when people will not endure sound teaching, but having itching ears they will accumulate for themselves teachers to suit their own likings, and will turn away from listening to the truth and wander into myths. As for you, always be steady, endure suffering, do the work of an evangelist, fulfill your ministry. (2 Tm 4:1–5)

Where did Timothy receive his authority to preach? How was he to know that what he preached was true? In both letters to Timothy, Paul reminded him of the source of his authority and assurance:

> Do not neglect the gift you have, which was given you by prophetic utterance when the elders laid their hands upon you. (1 Tm 4:14)

> For this reason I remind you to rekindle the gift of God that is within you through the laying on of my hands. (2 Tm 1:6)

> Follow the pattern of the sound words which you have heard from me, in the faith and love which are in Christ Jesus; guard the truth that has been entrusted to you by the Holy Spirit who dwells within us. (2 Tm 1:13–14)

We must not presume that with the Holy Spirit and the Bible alone, we have the authority to preach. Such a notion is not found here.

Keep in mind: Paul and Timothy had no written New Testament — only the Old Testament Scriptures and the apostolic deposit of faith passed orally from Jesus to His apostles and then on to their chosen successors. This reality is clearly seen in Paul's instructions to those under him. Their preaching was to be in line with what they had been taught by Paul: "So then, brethren, stand firm and hold to the traditions which you were taught by us, either by word of mouth or by letter" (2 Thes 2:15).

Paul then instructed the men under him, whom he had personally chosen and ordained, to continue this practice to ensure the accurate proclamation of the gospel in the future: "You then, my son, be strong in the grace that is in Christ Jesus, and what you have heard from me before many witnesses entrust to faithful men who will be able to teach others also" (2 Tm 2:1-2).

This notion of the necessary authority to preach through the apostolic succession, by the laying on of hands, was well understood and accepted in the early Church. Yet it took me about four years after my reception into the Catholic Church to realize fully the personal implications of this ancient practice.

I was attending the ordination of a close friend to the permanent diaconate. While our bishop was preaching and explaining the origins of the diaconate, he stated that during the first few centuries of the Church, especially during the days of intense persecution, the differences between bishops and local parish priests were sometimes indiscernible. This was the result of being scattered and at times under cover for fear of detection.

However, he noted, one clear distinction always set bishops apart from priests and deacons: Only the bishop had the authority to ordain. Only the bishop had the authority to lay hands on a man to give him the authority to preach.

I was cut to the quick. By whose authority did the men who laid their hands on me ordain me? By whom were they sent, so they could then send me? I realized that they actually had no authority to ordain me.

When Protestants threw out the fifteen-century-old tradition of the priesthood, they brought chaos into the Church. For this reason, when St. Francis de Sales began his work of trying to bring back home to the Church the Calvinists in Geneva, Switzerland, he began by distributing pamphlets door-to-door pointing out that the Protestant reformers and the preachers they had ordained had no authority to preach their new "gospel."

Hear his words in this first pamphlet, written with love for his separated brothers and sisters around the year 1594:

> First, then, your ministers had not the conditions required for the position which they sought to maintain, and the enterprise which they undertook. ... The office they claimed was that of ambassadors of Jesus Christ Our Lord; the affair they undertook was to declare a formal divorce between Our Lord and the ancient Church his Spouse; to arrange and conclude by words of present consent, as lawful procurators, a second and new marriage with this young madam, of better grace, said they, and more seemly than the other.
>
> For in effect, to stand up as a preacher of God's Word and pastor of souls — what is it but to call oneself ambassador and legate of Our Lord, according to that of the Apostle: We are therefore ambassadors for Christ? And to say that the whole of Christendom has failed, that the whole Church has erred, and all truth disappeared — what is this but to say that Our Lord has abandoned his Church, has broken the sacred tie of marriage he had contracted with her?
>
> And to put forward a new Church — is it not to attempt to thrust upon this sacred and holy Husband a second wife? This is what the ministers of the pretended church have undertaken; this is what they boast of having done; this

has been the aim of their discourses, their designs, their writings. But what an injustice have you not committed in believing them? How did you come to take their word so simply? How did you so lightly give them credit?

To be legates and ambassadors they should have been sent, they should have had letters of credit from him whom they boasted of being sent by. … Tell me, what business had you to hear them and believe them without having any assurance of their commission and of the approval of Our Lord, whose legates they called themselves? In a word, you have no justification for having quitted the ancient Church in which you were baptized, on the faith of preachers who had no legitimate mission from the Master.

Now you cannot be ignorant that they neither had, nor have, in any way at all, this mission. For if Our Lord had sent them, it would have been either mediately or immediately.

We say mission is given mediately when we are sent by one who has from God the power of sending, according to the order which he has appointed in his Church; and such was the mission of St. Denis into France by Clement and of Timothy by St. Paul. Immediate mission is when God himself commands and gives a charge, without the interposition of the ordinary authority which he has placed in the prelates and pastors of the Church: as St. Peter and the Apostles were sent, receiving from Our Lord's own mouth this commandment: Go ye into the whole world, and preach the gospel to every creature (Mk 16.15); and as Moses received his mission to Pharaoh and to the people of Israel.

But neither in the one nor in the other way have your ministers any mission. How then have they undertaken to preach? How shall they preach, says the Apostle, unless they be sent? (quoted in *The Catholic Controversy*, TAN Books, 1989, pp. 11–13)

I too write this in love — not merely to challenge the authority of non-Catholic ministers to preach, but to challenge them to examine the authority behind their preaching and ordination. If you are a Protestant minister, have you presumed something you shouldn't have? Have you taken upon yourself an unwarranted responsibility for which you will be eternally responsible?

I am one who found myself in this position and recognized that, although God had faithfully blessed and used my meager efforts, I had no authority to consider myself an ordained ambassador of Christ. I had misused those passages from Romans 10 to claim something for myself that I had no right to claim. I pray that God will forgive me for this presumption, and that He will lead those of you still caught in this presumption to hear the fullness of the truth and come home to His Church.

CHAPTER 8

Stand Firm and Hold to the Traditions

As a Protestant pastor I was committed to presenting the truth of Jesus Christ and His gospel. I took this mandate seriously and built my teaching and preaching upon the foundation of Scripture alone. I believed that what I was feeding my congregation was safely palatable.

As I look back now, I'm amazed at how blind I was. So many Scripture texts I unintentionally missed, conveniently avoided, or consciously explained away.

Some of these passages — such as Matthew 16:18–19, John 6:51–69, John 20:23, and 1 Timothy 3:15 — are fairly obvious to me now, since I've become Catholic. However, one particular text has become especially significant to me: "So then, brethren, stand firm and hold to the traditions which you were taught by us, either by word of mouth or by letter" (2 Thes 2:15).

To Paul and the Christians who received his letters, the touchstone for theological, doctrinal, and ecclesial truth was the *tradition*: the words and teachings being passed on, preserved, and revered, sometimes orally and sometimes in writing. Biblical passages similar to this one written to the Thessalonians, such as 1 Corinthians 11:2 and others, actually indicate that the readers were to accept the written testimonies *because* they were in agreement with the oral testimonies; the oral traditions were the authoritative template.

Most modern biblical scholarship has dismissed both the trustworthiness of early traditions and the validity of any original "deposit of faith." I have come to see that this development is the natural trajectory of the Protestant emphasis on Scripture *alone* as the only trustworthy testimony of early Christianity.

St. Paul and the other New Testament writers were moved to write most often because they needed to address specific, imminent problems that they could not correct in person. This historical reality has several important implications.

First, the New Testament authors probably took care of many problems personally that they never wrote about. Second, no doubt many things were going well that they never mentioned. Third, if they *could* have handled all the problems in person, we may have ended up with a very short New Testament!

For all these reasons, when Protestants limit themselves to the testimony of the written Word, they make themselves naïvely susceptible to the problems, and stubbornly resistant to the solutions, that in fact ecclesial tradition alone has preserved and addressed.

Sola scriptura actually exists nowhere in any Protestant denomination. In every denomination we encounter new traditions erected to fill the void left by the rejection of Sacred Tradition. When the validity of an authoritative deposit of faith is rejected, the basis for establishing any authority, even in Scripture, is short-circuited, leaving us right where modern scholarship has left us: as slaves to individual or scholarly opinion.

The tradition that St. Paul so often commanded the early Christians to cling to was the inspired truth that Jesus had promised the Church would receive through the guiding, protecting presence of the Holy Spirit (see John chapters 14–15). I have come to accept joyfully that reality. I believe that a portion of this Tradition became recorded in the written Word, but most remained present in the oral Tradition. For that reason, one of the primary reasons for the existence of the Church throughout the ages has been the protection and preservation of this truth.

I pray that we will remain faithful to St. Paul's command, actively doing our part to "stand firm and hold to the traditions," as we protect and defend the institution Christ established as the steward of these truths.

CHAPTER 9

Sola Scriptura: A Stony Path

Once upon a time there was an Ethiopian eunuch, a court official of Candace, Queen of the Ethiopians. He was in charge of all her treasure. He had come to Jerusalem to worship, and the Apostle Philip was led by an angel to go meet him. As the Ethiopian official was on his way back home, Philip found him riding in his chariot and reading the prophet Isaiah.

Now, of course, I'm not making this story up. It's found in Acts 8:26–40. Only a few details are given about the background of this African eunuch: what he specifically believed and why he had been drawn to travel all the way up to Jerusalem to worship. But apparently, while he was there, he must have stopped by the shop of a local Hebrew scribe and purchased a copy of the Book of Isaiah.

This scroll had to be hand-copied, for the printing press was still nearly fourteen centuries in the future. So it would have been quite rare and expensive. (It's important to realize that in those days, not everyone had copies of the Old Testament Scriptures lying around at home. That situation was not common until many centuries later.)

When Philip encountered the official, the angel led him to ask whether the African understood what he was reading. The eunuch's response indicates that his problem did not stem from being unable to read the language, which would have been either Hebrew or Greek (if it were the Septuagint version). No, the problem was one of interpretation, for he responded, "How can I [understand], unless someone guides me?" (Acts 8:31).

For anyone who claims that the Bible *alone* is sufficient, this account should stand as a significant stumbling block. Just consider what the Bible is so clearly teaching here.

The Ethiopian official, apparently a highly educated man, was reading one of the clearest prophecies from Isaiah about the Suffering Servant Messiah:

> As a sheep led to the slaughter
> or a lamb before its shearer is silent,
> so he opens not his mouth.
> In his humiliation justice was denied him.
> Who can describe his generation?
> For his life is taken up from the earth.
> (Acts 8:32–33, quoting Is 53:7–8)

The Ethiopian then asked Philip, "Please, about whom does the prophet say this, about himself or about someone else?"

Now let's pull ourselves away from the Ethiopian's specific question and Philip's response so we can recognize the significance of what was happening here. The written biblical prophecy was not sufficient to lead this man to Christ, or to faith and therefore salvation. A human witness, an interpreter, was needed.

Some might respond that Philip's answer, as well as those given by Sts. Paul, Peter, James, John, Matthew, Luke, and the others, became the New Testament, which explained the meaning of this and other Old Testament prophecies for any who would ever need an answer. But if this is true, then why are there still thousands upon thousands of sermons preached, commentaries written, seminary classes taught, and Bible studies conducted all over the world, if further explanation isn't necessary?

The reason is clear: Just as this highly motivated Ethiopian eunuch recognized, we cannot understand the eternal significance of the Scriptures unless "someone guides."

"But we've been given the Holy Spirit to provide this guidance," someone might respond. Then why so much confusion, contradiction, and conflict among Christians?

No. Just as the Apostle Philip so specifically illustrates, Jesus sent forth His hand-chosen and anointed apostolic band to "make disciples … teaching" the whole world about who He is and the salvation He offers (Mt 28:19–20).

The question at issue here is whether the Bible *alone* is truly sufficient for all matters of faith. Most Protestants accept this idea as an implicit dogma, and they have based most of their doctrinal apologetics on it, ever since Martin Luther made the following bold statement at the Diet of Worms:

> Unless I am convinced by the testimony of the Scriptures or by clear reason (for I do not trust either in the pope or in councils alone, since it is well known that they have often erred and contradicted themselves), I am bound by the Scriptures I have quoted and my conscience is captive to the Word of God. I cannot and I will not retract anything, since it is neither safe nor right to go against conscience. May God help me. Amen.

An entire book could be written to address the important implications of this statement, both obvious and hidden. Suffice it to say, however, that from this brash stand (in which

Luther was actually holding stubbornly to his own private interpretations of a select list of verses) the modern view has evolved that all we need is the Bible to know all we need to know about Jesus and salvation.

On the surface this position may sound gallant and faithful, as if we are rightly raising and praising the divinely inspired Word of God. But based on personal experience, I must admit to how blind I was, and how naïve this notion is, if not downright ridiculous. Like so many others who hold to *sola scriptura*, I was also blind to how we were actually giving precedence to the other two foundations upon which Luther had taken his stand: "reason" and "conscience," both of which can be darkened by sin.

With the clarion call of *sola scriptura*, Christians have been drawn into all kinds of theological and philosophical aberrations. It has led ultimately to unitarianism, universalism, double predestination, total depravity of the will, radical feminism, and the defense of divorce, contraception, abortion, euthanasia, and homosexual unions.

As an example of the problem of *sola scriptura*, consider carefully the implications of the following passage from Deuteronomy. As you do, remember that when Jesus confounded the Devil during his forty days in the desert, He relied upon the authority and truth of this book (see Dt 8:3; 6:16; and 6:13). When He summarized the Law, restating the Greatest Commandment, He again confirmed the authority of this and the other "books of Moses" (see Dt 6:5 and Lv 19:18). Also, remember that most Protestant scholars, preachers, and teachers build the doctrine of *sola scriptura* upon the fact that Jesus quoted from these books.

> "Everything that I command you you shall be careful to do; you shall not add to it or take from it.

"If a prophet arises among you, or a dreamer of dreams,
and gives you a sign or a wonder, and the sign or wonder
which he tells you comes to pass, and if he says, 'Let us go
after other gods,' which you have not known, 'and let us
serve them,' you shall not listen to the words of that prophet
or to that dreamer of dreams; for the Lord your God is test-
ing you, to know whether you love the Lord your God with
all your heart and with all your soul. You shall walk after
the Lord your God and fear him, and keep his commandments and obey his voice, and you shall serve him and cling
to him. *But that prophet or that dreamer of dreams shall be
put to death,* because he has taught rebellion against the
Lord your God, who brought you out of the land of Egypt
and redeemed you out of the house of bondage, to make
you leave the way in which the Lord your God commanded
you to walk. *So you shall purge the evil from the midst of you.*
(Dt 12:32–13:5; emphasis added)

Now imagine yourself the pastor of an independent Christian Bible church, responsible to no one but Jesus through the
Holy Spirit. How would you, or should you, interpret and apply this passage to your congregation? What should you do
with those prophets and dreamers in your midst who claim
private messages from God, who then attempt to pull people
from your congregation in directions different from where
you believe God is calling you?

Let's say you have chosen to teach your people the Trinitarian and Christological formulas of the third- and fourth-
century ecumenical councils, while these new leaders — confirmed by signs and wonders — are teaching that God is found
only in Jesus or in the Holy Spirit. What should you do with
these teachers of rebellion?

I suppose having them stoned would seem a bit violent to
those in our modern, "civilized" society. Yet this was the pre-
scribed punishment, described in Scripture: "You shall stone

him to death with stones, because he sought to draw you away from the Lord your God. ... And all Israel shall hear, and fear, and never again do any such wickedness as this among you" (Dt 13:10–11).

You can tell by the wording of this passage that a few leaders must have been flinging sheep instead of stones for this punishment. (Why else would Moses need to be redundant about emphasizing that stoning was to be done with stones?) More importantly, however, you can see that there would be great benefit to the future stability of your congregation if you heeded these instructions from God's Word.

Now you might say that, as the New Testament Church, you are not bound by these Old Testament Jewish regulations. However, though the Apostle Paul may have exhorted his followers to cease being slaves to "old Testament Jewish regulations," when push came to shove he confessed his unswerving loyalty to them: "But this I admit to you, that according to the Way, which they call a sect, I worship the God of our fathers, *believing everything laid down by the law or written in the prophets*" (Acts 24:14; emphasis added).

What will you tell your elders and congregation they should do with the schismatics in your midst? What about those of your congregation who follow them, for the Scriptures command that you stone them as well (see Dt 13:6–11)? And how will you handle any fights that may break out among your warring flock? The Scriptures are very strict about what must be done. (You *must* read Dt 25:11–12)

Now I'm not bringing these regulations to your attention because I believe we should rethink how we deal with schismatics or family squabbles. Rather I'm pointing out how dangerous the doctrine of *sola scriptura* can be and has been ever since it was first coined by the Protestant reformers of the fifteenth and sixteenth centuries.

When the wisdom and guidance of Sacred Tradition and the Church Magisterium were thrown to the wind, Christendom fell victim to "every wind of doctrine" (Eph 4:14). In fact it was in this context that Paul begged the Ephesian believers to "maintain the unity of the Spirit," recognizing that Christ had gifted His Body with apostles, prophets, evangelists, pastors, and teachers to enable the Church to "attain to the unity of the Faith" (Eph 4:1–16).

Now, granted, some of the men and women who have held these positions of Church leadership throughout history have done much to sever this unity. Some have made unity so downright uncomfortable that we could nearly justify breaking free to be all that Paul exhorted a Church to be. But then on what side of Deuteronomy 13 would we fall? And once we had successfully dodged all the stones, when might we need to start throwing stones of our own?

I became more sensitized to these dangers of *sola scriptura* when I first used the CHNetwork's pamphlet entitled *Read the Bible and Catechism in a Year*. (Ironically, I was the one who laid out the reading plan, but it was years before I had a chance actually to use it!) During the years of my Protestant seminary training and pastorates, I had read through the Bible from cover to cover several times, but this was to be the first time since becoming a Catholic. In the process, my eyes were newly opened to the vast number of scripture passages that can pose grave difficulties for modern interpreters.

As I ponder my years as a Protestant pastor, I'm now much more aware of how I unconsciously divided Bible passages into two categories: those that were easily interpreted and preached (such as Jn 3:16, Rom 8:28, or Gal 2:20) and those that needed qualifying explanations (such as Matt 16:16–19, Jn 6:51–69, Heb 6:4–6, and Jas 2:24). I have come to realize that many of us Protestant clergy had an unspoken way of dealing with difficult, uncomfortable verses such as those in the latter list. We'd essentially let them sit until we heard or read someone we highly respected, and who, having passed the litmus tests of our other accepted dogmas, gave a plausible, believable, repeatable answer. This we then memorized and added to our list of quick knee-jerk responses.

The Westminster Confession, written in 1646 — the primary confession upon which I built my Presbyterian Calvinist faith — specified how Calvin and his co-religionists had explained we should deal with "difficult" scriptural passages: Scripture is to be explained by other scriptural texts. A less clear text is to be clarified by a more clear text.

Even so, there's a problem with this approach, which I didn't see for many years. How are we to determine for certain which of two texts is less clear, and which is more clear? Calvinists and Arminians, for example, have contradictory opinions about which verses relating to the "freedom of the will" are clear or unclear. So which are to be used to explain the others?

Whether you are Catholic or Protestant, I strongly encourage you to read carefully through the entire Bible, even those passages that are a bit tedious. As you do so, be sure to note the many, many verses that are not so easily explained at first glance. When you do, I pray you will grow to appreciate with great thanksgiving how gracious and loving Christ our Savior was when He gave us the Church guided by His Spirit. Obedience to her might keep us all from becoming candidates for stoning!

CHAPTER 10

Ten Verses I Never Saw

One of the more common experiences of Protestant converts to the Catholic Church is the discovery of verses "we never saw." Even after years of studying, preaching, and teaching the Bible, sometimes from cover to cover, all of a sudden a verse "we never saw" appears as if by magic and becomes an "Aha!" mind-opening, life-altering messenger of change that threatens our spiritual status quo.

Sometimes it's just recognizing an alternate, clearer meaning of a familiar verse. But often, as with some of the verses mentioned below, it seems as if some Catholic had sneaked in during the night and somehow put that verse there in the text!

The list of these surprise verses is endless, depending on a convert's former religious tradition. But the following are a few key verses that helped turn my heart toward home.

1 **Proverbs 3:5–6**
Trust in the Lord with all your heart,
and do not rely on your own insight.

> In all your ways acknowledge him,
> and he will make straight your paths.

Ever since my adult reawakening (read "born again" experience) at age 21, this proverb has been my "life verse." It rang true as a guide for all aspects of my life and ministry. But then during my nine years as a Presbyterian minister, I became desperately frustrated by the confusion of Protestantism.

I loved Jesus and believed that the Word of God was the one trustworthy, infallible rule of faith. But so did lots of the non-Presbyterian ministers and laymen I knew: Methodists, Baptists, Lutherans, Pentecostals, Congregationalists, and others. The problem was that we came up with sometimes radically different conclusions from the same verses.

With this particular, most favorite verse, for example, the questions grew over time: How do you "trust in the Lord with all your heart"? How can you make sure you're not "leaning on your own understanding"? We all had different opinions and lists of requirements.

How can you be certain that "in all your ways [you] acknowledge him" rather than using this as an excuse to advance your own agenda? And how can you be certain that the choices you have made were truly God's efforts to make "straight your paths" — when it may actually be the case that you are just using this verse to blame Him for your mistakes?

A verse I had always trusted suddenly became nebulous, immeasurable, and unreachable.

2 1 Timothy 3:14-15

I hope to come to you soon, but I am writing these instructions to you so that, if I am delayed, you may know how one ought to behave in the household of God, which is the church of the living God, the pillar and bulwark of the truth.

I've mentioned this verse several times already in this book because this was the key "verse I never saw" that started my journey home to the Church. Dr. Scott Hahn pulled this one on me.

"So, Marc, what is the pillar and foundation of truth?" he asked.

I answered, "The Bible, of course."

"Oh, yeah? But what does the Bible say?"

"What do you mean?"

When Scott told me to look up this verse, I suspected nothing. I had taught and preached through First Timothy many times. But when I read this verse, it was as if it had suddenly appeared from nowhere, and my jaw dropped.

The Church? Not the Bible? This realization alone sent my mind and essentially my whole life reeling. It didn't immediately direct my attention toward the Catholic Church; rather, it made my situation worse, for I had never considered any church to have this corner on truth. The question of *which* church was one I was not ready to broach.

3 2 Timothy 3:14-17
But as for you, continue in what you have learned and have firmly believed, knowing from whom you learned it and how from childhood you have been acquainted with the sacred writings which are able to instruct you for salvation through faith in Christ Jesus.

All scripture is inspired by God and profitable for teaching, for reproof, for correction, and for training in righteousness, that the man of God may be complete, equipped for every good work.

I and others had always turned to the second paragraph above (verses 16–17) to buttress our belief in *sola scriptura*. So to this verse I quickly turned my attention. Among many truths, three especially important ones became very clear, for the first time.

First, when Paul used the term "Scripture" in this verse, he could only have meant what we call the Old Testament. Only a portion of the New Testament documents had been written at that point, and the New Testament canon would not be established for another three hundred years!

Second, "all" Scripture does not mean "only" Scripture, nor specifically what we have in our modern Bibles.

Third, the emphasis in the context of this passage (verses 14–15) is the trustworthiness of the oral tradition Timothy had received from his mother and others — not *sola scriptura!*

4 2 Thessalonians 2:15

So then, brethren, stand firm and hold to the traditions which you were taught by us, either by word of mouth or by letter.

"Traditions"? This was a word we Protestants avoided like the swine flu. Yet our lives and theologies were steeped in traditions, whether or not we recognized or labeled them this way.

The traditions that these early Christians were to hold fast to were not just the written letters and Gospels that would eventually make up the New Testament. They also included elements of the oral tradition.

Even more significantly, the context of Paul's letters indicates that his normal, preferred way of passing along "what he had received" was oral. His written letters were, from his perspective, an accidental, sometimes unplanned add-on, dealing with immediate problems — leaving unsaid so much of what his readers had learned through oral teaching.

5 Matthew 16:13-19

Now when Jesus came into the district of Caesarea Philippi, he asked his disciples, "Who do men say that the Son of

man is?" And they said, "Some say John the Baptist, others
say Elijah, and others Jeremiah or one of the prophets." He
said to them, "But who do you say that I am?" Simon Peter
replied, "You are the Christ, the Son of the living God."

And Jesus answered him, "Blessed are you, Simon Bar-Jona!
For flesh and blood has not revealed this to you, but my
Father who is in heaven. And I tell you, you are Peter, and
on this rock I will build my church, and the powers of death
shall not prevail against it. I will give you the keys of the
kingdom of heaven, and whatever you bind on earth shall
be bound in heaven, and whatever you loose on earth shall
be loosed in heaven."

There is so much to discuss in this verse, so much I never
saw. I always knew that Catholics used this passage to argue
Petrine authority, but I wasn't convinced. To the naïvely ignorant, the English words "Peter" and "rock" are so different that
it seemed obvious to me that Jesus was referring to the faith
Simon Peter received as a gift from the Father.

For the more informed seminary-educated Bible students,
like me, the key was in the original Greek. The English name
"Peter" is the translation of *petros*, which I was taught meant
"little pebble," and "rock" is the translation of *petra*, which I was
taught meant "large boulder." It seemed an obvious disconnect,
so for years I taught specifically against Petrine authority.

Then, with some embarrassment I came to recognize,
through the witness of various Catholic apologists, the implications of an historical fact I knew all along: Behind the Greek
was the Aramaic that Jesus originally spoke, in which the word
for "Peter" and "rock" are identical — *kepha*. Once I saw that
Jesus had said essentially, "You are *kepha*, and on this *kepha* I
will build my Church," I knew I was in trouble.

53

6 **Revelation 14:13**
And I heard a voice from heaven saying, "Write this:
Blessed are the dead who die in the Lord henceforth."
"Blessed indeed," says the Spirit, "that they may rest from
their labors, for their deeds follow them!"

For years, as a Calvinist preacher I recited this verse at every funeral graveside service. I believed and taught *sola fide* ("faith alone"), discounting any place for works in the process of our salvation. But then, after my last funeral service as a minister, a family member of the deceased cornered me.

He asked, with a tremble in his voice, "What did you mean that Bill's deeds follow him?" I don't remember my response, but this was the first time I became aware of what I had been saying. This incident began a long study of what the New Testament and then the early Church Fathers taught about the mysterious but necessary synergistic connection between our faith and our obedience of faith (works).

7 **Romans 10:14-15**
But how are men to call upon him in whom they have not
believed? And how are they to believe in him of whom
they have never heard? And how are they to hear without
a preacher? And how can men preach unless they are sent?
As it is written, "How beautiful are the feet of those who
preach good news!"

I had always used these verses to champion the central importance of preaching and to defend my decision to give up my engineering career for the great privilege of becoming a preacher of the gospel. I was never bothered by the last phrase about the need of being "sent," because I could point to my ordination, where a gaggle of local ministers, elders, deacons, and laymen had laid their hands on my sweaty head to send me forth in the name of Jesus.

Nevertheless, my reading of the history and writings of the early Church Fathers and my rereading of the scriptural context of Paul's letters shed new light on this passage. I came to realize that Paul emphasized the necessity of being "sent" because the occasion of his letters was to combat the negative, heretical influences of self-appointed false teachers.

I had never thought of myself as a false teacher. But by what authority did those people send me forth? Who sent them? In this insight, I came to understand the importance of apostolic (literally, "those who have been sent") succession.

8 John 15:4 and 6:56

Abide in me, and I in you. As the branch cannot bear fruit by itself, unless it abides in the vine, neither can you, unless you abide in me. (15:4)

He who eats my flesh and drinks my blood abides in me, and I in him. (6:56)

The book of the Bible I used most often in preaching was the Gospel of John. The chapter from John that I used most often in preaching was chapter 15, the analogy of the vine and the branches. I bombarded my congregations with the need to "abide" or "remain" in Christ.

But what does this mean? I always had an answer, but then I looked closely for the first time at the only verse where Jesus Himself defines clearly what we must do to abide in Him. I was floored.

"He who eats my flesh and drinks my blood *abides in me and I in him.*" This verse led me to study a boatload of other verses in John 6 that I had never "seen" before. In the end, with regard to accepting Jesus at His word on the Eucharist, I found only one answer: "Where else can we go? Only you have the words of eternal life."

9 Colossians 1:24
Now I rejoice in my sufferings for your sake, and in my
flesh I complete what is lacking in Christ's afflictions for the
sake of his body, that is, the church.

I don't know whether I purposely avoided this verse or just blindly missed it, but for the first forty years of my life I never really "saw" it. And to be honest, when I finally saw it, I still didn't know what to do with it. Nothing in my Lutheran, Congregationalist, or Presbyterian backgrounds helped me understand how I or anyone could rejoice in suffering, and especially why anything was needed to complete the suffering of Christ — for I believed that nothing there was lacking!

Christ's suffering, death, and resurrection were sufficient and complete! To say anything else, I believed, was to attack the omnipotent completeness of God's sovereign grace. But then again, this was the Apostle Paul speaking in inerrant, infallible Scripture. And we were to imitate him as he imitated Jesus.

Finally, I read an apostolic letter by Pope John Paul II called *Salvifici Doloris,* "On the Christian Meaning of Human Suffering." It opened my eyes to a beautiful mystery that is recognized by the ancient Catholic understanding of redemptive suffering.

10 Luke 1:46-49
And Mary said, "My soul magnifies the Lord, and my spirit
rejoices in God my Savior, for he has regarded the low es-
tate of his handmaiden. For behold, henceforth all generations will call me blessed; for he who is mighty has done
great things for me, and holy is his name."

The most difficult hurdle for so many Protestant converts to get over is our Blessed Mother Mary. For most of my life, the only time Mary came into the picture was at Christmas — and dare I say, as a statue!

I never referred to her as "blessed." Yet Scripture says all generations will call her blessed. Why didn't I?

This question led me to see other verses for the first time, including John 19:26–27. There I read that, from the cross, Jesus gave His mother into the keeping of John, rather than any supposed siblings. By grace I began, in imitation of my Lord and Savior and eternal brother Jesus, to recognize Mary, too, as my blessed loving Mother.

CHAPTER 11

The Church Fathers I Never Saw

Scripture verses aren't the only kind of text I somehow "never saw" before I started on the journey home to the Catholic Church. I also missed a number of important passages in the writings of the Church Fathers. This experience seems to be nearly universal among converts, who often note how reading the Fathers, either for the first time or for the first time with awareness, convinced them that the early Church was amazingly Catholic and certainly not Protestant!

With this experience in mind, here's a small sampling of significant quotes from these early Christian writers that demonstrate the presence of Catholic teaching and practice. The list could be almost endless, but the following passages in particular were influential in my own conversion.

> Our apostles knew through our Lord Jesus Christ that there would be strife for the office of bishop. For this reason, therefore, having received perfect foreknowledge, they

appointed those who have already been mentioned, and afterwards added the further provision that, if they should die, other approved men should succeed to their ministry.

St. Clement of Rome
Letter to the Corinthians, 44:1–2, c. A.D. 95

The majority of conservative scholars throughout Christian history — whether Catholic, Orthodox, or Protestant — have affirmed that the author of these words was the bishop of Rome, probably the fourth, with St. Peter being the first. Certainly what he wrote here did not describe any form of Protestantism I knew.

The author implies that the Apostles intended for the Church to be led by bishops who would then be succeeded by other bishops, not individuals who merely and subjectively "sensed" that God was calling them into ministry or to start their own church. Nor does it allow for a random group of believers to bond together and elect their leader. In this very early passage, written in the generation that immediately followed the Apostles, we find the assumption of a continuous apostolic succession.

> You must follow the bishop as Jesus Christ follows the
> Father, and the presbytery as you would the Apostles.
> Reverence the deacons as you would the command of God.
> Let no one do anything of concern to the Church without
> the bishop. Let that be considered a valid Eucharist which
> is celebrated by the bishop, or by one whom he appoints.
> Wherever the bishop appears, let the people be there, just as
> wherever Jesus Christ is, there is the Catholic Church.

St. Ignatius of Antioch
Letter to the Smyrnaeans, 8:1–2, A.D. 107

There is much here that is certainly not Protestant. Abandoning the bishop, his presbytery of priests, and his deacons meant abandoning the "Catholic Church" (the first recorded use of this title). And what is the significance of a "valid" Eucharist? Does this imply that there were Christians celebrating the Eucharist, or maybe calling it the Lord's Supper, on their own apart from a bishop's permission or authority? If the rite were only "symbolic," then what difference would it make?

> The Church, having received this preaching and this faith, although she is disseminated throughout the whole world, yet guarded it, as if she occupied but one house. She likewise believes these things just as if she had but one soul and one and the same heart and harmoniously she proclaims them and teaches them and hands them down, as if she possessed but one mouth. For, while the languages of the world are diverse, nevertheless, the authority of the Tradition is one and the same.
>
> **St. Irenaeus**
> *Against Heresies*, 1, 10, 2, c. A.D. 190

Does this passage form a reasonable basis for the trajectory of today's thousands of independent denominations, each with their own set of beliefs and practices? Or does it rather reveal an assumption by St. Irenaeus that there was one Church, with "one soul and one and the same heart," spread out as far as the one gospel message (the Tradition) had reached?

> They abstain from the Eucharist and from prayer, because they do not confess that the Eucharist is the Flesh of our Savior Jesus Christ, Flesh which suffered for our sins and which the Father, in His goodness, raised up again.
>
> **St. Ignatius of Antioch**
> *Letter to the Smyrnaeans*, 7:1, A.D. 107

> We call this food Eucharist; and no one else is permitted
> to partake of it, except one who believes our teaching to be
> true and who has been washed in the washing which is for
> the remission of sins and for regeneration, and is thereby
> living as Christ has enjoined. For not as common bread nor
> common drink do we receive these; but since Jesus Christ
> our Savior was made incarnate by the word of God and had
> both flesh and blood for our salvation, so too, as we have
> been taught, the food which has been made into the Eucha-
> rist by the Eucharistic prayer set down by Him, and by the
> change of which our blood and flesh is nurtured, is both the
> flesh and the blood of that incarnated Jesus.

St. Justin Martyr
First Apology, 66, A.D. 151

Everything in these two passages conforms to Catholic
doctrine and practice concerning Baptism, the Eucharist, and
the acceptance of Church teaching for reception of the sacraments. As a Protestant, I had disavowed nearly all this teaching, preaching against it and explaining it otherwise.

The significance of the following quote from St. Clement,
the fourth bishop of Rome, is this: Why is the bishop of Rome,
Italy, expecting obedience of a church in Corinth, Greece?
Though Greece at this time was under Roman control, still
there was no reason to expect a leader of a religious sect in
Rome to have any clout over a similar group of religious sec-
tarians in Greece — unless that leader was a bishop with authority over them.

> Owing to the sudden and repeated calamities and misfor-
> tunes which have befallen us, we must acknowledge that
> we have been somewhat tardy in turning our attention to
> the matters in dispute among you, beloved. … Accept our
> counsel, and you will have nothing to regret. … If anyone
> disobey the things which have been said by Him through
> us, let them know that they will involve themselves in

> transgression and in no small danger. ... You will afford us
> joy and gladness if, being obedient to the things which we
> have written through the Holy Spirit, you will root out the
> wicked passion of jealousy.

St. Clement of Rome
Letter to the Corinthians, 1: 58–59, 63, A.D. 80

St. Ignatius, bishop of Antioch, who was from the East, wrote seven letters to seven key early churches. But it was only in his letter to the church in Rome that he expressed such exalted praise of the bishop:

> Ignatius ... to the church also which holds the presidency
> in the place of the country of the Romans, worthy of God,
> worthy of honor, worthy of blessing, worthy of praise, wor-
> thy of success, worthy of sanctification, and, because you
> hold the presidency in love, named after Christ and named
> after the Father.

St. Ignatius of Antioch
Letter to the Romans, 1:1, A.D. 110

St. Irenaeus, a bishop from the region of France who learned his faith from St. Polycarp, who learned his faith from the Apostle John, demonstrates in the following passage the assumption of his day: All churches must agree with the Church of Rome.

> It is possible, then, for every Church, who may wish to
> know the truth, to contemplate the tradition of the Apostles
> which has been made known throughout the whole world.
> And we are in a position to enumerate those who were in-
> stituted bishops by the Apostles, and their successors to our
> own times. ... But since it would be too long to enumerate
> in such a volume as this the successions of all the churches,
> we shall confound all those who, in whatever manner,
> whether through self-satisfaction or vainglory, or through
> blindness and wicked opinion, assemble other than where

it is proper, by pointing out here the successions of the bishops of the greatest and most ancient Church known to all, founded and organized at Rome by the two most glorious Apostles, Peter and Paul, that Church which has the tradition and the faith which comes down to us after having been announced to men by the Apostles. For with this Church, because of its superior origin, all churches must agree, that is, all the faithful in the whole world; and it is in her that the faithful everywhere have maintained the apostolic tradition.

St. Irenaeus
Against Heresies, 3, 3, 1–2, c. A.D. 190

How would a Protestant have to rewrite such a passage to make it conform to Protestant teaching?

In the next quote, St. Cyprian of Carthage, a third-century African bishop, clearly and firmly defended the primacy of the Bishop of Rome:

The Lord says to Peter: "I say to you," He says, "that you are Peter, and upon this rock I will build my Church.' ... On him He builds the Church, and to him He gives the command to feed the sheep; and although He assigns a like power to all the Apostles, yet He founded a single chair, and He established by His own authority a source and an intrinsic reason for that unity. Indeed, the others were that also which Peter was; but a primacy is given to Peter, whereby it is made clear that there is but one Church and one chair. So too, all are shepherds, and the flock is shown to be one, fed by all the Apostles in single-minded accord. If someone does not hold fast to this unity of Peter, can he imagine that he still holds the faith? If he desert the chair of Peter upon whom the Church was built, can he still be confident that he is in the Church?

St. Cyprian of Carthage
The Unity of the Catholic Church, A.D. 251

The celebrated nineteenth-century English convert John Henry Cardinal Newman (1801–1890) made an important observation about this statement in his *Essay on the Development of Doctrine:* This defense of the primacy of the bishop of Rome, expressed rhetorically and not defensively, predates by nearly one hundred years the definitions of the Trinity and the divinity of Christ by ecumenical councils!

Consider these two quotes from two highly influential churchmen of the fourth century addressing the sacrilege of schism from the Church established by Jesus in His apostles, centered on St. Peter:

> Those who do not have the succession of Peter do not hold the chair of Peter, which they rend by wicked schism; and this, too, they do, wickedly denying that sins can be forgiven even in the Church, whereas it was said to Peter: "I will give you the keys of the kingdom of heaven, and whatever you bind on earth shall be bound also in heaven, and whatever you loose on earth shall be loosed also in heaven." And the vessel of divine election himself said: "If you have forgiven anything to any one, I forgive also, for what I have forgiven I have done for your sakes in the person of Christ.
>
> **St. Ambrose of Milan**
> *On Penance*, I:VII, 33, c. A.D. 390
>
> There is nothing more serious than the sacrilege of schism because there is no just cause for severing the unity of the Church.
>
> **St. Augustine**
> *Treatise on Baptism Against the Donatists*, V, 1, A.D. 400

Finally, this last quote from the early second century beckons to those outside the Church to come home:

> For as many as are of God and of Jesus Christ are also with the bishop. And as many as shall, in the exercise of repen-

tance, return into the unity of the Church, these, too, shall belong to God, that they may live according to Jesus Christ. Do not err, my brethren. If any man follows him that makes a schism in the Church, he shall not inherit the kingdom of God. If any one walks according to a strange opinion, he agrees not with the passion of Christ.

St. Ignatius of Antioch
Letter to the Philadelphians, 3.2, c. A.D. 110

CHAPTER 12

"As the Good Book Says!"

Over the years my sons have had roles in several musical productions with our local community theatre. Once my oldest son, Jon Marc, was asked to play the rabbi's son in the wonderful musical *Fiddler on the Roof,* a story set in a Jewish village in Russia at the turn of the last century. Our middle son, Peter, had the role of a village youth.

After a week of rehearsals, they had not yet found someone to play Perchik, the socialist student who wins the hand of Hodel, the second daughter of the story's main protagonist, Tevye. One Sunday afternoon, I made the mistake of helping out by reading the part. Sure enough, I became Perchik.

I wasn't pursuing this role. Lord knows I have more than enough to do without getting involved in a major stage production! But with hindsight I now know that it was surely God's plan, because it was such an enriching experience. Let me explain.

First, after weeks of listening to the lines of Tevye (recited by a seventy-nine-year-old Jewish judge who was playing the role for the seventh time), I became convinced that there is no greater model for intimate, personal prayer than the devotional habits of this Russian Jewish character. Rent the DVD, watch, and learn. Tevye believes deeply in the Lord; he lives by the Good Book and talks with God out of an awesome respect, even when he complains. I wish we all prayed both our spontaneous and our formal prayers as intimately and sincerely as he does.

"On the other hand" (a phrase used many times by this faithful Jew), this play provides an interesting illustration of the problem that comes from merely private interpretation of both Tradition and the Scriptures.

Tevye is fond of quoting Scripture to make a point, and he always introduces such a quote with the words, "As the Good Book says …" On one occasion, while praying, he even tries to make a point to God by quoting the Scripture.

"As the Good Book says …" he begins. Then he catches himself as he realizes the irony of talking to the Lord that way. So he continues: "But who am *I* to tell *You* what the Good Book says?"

One of the running gags in the story is the interesting spin put on the words of the Good Book by both Tevye and the local rabbi. Sometimes Tevye even imputes to Scripture words that aren't there. (Does that sound familiar?)

One of my favorite examples of this kind of humor comes when Tevye states, "As the Good Book says, 'When a poor man eats a chicken, one of them is sick.'" The rabbi's son (played by my son Jon Marc) replies, "Where does the Good Book say that?" And Tevye replies, "I don't know, but somewhere it says something about a chicken!"

Nowhere is the danger of private interpretation more evident than in the scene where my character teaches Tevye's two innocent young daughters about the "clear" meaning of the biblical story of Laban and Jacob. And what might that meaning be? "One must never trust an employer!"

In a sense, the entire play is about how a family is to live out the truths of Scripture and Tradition in the midst of pressures from society and culture.

The most riveting image of the play is that of a fiddler playing precariously on the peak of a roof. His situation is a visual metaphor for the Jewish family — and the entire Jewish people. They must work to maintain their balance as they "play" the "music" of life, taking their stand on the security of long-held beliefs and customs while trying to avoid the slippery slopes of untested ways.

How many Protestant Christians, I sometimes wonder, find themselves in a similar situation? They are trying to live their lives and bring up their children based on what they *think* God is teaching them through the Bible *alone*, through the interpretations of their local minister, or through the unexamined traditions of their particular denomination. But they find those private interpretations to be confusing and contradictory, a difficult place to stand without losing balance.

There's a message in this play for Catholics as well who practice the rules and rituals of their faith without knowing the reasons why. For when the surrounding culture or even members of our families challenge our beliefs (as happened in the play), do we understand our Catholic faith enough to stand firm on what is true?

In the play, Tevye takes his stand on a tradition that, by the end, has crumbled under the weight of his circumstances. In Protestant practice, the tradition of Bible *alone* is maintained as the only firm place to stand. But under the weight of rationalism, individualism, and indifferentism, that tradition also crumbles.

Thank God that He gave us the Church, guided, protected, and preserved by the Holy Spirit, to help us understand how to live our lives under the guidance of both Tradition and Scripture. Now if we can only be humble and submissive enough to listen and obey joyfully!

Oh, and I learned one last important personal lesson from *Fiddler on the Roof*. After five performances in which I had portrayed my role with few noticeable flaws (and, might I add, with much acclaim), the good Lord brought me back down to earth — just in case I had any fleeting ideas that I should quit my day job and head off to Hollywood. In the sixth and final performance, in the scene where my character is persuading the two youngest daughters that the Bible teaches socialist ideals, the Lord had some fun with me.

The younger children exited, leaving me with their two older sisters, Hodel and Chava. I was to sit on a small bench to read, awaiting Hodel's mild rebuke. As I sat down and listened to her say, "That was a very interesting interpretation!" the bench suddenly crumbled beneath my weight.

I didn't merely fall backwards. Both of my feet went up into the air, reminiscent of a Chevy Chase pratfall. Scrambling up as quickly as a fifty-year-old can, I noticed that Hodel and Chava were struggling to keep from splitting their sides laughing.

Regaining my composure, I responded, "Not as interesting as that fall!" and then went on with the scene as if nothing had happened. The moral of this story: Next time they need to find a lighter Perchik!

CHAPTER 13

The Problem With Protestantism: It Preaches!

Stand in the middle of an average-size American town, and you will be surrounded by Christian churches of every conceivable denomination, positioned sometimes right across from each other or on opposite street corners. Is there something wrong with this picture?

I know that nearly every convert to the Catholic faith has faced this conundrum, but what about adherents of other Christian traditions? The data, from Protestant sources, indicates that there are over thirty thousand such groups — some quite large, with hundreds of local congregations, while hundreds of others have only a few devoted members. Protestant sources also claim that this number continues to grow at the rate of one new church every five days!

Doesn't this situation make you pause even for a moment? This is surely a far cry from the unity Jesus intended and prayed for in John 17, and from the "one holy, Catholic, and apostolic Church" defined at the Council of Nicaea.

The first congregation I served as a Presbyterian pastor was called Second Presbyterian Church. First Presbyterian was one block away, and the two existed because of a split that had occurred nearly 150 years earlier over whether a particular baby who had died unbaptized was going to heaven or hell. The pastor and half of the congregation voted for hell; the dissenting half voted for heaven and left to form their own congregation a block away.

Which group was right, how does one determine this, and were they correct in splitting over this issue?

Within easy walking distance of these two now-speaking-yet-still-divided Presbyterian congregations stood:

- a United Methodist church (which originally was an Evangelical United Brethren church before the merger)

- a Lutheran church (now Evangelical Lutheran Church of America after a different merger)

- an Episcopal church (the American version of the Anglican Church, started after the break caused by the American Revolution)

- a small Free Methodist church (one branch of the Wesleyan tradition)

- a Baptist church (American Baptist as opposed to Southern Baptist, Freewill Baptist, or Independent Baptist)

- a Salvation Army church

- an independent Bible church, with a name something like "Christian Fellowship Church."

Is this collection of divided voices what Jesus hoped and prayed for?

Many have tried to cover up this apparent disunity by claiming that denominationalism is somehow God's plan, almost as if a strange form of "transubstantiation" has occurred in the Church itself: Under the appearance of disunity exists the real substance of an invisible unity. Yet Jesus said that the unity of His followers would be visible in the Apostles and their disciples, and especially in their love for one another (see Jn 13).

Our disunity is at least a result of our inability to love those who think differently, so let's not blame God for the results of our pride.

But why are there so many divergent Christian groups, especially when most of them are founded on the idea that the Bible *alone* is sufficient to lead us into all truth? Again let's not blame the inspired, inerrant Word of God for this proliferating confusion. I think the problem stems from the basic fact that the words of Scripture are so powerfully *preachable*. Sometimes a great blessing, when misused, can lead to a curse!

You can take a verse such as John 3:16 — "For God so loved the world that he gave his only begotten son, that whoever believes in him should not perish but have eternal life" — and preach it! If the preacher is particularly skilled at preaching, and is pleasing to the eyes; and if what he or she has to say seems to be food for an ailing soul and full of wisdom (see Gn 3:6); then people will follow in droves! Sad to say, though, some self-proclaimed preachers take the fact of "people following" as a confirmation that what they have preached must be true.

The history of Christianity is deluged with preachers who have put together their own new collection of Bible verses and consequently preached themselves and their followers into a new denomination or sect. For example, by combining one specific collection of apocalyptic verses, the Bible teacher James

Darby established a whole new strand of Protestantism that adopted the historically novel idea of an impending "rapture."

Combining another set of verses that emphasized "by His stripes we are healed" and "whatever you ask in my name I will do for you," many have preached themselves and their followers quite nicely into large, growing sects believing that anyone with sufficient faith should be healthy and rich.

Combining a totally different set of Bible verses that focus on a Christian's responsibility to feed, clothe, and care for the poor, many others follow a social gospel. Combining yet another collection of carefully chosen verses, this time emphasizing the total depravity of all humankind and the sovereignty of God, many have preached thousands of people into Lutheranism or Calvinism or one of their spin-offs. And using the same inspired Bible, Methodists, Baptists, Pentecostals, Nazarenes, Congregationalists, Episcopalians, and even Unitarian-Universalists have each emphasized their own selection of key verses and preached themselves into independent existence.

All these groups, and many more, claim that the Bible is the only God-given source of truth. Yet they can't find agreement with one another in their preaching.

It seems obvious, at least to me, that just because a notion is *preachable* doesn't make it true. Yet the average person, with all the usual needs and feelings of spiritual hunger, can easily be swayed to believe otherwise.

In the Broadway musical *The Music Man* we encounter a vivid portrayal of this very phenomenon in the guise of a musical instruments salesman. How do you sell something to people that they neither need nor want? The music man, through his winsome homiletic skills, convinced an entire town not only that there was "trouble in River City," but that what he had to sell was the very answer they needed.

Before he was done, every parent in town had purchased an instrument and a uniform. And even in the end, when the beauty of the uniforms couldn't cover up the fact that the kids couldn't play a lick, his charismatic preaching was able to convince them that all that mattered was for their children to look great in uniforms.

Thousands, even millions, of sincere people have followed charismatic "music men" into aberrant forms of Christianity because what these winsome preachers had formulated on their own from Scripture was convincingly *preachable*. Here's the great danger: The preacher himself can become so convinced and excited about what he has "discovered" that he can grow blind to the fact that what he is preaching is totally brand new, with only a fleeting connection to the truth Jesus delivered to His apostles.

Maybe the most common characteristic of these man-made religions is that they present an easy gospel, one without suffering or effort, and overflowing with guarantees. These new theologies have nothing like that proclaimed by the great preacher St. Francis de Sales (1567–1622), who devoted his life to bringing back those who had been lured away into new theologies:

> "For you have need for patience that, doing the will of God, you may receive the promise," says the apostle (Heb 10.36). True, for our Savior himself has declared, "By your patience you will win your souls" (Luke 21.19). It is man's great happiness to possess his own soul … and the more perfect our patience the more completely do we possess our souls. We must often recall that our Lord has saved us by his suffering and endurance and that we must work out our salvation by sufferings and afflictions, enduring with all possible meekness the injuries, denials, and discomforts we meet." *(Introduction to the Devout Life, III, 3)*

How many of the more than thirty thousand Christian groups that exist today, and are expanding exponentially, have kept and proclaim the fullness of the gospel message, with both its promises and demands? I dare say, and ask your patience for my boldness, that through all of my searching and preaching, I have found this fullness only in the teachings of the Catholic Church, a two-thousand-year-old Church whose message is truly *preachable*!

CHAPTER 14

How to Make the Best Coffee by Dr. Always Fidgeting

Want to ensure that you'll start your day with only the best possible coffee?

The modern rage is coffee. Who would have thought twenty years ago that anyone would pay $3.50 a cup! But everywhere there are outlets enticing our sophisticated lust for a more flavorful, more jolting cup of java (as the more sophisticated call it).

But what really makes one cup of coffee better than another? Many opinions compete in answer to this crucial question. Over the past ten years, I have had the privilege of traveling the world. As a result, I have tasted the full range of brews, from the best to the worst, and now out of sheer love for my fellow man, I share this knowledge with you. You need search no further for the answer.

The key to making the best coffee is not primarily a function of the exotic location where the beans are cultivated; or how they were dried or decaffeinated; or what might be their grind, water purity, or brewing temperature; or how long the coffee has remained cooking on the burner. No, all these factors may influence the taste or potency, but none is the main factor in producing a truly superior cup of java.

The key to good coffee — are you ready — is using a fresh filter! I don't mean merely using a clean filter with each new brew, or choosing between bleached, unbleached, or environmentally sensitive recycled paper, though these choices play a major factor. No, I mean this: Do you keep your filters *fresh?*

Usually filters come in packets of fifty or a hundred and generally in a box or plastic bag. You may never have thought of this, but as with potato chips, crackers, or cookies, keeping the bag sealed, once opened, makes all the difference in the world! Would you eat a chip or cracker from a bag that's been left open for weeks? Of course not! And since coffee filters are processed from cellulose, which is plant matter not unlike potatoes or wheat, it's only reasonable to expect that fresh filters make better coffee than stale filters.

Why this is so remains a mystery, though renowned researcher Dr. Putn Juan Ovahonyi believes that the oxidation that results from extended exposure to air causes a shift in the molecular structure of one of the side-chains of the cellulose molecule, which in turn forms a zwitterion linkage with two of the naturally occurring amino acids in coffee beans. These amino acids, which produce the flavors sought after by discerning coffee drinkers, are subsequently extracted from the brewing coffee into the filter, leaving the coffee with what researchers technically label a "cardboard" taste.

More research is needed, of course, but since every day of our lives begins with and is sustained by that essential cup of coffee, and since our alertness, our effectiveness, even our compatibility with family, friends, and coworkers depends upon the coffee we drink, would you risk any of this by failing to make a little extra effort every day to ensure that your coffee filters are kept fresh and supple?

And since this is so crucial to every area of your life — physical, emotional, relational, and spiritual — why trust this matter to the less-than-adequate containers provided by the filter manufacturers? Isn't it reasonable that they want the un-informed public to allow their filters to go stale so they are forced to buy more and more filters?

Well, you need worry no longer about getting anything less than the best morning coffee by storing your filters in the vacuum-sealed, liquid-nitrogen-cooled, solar-powered St. Yakuma's Coffee Minisculator, or SAYACOMIN for short. The SAYACOMIN, guaranteed to keep your coffee filters at the ideal temperature and humidity for nothing short of the best coffee you ever tasted, can be yours for only ten payments of $19.95.

And if you act now and contact us within the next ten minutes, then you are gullible enough to believe almost any-thing proffered by today's "answer to all your worries," self-proclaimed, self-appointed Bible preachers.

Just because something sounds feasible from someone be-lievable doesn't make it reasonable.

CHAPTER 15

Does Faith Replace the Law?

The Apostle Paul wrote to the Galatians: "A person is not justified by works of the law but through faith in Jesus Christ" (Gal 2:16). Following the lead of the Protestant reformer Martin Luther, millions of Christians have set faith in Christ over and against obedience to the law, as if one supplants the other.

Nevertheless, this "faith versus law" idea is a false opposition that has led to much chaos and confusion in Christendom. Neither Jesus nor St. Paul ever even implied that once we have faith we no longer need to obey the laws of God.

In Matthew 5:17-20, Jesus said:

> Do not think that I have come to abolish the law and the prophets. I have come not to abolish them but to fulfill them. For truly, I say to you, until heaven and earth pass away, not an iota, not a dot, will pass from the law until all is accomplished. Whoever then relaxes one of the least of these commandments and teaches men so, shall be called least in the kingdom of heaven; but he who does them and teaches them shall be called great in the kingdom of heaven.

Note the implication of Jesus' warning here: We must avoid preachers who claim that He, His apostles, His Church, or His Word have said that we no longer need to be obedient to the commandments of God — but should instead live by "faith alone."

For his part, St. Paul announced: "I worship the God of our fathers, believing everything laid down by the law or written in the prophets" (Acts 24:14). So what should we think about the Apostles' apparent denigration of the law? Consider a useful analogy.

We are called to be obedient to the laws of our nation, state, and community, unless they contradict the laws of God. When we add up these civil laws, regulations, and rules, our lives may seem quite constrained. We might even grow bitter about this constraint, complaining how impossible it is to keep these laws perfectly (especially if we're in a hurry while driving).

Influenced by such bitterness, we might develop an attitude in which we strive to be obedient to all these laws even while we resent those who implement and enforce them. We might even believe that we're faithful, loyal citizens just because we haven't broken any major laws — or at least haven't been caught doing so — while at the same time only giving lip service to the institutions and people who rule over us.

A similar thing happened among the ancient Israelites. Following God's laws had become more important to many of them than loving God, and St. Paul's conversion was at least in part a reaction to this situation.

Now apply Luther's interpretation of Paul — rejecting the law as if it were opposed to faith — to our lives as American citizens. To do so would mean we must love and have faith in our government and her leaders while ignoring their laws. "I'm unable to follow the laws because of my sinfulness, my weakness of character and self-control," we would have to conclude. "So I'll have faith in the righteousness of my local representative, which will shield me from incarceration!"

Obviously, that approach wouldn't work in our life as citizens of this country. Nor does it work in our spiritual life as citizens of God's kingdom.

As St. Paul explains, the laws that God gave His people served as a custodian, guiding and protecting them on their journey of faith until, through Christ, they received salvation and the grace to fulfill the law (see Gal 3:24). But the laws themselves were never to be ignored or cast aside.

They could, however, be altered under the guidance of God. Just as we find in the Old Testament that God sometimes led His hand-chosen leaders to adjust the laws, so in the New Testament we find that God has sometimes led His Church to adjust the laws to which we must remain obedient (see Acts 15).

Our faith in Christ never frees us from this obligation. But by the grace we receive through faith, we're empowered, and humbled, to grow in holiness as we embrace the laws of God.

CHAPTER 16

My Journey to the Eucharist

In my journey of faith, the Lord has brought me through a wide range of Christian traditions, each of which had a different view of the Lord's Supper.

I was baptized, catechized, and confirmed a Lutheran, so I was basically weaned on the Lutheran view of *consubstantiation*. According to this traditional Lutheran teaching, at the Lord's Supper the real substance of Christ's Body and Blood are present *alongside* the substance of the bread and wine. This of course differs from the Catholic doctrine of *transubstantiation*, which tells us that in a valid Eucharist, the substance of the bread and wine is *changed into* the substance of Christ's Body and Blood. In Lutheran teaching, Christ is truly present in Communion, but the substance of the bread and wine remains as well.

The first Sunday of every month, we would process forward and kneel at the front altar to receive a piece of cubed bread and to drink wine from small individual cups. I vaguely remember being taught that I was truly receiving Jesus, but I honestly don't remember taking the Sacrament very seriously. It was more a rite of passage for me, a sign that I had become a full-fledged adult member of the church.

I don't think I ever gave much thought to the notion that Jesus was present in the cubed pieces of white bread and the wine, nor was this what I was actually taught. The residual bread and wine after worship were certainly not treated as if Jesus were actually present in them, nor would it ever have come to our minds to "adore" these elements, since they had remained just bread and wine.

After abandoning my Christian faith several years into college, I had an adult conversion experience as a Congregationalist. In that tradition, again once a month, we celebrated the Lord's Supper. But we passed down the pews plates of cubed bread and small cups of non-alcoholic grape juice.

This ritual, we believed, was merely a memorial meal in which we celebrated Christ's sacrifice for our sins. There was no implication whatsoever that Jesus was truly present in the bread and juice. The minister stressed instead that He was there in our hearts through the presence of the Holy Spirit.

At the interdenominational, evangelical seminary I attended, our classes taught a wide diversity of views. The professors placed no weight on any particular interpretation, primarily because there were so many different positions held by the more than thirty different denominations represented.

Later as an ordained Presbyterian minister, I celebrated the "Table of the Lord," much as we had as Congregationalists. In this denomination, however, we taught that Jesus was present in a unique way in Communion, through our faith.

As I compare these various traditions of my past to what I have come to believe as a Catholic, several conclusions occur to me.

First, it is much more clear to me now than it ever was before how confusing and contradictory are the great variety of views that have arisen since the Reformation. Before the Reformation a single view of the Eucharist had been almost unanimously accepted by Christians in all ages, in all languages, in all cultures, at all times. Since the Reformation so many different views have arisen that among non-Catholic Christians, the Lord's Supper is generally not all that important.

My challenge to any Protestant Christian is to examine closely the history of this sacrament. Examine the primary sources of the first fifteen centuries of Christianity. What you will learn, among many things, is that the Eucharist has always been considered the essential center of Christian worship and life.

In trying to remember the gist of some of the arguments I formerly used against the Catholic view of transubstantiation, I checked a few of my old systematic theology books. In each case the authors gave similar arguments, but one in particular made the Catholic literal view a moot point. For instance, here is the brief argument given by Louis Berkhof in his *Systematic Theology* (Eerdmans, 1939), the preferred text on the subject at my evangelical seminary:

> The Church of Rome makes the [linking verb] "is" emphatic. Jesus meant to say that what He held in His hands was really His body, though it looked and tasted like bread. But this is a thoroughly untenable position. In all probability Jesus spoke Aramaic and used no copula at all. And while He stood before the disciples in the body, He could not very well say to His disciples in all seriousness that He held His body in His hand. Moreover, even on the Roman Catholic view, He could not truthfully say, "This is my body," but could only say, "This is now becoming my body" (p. 649).

I once hung on every word written by Professor Berkhof. But now I find it remarkable that, in but three sentences, he quickly and matter-of-factly wrote off as "thoroughly untenable" nearly two thousand years of consistent Catholic testimony.

In response, we might note first that it is true both the Hebrew and Aramaic languages do not use a word for what reads here in English as the verb "is." However, giving Professor Berkhof the benefit of the doubt and presuming he was much too busy and pressed to check his sources, we should note that anyone who has studied Hebrew knows that even though this is true, it doesn't mean what Berkhof and others conclude. The truth is that in statements such as "David is king" or "This is my body," where the present tense uses only juxtaposed nouns or demonstrative pronouns, the "is" is very strongly presumed. It is only with other tenses, such as past or future, where a specific form of the verb meaning "to be" is added.

Berkhof and others have drawn a false theological conclusion from a grammatical construct. We find a similar presumption of meaning in certain English constructions, such as when we say, "Butch is my dog, and Rover, too." We don't need to say "is" in the second clause to know it is there. The same was true in the Hebrew and Aramaic constructions.

I find it also remarkable — and again I give them the benefit of busyness and pressed deadlines — that some of the same anti-Catholic authors who make the above claim also hang their hat on the distinctions in the Greek text of Matthew 16:18. As I noted in an earlier chapter, they fail to mention that the same Aramaic that Jesus would have spoken (which lies behind the Greek) had only one word for "rock," *kepha*. So their forced distinction between "You are *Peter*" (Greek *Petros*, masculine, meaning "small pebble") and "on this *rock*" (*Petra*, feminine, "rock") is *truly* "thoroughly untenable."

In the latter part of Professor Berkhof's disclaimer, he is really basing his argument on a weak form of rationalism, which carries no particular weight or authority; it is merely his opinion. A similar argument could be made for many miraculous realities: "This can't be God standing before me!" a first-century Jew may have exclaimed. "God is omnipotent, omnipresent, and omniscient, yet you say this dirty, sweaty Galilean man standing before me, who bleeds and weeps and doesn't know the time of his Second Coming, is God? You can't be serious!"

Based on the most literal interpretation of Sacred Scripture, the witness of the Apostles and the early Church Fathers, and the writings of faithful Catholic teachers throughout the centuries, I have concluded that the Catholic belief in the Real Presence of the Body and Blood, Soul and Divinity of Jesus Christ in the Eucharist is a reasonable conclusion. Catholics accept this dogma by faith — not faith in philosophy and reason, but faith in the words of Jesus. He said that He would give His Holy Spirit to the Church to lead her into all truth, and that the gates of hell would not prevail against her (see Jn 6:13; Mt 16:18).

Catholics believe transubstantiation is possible because they believe that for God nothing is impossible (see Lk 1:37). And they also believe, as Proverbs 3:5 insists, that we must not rely on our own understanding — for we may find that, because of our busyness and our pressed deadlines, we have merely accepted the opinions of other busy people, and have all along been wrong.

CHAPTER 17

The Winnowing Effect of the Eucharist

I'm assuming at least three types of readers for this book: those who are presently on the journey considering the Catholic faith, those who have already made it "home," and those who are praying for both, lifelong Catholics who are partners in this work. It's also possible, of course, that some non-inquiring, non-Catholics might be reading, and they might be wondering what could possibly compel otherwise happy non-Catholic Christians to consider and then convert to the Catholic faith?

Surprisingly, these converts have many, many reasons. But one of the most important is found in John 6. In fact, all of chapter 6 — not just those controversial verses in the 50s — directly addresses why so many have concluded they must become Catholic, for one of the primary themes of this powerful chapter is winnowing: thinning down the crowd to those who truly believe.

John 6 begins with the miraculous feeding of the five thousand. As a result, "when the people saw the sign which he had done, they said, 'This is indeed the prophet who is to come into the world!'" (Jn 6:14). So the chapter begins with a large crowd of people who, with the courage of "group think," proclaim their faith in Jesus.

But Jesus wasn't convinced. The next day, when He was preaching in the synagogue at Capernaum (see Jn 6:59), He posed the subject that would serve to winnow down this crowd:

> Jesus answered them, "Truly, truly, I say to you, you seek me, not because you saw signs, but because you ate your fill of the loaves. Do not labor for the food which perishes, but for the food which endures to eternal life, which the Son of man will give to you; for on him has God the Father set his seal." (Jn 6:26–27)

In response, the crowd, or at least one or two of their spokesmen, asked the age-old question, "What must we do, to be doing the works of God?" (Jn 6:28).

As Jews, the crowd had an age-old answer to this question. But people are always seeking an easier answer than the one they already have. So Jesus gave them an answer they didn't expect. He essentially drew a line in the sand, based on their very exclamation of faith, and dared them to cross it: "This is the work of God, that you believe in him whom he has sent" (Jn 6:29).

The crowd responded: "Then what sign do you do, that we may see, and believe you? What work do you perform? Our fathers ate the manna in the wilderness; as it is written, 'He gave them bread from heaven to eat'" (Jn 6:30–31).

This seems like an amazingly sophisticated response for your average uneducated rural Jewish audience. They even quoted the prophet Nehemiah (see Neh 9:15). Could one of the Pharisees, buried in the crowd, have been taunting Jesus, trying to trick Him into blasphemy?

Jesus, knowing what is in the hearts of men (as John tells us earlier), responded not flippantly, but with His most serious form of proclamation: "Truly, truly, I say to you, it was not Moses who gave you the bread from heaven; my Father gives you the true bread from heaven. For the bread of God is that which comes down from heaven, and gives life to the world" (Jn 8:32–33).

It's possible that before the Pharisee could wrap his mind around this statement to make another theological response, several commoners from the crowd, like the woman at the well, cried out in earnest, "Lord, give us this bread always" (Jn 6:34). This request may actually have offended the Pharisees and scribes, who considered themselves the ones to whom the crowd should come for spiritual food. But before they could answer, Jesus responded:

> *I am the bread of life; he who comes to me shall not hunger,*
> *and he who believes in me shall never thirst.* But I said to you
> that you have seen me and yet do not believe. All that the
> Father gives me will come to me; and him who comes to
> me I will not cast out. For I have come down from heaven,
> not to do my own will, but the will of him who sent me;
> and this is the will of him who sent me, that I should lose
> nothing of all that he has given me, but raise it up at the last
> day. *For this is the will of my Father, that every one who sees*
> *the Son and believes in him should have eternal life; and I will*
> *raise him up at the last day.* (Jn 6:35–40, emphasis added
> here and in the following passages)

Here was an answer none within hearing ever expected. Imagine, if you have a comedic imagination, a thousand people standing with their jaws to the ground. This is the last we hear of the crowd. This was more than they could handle. The winnowing process had begun, leaving only "the Jews" (that is, the Pharisees and Scribes) and those who had declared themselves "the disciples of Jesus."

The Pharisees and scribes huddled up and "murmured at him, *because he said, 'I am the bread which came down from heaven.'* They said, 'Is not this Jesus, the son of Joseph, whose father and mother we know? How does he now say, "I have come down from heaven"?'" (Jn 6:41–42).

But you can't keep anything from Jesus. Often it was reported that He knew what people were whispering. Here was His first opportunity to correct any misunderstanding they might have concerning His words. But He didn't. Instead, He stated:

> Do not murmur among yourselves. No one can come to me unless the Father who sent me draws him; and I will raise him up at the last day. … Truly, truly, I say to you, he who believes has eternal life. *I am the bread of life.* Your fathers ate the manna in the wilderness, and they died. *This is the bread which comes down from heaven, that a man may eat of it and not die. I am the living bread which came down from heaven; if any one eats of this bread, he will live for ever; and the bread which I shall give for the life of the world is my flesh.* (Jn 6:43–51)

Startled, the Pharisees and Scribes probably pulled in their huddle even tighter and "disputed among themselves, saying, *'How can this man give us his flesh to eat?'*" (Jn 6:52). They expressed in whispers what the crowd had found revolting. Jesus was not speaking figuratively: His words meant exactly what He said.

Presuming that Jesus again heard their murmurings, He had a second opportunity to soften any misunderstandings. But instead He couldn't have piled it on deeper:

Truly, truly, I say to you, unless you eat the flesh of the Son
of man and drink his blood, you have no life in you; he who
eats my flesh and drinks my blood has eternal life, and I
will raise him up at the last day. For my flesh is food indeed,
and my blood is drink indeed. He who eats my flesh and
drinks my blood abides in me, and I in him. As the living
Father sent me, and I live because of the Father, so he who
eats me will live because of me. This is the bread which
came down from heaven, not such as the fathers ate and
died; he who eats this bread will live for ever. (Jn 6:53–59)

From this point on in chapter 6, we hear nothing more of
the Pharisees and scribes. They have huddled somewhere else
to fine-tune their plot against Jesus, leaving only Jesus' disciples.

Apparently some of the disciples, however, were not happy
with the boldness of His words: "Many of his disciples, when
they heard it, said, 'This is a hard saying; who can listen to it?'"
(Jn 6:60). Once again, Jesus knew "in himself that his disciples
murmured at it" (Jn 6:61), and with His friends, He now had an
intimate opportunity to straighten out any misunderstandings.

In other circumstances, Jesus had admitted to His followers that to the crowd He often spoke in parables while to them
He was straightforward, sharing with them the secrets of the
kingdom of God (see Lk 8:9–10). So then, as with the parable
of the sower He once had taught, He could have given them
the keys to the symbolism of what He was saying.

But He wasn't speaking in symbols. To His friends He said,
perhaps with growing frustration:

Do you take offense at this? Then what if you were to see
the Son of man ascending where he was before? It is the
spirit that gives life, the flesh is of no avail; the words that I
have spoken to you are spirit and life. But there are some of
you that do not believe. (Jn 6:61–64)

91

I used to argue that here Jesus was admitting that He was only speaking in images and not literally. But nowhere else in Scripture does Jesus use the word "spirit" to mean "symbol." When He said, for example, that "God is spirit and those who worship him must worship in spirit and truth" (Jn 4:24), was he saying that God is only a symbol, or that our worship is to be only symbolic? When he said, "Truly, truly, I say to you, unless one is born of water and the Spirit, he cannot enter the kingdom of God" (Jn 3:5), was He only speaking figuratively?

Hardly. But in any case, on this occasion, even His closest friends did not understand Him to be speaking figuratively, for we read: "After this many of his disciples drew back and no longer went about with him" (Jn 6:66).

The winnowing process separated those who accepted Jesus at His word about eating His Body and drinking His Blood from those who refused to accept this teaching. It had reduced the large crowd down to twelve, and even to the Twelve, Jesus said, "Do you also wish to go away?" (Jn 6: 67).

The winnowing process had not ended, for only one of these spoke up: "Simon Peter answered him, 'Lord, to whom shall we go? You have the words of eternal life; and we have believed, and have come to know, that you are the Holy One of God'" (Jn 6:68–69).

Three quick points we should note in closing.

First, is there any wonder that Jesus chose Simon Peter upon whom to build His Church? Here Peter models for us "the obedience of faith" (Rom 1:5), even when we do not fully understand, even when our senses tell us something different from what Jesus is calling us to believe. Let's face it: How hard must it have been for Simon Peter to believe that the plain human being standing before him was "the Holy One of God"?

Second, if we want truth and we recognize, through the teaching of St. Paul, that the Church, "the pillar and bulwark of the truth" (1 Tim 3:15), is the very "body of Christ" (1 Cor 12; Eph 4:4–15), then "to whom shall we go?"

Finally, with whom in Jesus' audience do you identify: the crowd? the Jewish leaders? the wider circle of disciples who left because they found Jesus' teachings too hard to stomach? the eleven who sat in silence unwilling to commit themselves?

Or do you identify with Simon Peter, who, at least in this instance, allowed faith to seek understanding? Where are you in the winnowing process?

CHAPTER 18

St. Paul on Lent

Did St. Paul have anything to say about observing the disciplines of Lent? It's generally accepted that the specific practice of the forty days of Lent leading up to Easter was a later development in the life of the Church, so in this sense we shouldn't expect him to have said anything about it. But more in general, did St. Paul say anything about observing seasons of fasting and self-denial?

Returning for a moment to my past as a Calvinist Presbyterian pastor, I can assure you that I would have answered this question in this way: "Yes, he certainly did! He would have said, 'Don't!'" As I'm sure some of you, with similar backgrounds, have also done, I would have based my opinion on a carefully selected and arranged sampling of Scripture passages. Let's look at a few of them.

I would have begun with a passage from Galatians. St. Paul was troubled that the Galatian Christians were following "false gospels," and one sign of this tendency was that they were falling back into observing superstitious rituals:

Formerly, when you did not know God, you were in bondage to beings that by nature are no gods; but now that you
have come to know God, or rather to be known by God,
how can you turn back again to the weak and beggarly
elemental spirits, whose slaves you want to be once more?
You observe days, and months, and seasons, and years! I am
afraid I have labored over you in vain. (Gal 4:8–11, emphasis
added here and in following passages)

I would have preached that St. Paul was warning against
observing special days as a form of religious discipline, calling
it a useless vanity.

To the Christians at Colossae, the Apostle had a similar
concern and warning:

Therefore let no one pass judgment on you in questions of
food and drink or with regard to a festival or a new moon
or a sabbath. These are only a shadow of what is to come;
but the substance belongs to Christ. Let no one disqualify
you, insisting on self-abasement and worship of angels, taking his stand on visions. ... Why do you submit to regulations, "Do not handle, Do not taste, Do not touch" (referring to things which all perish as they are used), according
to human precepts and doctrines? These have indeed an
appearance of wisdom in promoting rigor of devotion and
self-abasement and severity to the body, but they are of no
value in checking the indulgence of the flesh. (Col 2:16–23)

Whoa! Sure sounds like St. Paul was telling the first-generation Christians to turn away from and reject leaders who
impose ritualistic regulations upon them that restricted their
eating or schedules.

In his letter to the Romans, he inserted himself between
believers who were judging each other with regard to their
differing standards of eating and piety. His answer was this:
"Let every one be fully convinced in his own mind. ... For the

kingdom of God is not food and drink but righteousness and peace and joy in the Holy Spirit" (Rom 14:1–17).

I would have preached that here St. Paul was saying this is simply a matter of individual conscience! What we eat or don't eat, or when, is not as important as being righteous (that is, holy). For it's only through being holy that we can experience "peace and joy in the Holy Spirit."

To his spiritual son, Timothy, the Apostle warned that someday in the future, false teachers would add such restrictive regulations to the faith and make them mandatory. As a Presbyterian pastor, I would have quipped, "Does the following sound familiar?"

> Now the Spirit expressly says that in later times some will
> depart from the faith by giving heed to deceitful spirits
> and doctrines of demons, through the pretensions of liars
> whose consciences are seared, *who forbid marriage and
> enjoin abstinence from foods which God created to be received
> with thanksgiving by those who believe and know the truth.*
> For everything created by God is good, and nothing is to
> be rejected if it is received with thanksgiving; for then it is
> consecrated by the word of God and prayer. (1 Tim 4:1–4)

I actually taught that this verse warned prophetically against churches such as the Roman Catholic Church, which I believed controlled the lives of their members through the imposition of unnecessary disciplines. (I realize now, of course, that St. Paul was probably referring here to the early Gnostic heretics, some of whom forbade both marriage and the eating of any meat because they taught that the entire material world was inherently evil, created by a lesser but evil god.)

I could note more verses that were a part of my position's arsenal. Together, these seemed to me to teach that a Church that imposes these constrictive disciplines is one that should not be followed; that these disciplines are mere vanity and do not make us more holy; and that what is truly important is just imitating and following Jesus.

This, at least, is what I used to believe and teach.

Then, however, I discovered the significance of what St. Paul taught in the verses preceding those quoted in 1 Timothy:

> I hope to come to you soon, but *I am writing these instructions to you so that, if I am delayed, you may know how one ought to behave in the household of God, which is the church of the living God, the pillar and bulwark of the truth.* (1 Tim 3:14–15)

Two important truths are expressed here. First, the trustworthy source of truth is not Scripture alone nor our individual consciences, but the Church. Second, St. Paul, as one of the highest leaders in the Church, recognized that he had the authority from Christ to teach Christians how they "ought to behave in the household of God."

The Church and her leaders, guided by the Holy Spirit (as Jesus promised in John chapters 14–16), have always recognized that in our battle against sin, our sin-damaged wills need to be disciplined. We strengthen our will to resist difficult temptations by choosing to abstain for a time from good things.

The early Church recognized this reality. When the apostolic leaders were forced to decide which disciplines from their Jewish past must be imposed upon Gentile converts (such as circumcision), they didn't merely throw everything out and tell the new converts just to decide for themselves. Rather the leaders, recognizing their responsibilities under the Holy Spirit to guide the Church, gave a list of regulations which were then to be communicated to all the local churches:

> We have therefore sent Judas and Silas, who themselves will tell you the same things by word of mouth. *For it has*

> *seemed good to the Holy Spirit and to us to lay upon you no*
> *greater burden than these necessary things: that you abstain*
> *from what has been sacrificed to idols and from blood and*
> *from what is strangled and from unchastity. If you keep your-*
> *selves from these, you will do well.* (Acts 15: 27–29)

Now we know, from the rest of the New Testament and the writings of the early Church Fathers, that these were not literally "all" that was now required of them. Rather, they were new regulations covering certain dietary disciplines. The point, however, is that this incident demonstrates that the Church has always recognized its responsibility, under the Holy Spirit, to place boundaries on our lives, which include moral as well as spiritual disciplines. In this case the Church, led by the Apostles themselves, even found it necessary to "enjoin abstinence from [particular] foods which God created" for legitimate spiritual reasons!

Constrictive rules and regulations of a season such as Lent did not merely evolve over the ages through the "unnatural seclusion of angry, repressed monks" (as I used to teach). Rather, they came from Jesus himself. In the Sermon on the Mount, He spoke long and directly about times when His followers would "give alms … pray … fast" (Mt 6:2–18).

Our Lord wasn't saying that these acts were vain or unimportant. Instead, He assumed that all His followers would continue to practice such age-old disciplines. What He warned against was the vanity of doing these things inappropriately, either to impress other people or to think that in doing them we somehow obligate God to reward us.

All the disciplines of Lent — examining our lives; giving up specific good things for the goal of self-discipline; gathering together for penance, worship, and adoration — are exactly in line with what St. Paul taught: "Let every one be fully convinced in his own mind. … For the kingdom of God is not food and drink but righteousness and peace and joy in the Holy Spirit" (Rom 14:1–17).

The acts themselves are not the most important thing. What's important is how they help us to become more fully convinced in our own minds of the truth of Jesus Christ our Lord and of His Church, His Body, in which we became full members through baptism. Through these disciplines of Lent we can grow by grace in "righteousness and peace and joy in the Holy Spirit."

CHAPTER 19

Can I Trust My Conscience?

In the sixteenth century two celebrated spiritual leaders, Martin Luther and St. Thomas More, stood on opposite sides of the religious debates of their day. Ironically, they took their stand on the same principle: an appeal to conscience.

Luther died outside the Catholic Church because he claimed that his conscience compelled him to oppose the Church. More died a martyr because he insisted that his conscience forbade him to oppose the Church.

Today the cry to stand on conscience, especially with regard to socially contentious issues, is heard more and more among Catholics and others as well. Yet just as it was in the time of Luther and More, the conclusions drawn according to individual conscience are often contradictory. How is it, then, that trusting one's conscience seems both perennially essential, yet dangerously unreliable?

Consider this analogy. I'm 6 feet 4 inches tall. Most people consider me tall, but in my mind's eye I'm just average height.

In fact, whenever I encounter others of my height, I think of them as taller than I am.

For most of my life, you see, my normal line of vision has tilted down slightly as I look into the faces of family and friends. What seems, then, to be "level" or "normal" in my mind is skewed slightly downward.

My perception of height is thus not objectively accurate, but instead rather subjective, relative to my experience. If I had spent my life with mostly taller people or mostly shorter people, I would probably have become accustomed either way to think of myself, in my mind's eye, as their height.

Given this situation, if I were to stand before a large mirror alongside others, I'd be surprised at what appears there. No doubt I would then look around for a reliable measuring instrument, some kind of yardstick, to determine accurately how my height compares objectively to that of the others. Only then could I correct that warped lifelong perception of myself and others.

In a similar way, the perception of right and wrong that we call our conscience can become untrustworthy. Over the years, it tends to adjust to the world around us, in ways to which we are dangerously blind. Sometimes our conscience bends to be more like those whom we admire or who admire us. Sometimes it bends away from those whom we dislike or who dislike us.

Either way, our conscience may end up skewed in ways we don't recognize. The Scripture recognizes this problem when it speaks of consciences that are "weak," "wounded," "branded" or "tainted" (see 1 Cor 8:7–12; 1 Tm 4:2; Ti 1:15).

So how do we gain a trustworthy conscience, a vision of right and wrong that is accurate? Most people are unwilling to examine and correct their consciences until they become aware, through direct confrontation with another person's conscience or some other "Aha!" experience, that "there's something wrong with this picture!" Such an experience is like standing before the mirror.

Having recognized the problem, we must regularly examine and form our conscience by using a reliable moral "yardstick" — an objective means of measuring what is right and wrong. But practically speaking, what kind of yardstick is available?

Luther claimed that we must use Scripture *alone* to form conscience. But we need only observe the chaos of Christian opinions on critical moral issues to see that Luther's *sola scriptura* principle has proven perpetually untrustworthy as a means of forming conscience. Merely private scriptural interpretation is simply too subjective.

Others say that the best way to form conscience is to ask "WWJD?" ("What would Jesus do?") Yet this approach can be just as subjective and shaky as *sola scriptura*. We need the living voice of Christ in His Church, speaking into our contemporary situation and addressing our moral concerns.

Rather than asking, "What *would* Jesus do?" we should ask, "What *did* Jesus do?" What did He do to provide us with an objective means to measure truth and form a faithful conscience?

The answer, of course, is that He gave us as a trustworthy yardstick "the Church of the living God, the pillar and foundation of truth" (1 Tm 3:15). If we make it a habit to study and embrace the Church's precepts, and all the authoritative moral teachings of her Magisterium, we'll form a conscience on which we can confidently take our stand.

CHAPTER 20

Some Thoughts About Mary

As a Protestant pastor I was uncomfortable with many Catholic teachings and traditions. In reflection now, when I compile all the kinds of objections to the Church that I had — objections I often passed along to my congregations — I can see that they all coalesce into basically one complaint.

It's the most common objection I now receive from non-Catholics about most any Catholic teaching: "Where does it teach this in Scripture?" And the objection often has to do with Mary.

"Show me in Scripture where I have to believe that Mary was conceived immaculately ... or that she was assumed into heaven ... or that I can pray to her, asking for her intercession as 'Mother of all Graces'?" For me, as for many evangelical converts, the last and most insurmountable hurdle to cross was Mary.

First, allow me to say that I am still sympathetic to the question, "Where does it teach this in Scripture?" After all, I was a Protestant for forty years and a pastor for more than nine, and I remain an avid though admittedly inadequate student of Scripture. Whenever I consider a teaching of the Catholic Church that is based predominantly on Sacred Tradition, a little yellow flag still rises up within my own conscience. I still tend to feel a bit more comfortable when I can clearly point to a chapter and verse.

Nevertheless, with regard to the teachings about Mary in particular, I came to three important conclusions. First, what I discovered in my own journey was that most of the teachings about Mary do have strong foundations in Scripture. If they're not directly addressed, they can at least be logically deduced through scriptural reasoning.

Second, I learned that the idea that "Christian teachings are true only if found in Scripture" is in fact a modern tradition. Throughout Christian history, the Scriptures were always a foundation in defense of Christian truth, as can be seen in the writings of the early Church Fathers or the great Doctors of the Church. Never, however, do we find these Christian writers demanding that a particular doctrine be proved solely from Scripture. Such an expectation arose only during the Protestant Reformation, when the authority of both the Church's Magisterium and Sacred Tradition were set aside as foundations for Christian truth.

Perhaps most telling is the fact that Scripture itself never makes such a demand. Nowhere can we find in Scripture the phrase, "It must be proven solely from Scripture."

Let's take another Christian doctrine, such as the Trinity. With Scripture alone, and no other traditional or doctrinal presumptions, you cannot decisively end up with the orthodox understanding of the Trinity as defined in the Council of Nicaea. You can, in fact, come up with any number of explanations of how God the Father, the Lord Jesus Christ, and the Holy Spirit coexist and relate (and early heretics did just that).

Beginning from the Council's decisive definition of the Trinity, however, you can return to Scripture and see how this dogma is clearly illustrated in the truths of Scripture. The same is true for the dogmas about Mary. The traditional teachings of the Church make sense out of the scriptural data we find about Mary.

Third, I came to realize that much of what I was taught about the Catholic Church was not true. Sadly, too few Protestants have ever read anything about the Catholic Church written by a Catholic.

Consider this: Suppose you are a Methodist Christian. If you heard that I was teaching a class in my Catholic parish about what Methodists believe, using a book written by Catholics, wouldn't you object, insisting that I use a book written by a faithful Methodist? Shouldn't Catholics expect the same from Protestants?

Please be careful. There are many books, old and new, saying strange things about the Catholic Church, building amazing tales on half-truths. If you truly want to understand what the Catholic Church teaches about Mary and other doctrines and practices, then consider reading books by authors who love Jesus Christ and who desire to present the Catholic Church faithfully and truly. Try starting with the Catechism!

CHAPTER 21

Do Our Separated Brethren Need to Come Home?

Do our separated brethren need to come home? Just asking this question sometimes ruffles feathers, among both Protestants and Catholics. Today the growing opinion seems to be that, since many Catholic teachers no longer stress *"extra ecclesia nulla salus"* ("outside the Church there is no salvation"), our separated brethren should contentedly stay right where they are.

Many have misinterpreted the Church's statement that non-Catholic Christian churches and denominations *can* be a means of salvation to mean that they *are* means of salvation. There's a wide chasm between these two statements! The first emphasizes the loving mercy of God; the second implies that the Catholic Church no longer matters: "Heaven has many, many doors, and any church is a good port in the storm."

We have many reasons to justify helping our separated brethren "come home" to the Church. But one particular reason even the most sincere non-Catholic needs to come home to the Church became exceedingly clear to me while rereading Fr. Thomas Dubay's important book *Fire Within* (Ignatius, 1989). This book is a must read.

In the context of discussing the transforming union with God — the highest level of spiritual intimacy we can attain this side of heaven — he writes: "If we did not have the mystic's teaching about the loftiest prayer, we would be at a loss to explain a great deal of Scripture" (p. 195).

Did you catch the significance of this statement? Consider the following Scripture verses:

> We all, with unveiled face, beholding the glory of the Lord, are being changed into his likeness from one degree of glory to another. (2 Cor 3:18)

> For our sake he made him to be sin who knew no sin, so that in him we might become the righteousness of God. (2 Cor 5:21)

> ... that you may be filled with all the fullness of God. (Eph 3:19)

> … that … you may ... become partakers of the divine nature. (2 Pt 1:4)

And lest we forget:

> You, therefore, must be perfect as your heavenly Father is perfect. (Mt 5:48)

The list goes on and on of Scripture verses whose meaning is not obvious, and which have consequently led to a myriad of conflicting conclusions. Fr. Dubay and other Catholic mystics point out two truths about these texts.

First, many of them refer to a much higher and more demanding — that is, more sacrificial — spiritual life than most of us might otherwise imagine. Second, without trustworthy spiritual guidance, we can be led on potentially damning spiritual wild-goose chases if we rely solely on our private interpretation or that of some charismatic personality.

What, for example, does it truly mean to be "born again," to "abide in Christ," to "have Christ dwelling in your heart," to "have eternal life," or to be "filled with the Holy Spirit"? Think of the wide range of interpretations of these texts and how these have spawned a wide world of religious craziness! All it takes is just one evening watching certain Protestant television channels, where hour after hour the preaching of each program contradicts at some points the preaching of the previous one.

What does it mean, after all, to have a "personal relationship with Jesus Christ"? Isn't this exactly what Catholic mystical writers, such as St. John of the Cross, St. Teresa of Avila, and Fr. Dubay, are trying to teach us?

Father Dubay writes:

> Our being filled with God is, of course, the reason for everything else in the economy of salvation … the transforming union is likewise the purpose of all else in the Church. The Eucharist itself, the Sacrament of all Sacraments, is, according to the Word of the Lord, aimed at producing eternal life here on earth. Jesus declares that whoever eats His flesh and drinks His blood *has* eternal life (Jn 6:54–56). It is a life that is to be abundant to the full (Jn 10:10). The fullness is the Transformation; there is no other. (*Fire Within*, pp. 196–197)

When Catholics reach out to their separated brothers and sisters, they are not passing judgment on anyone's place in salvation. They are reaching out because they want them to have a true and authentic personal relationship with Jesus Christ, not one based on their best guess about what some Scripture text means.

Sadly, though, coming home to the Catholic Church does not in and of itself ensure an understanding and reception of the fullness. That requires a receptive and repentant heart and mind; an obedient spirit willing to be nurtured and led by God's appointed leaders; and a diligent desire to do whatever is necessary to grow closer to God in prayer and love.

In a two-edged statement that both states a fact and issues a warning, Fr. Dubay continues:

> In this Mystical Body of Christ [the Eucharist] we are to find our fulfillment, not something less. Thus all structures in the Church — institutions, priesthood, curias, chancery offices, books, and candles, and all else — are aimed at producing this abundance of life, this utter immersion in triune splendor, this transforming union. (*Fire Within*, p. 197)

It is precisely because many of us know from personal experience how easy it is to misinterpret and misapply some Scripture texts in relation to worship, church government, and other aspects of ministry that we reach out to friends and family outside the Church. We do this in the name of Christ and His Church, not in passing judgment, but because we ourselves have come to discover the "blessed assurance" of having a Spirit-guided Teacher we can trust.

CHAPTER 22

Four Significant Events

Four significant events occurred within a span of three days in the fall of 2004. One was the election of a U.S. president (November 2); the other three were religious events: for Catholics, All Saints' and All Souls' Days (November 1 and 2), and for Protestants, Reformation Sunday (October 31). Some parallels between the political event and the religious events are instructive.

In the days leading up to the election, the two parties and their respective campaign propaganda machines had presented drastically contradicting caricatures of the opposing candidates. Mind you, as I write I am being careful to avoid any partisan issues. But I can say that often during the preceding months, I had been lividly outraged by the ways the party opposing the candidate I supported purposely misrepresented him.

I'd hear a campaign speech or a radio ad proclaiming twisted information that I figured anyone in their right mind would know was false. Yet friends and family who were lifelong members of the opposing party thought the exact opposite: They accepted without question their party's line and were equally appalled by everything my party proclaimed. The situation was a chaos of conflicting countercurrents of spin.

A similar conflicting spin forms the basis for the conjunction of the three religious events. As a Presbyterian pastor, I led many celebrations of Reformation Sunday, the last being the most vivid.

Reformed church furnishings typically reflect an ideal of iconoclasm. But the church sanctuary I "inherited" when I was hired displayed prominently large stone relief portraits of six major Protestant reformers. As I gazed out from my pulpit, I was buttressed by the faces of Luther, Melanchthon, Zwingli, Calvin, Knox, and Huss.

Every year I would take this Sunday to remind my congregation of the Protestant understanding of Church history, reinforcing why our denomination existed and why we were different from the other denominations that surrounded us. The following is an example of this kind of Protestant explanation of the Reformation event that I quote from a Lutheran Internet site. Pay attention carefully to the loaded language and the spin. How many phrases can you underline that betray an inaccurate or incomplete understanding of history?

> The Reformation in church history designates the movement in the 16th century which aimed to restore the Church founded by Jesus Christ, deformed in the course of centuries, chiefly by the Papacy, to its early normal condition. ...

> The history of the many church Councils shows that the Papacy and hierarchy were opposed to reform. ... Into this era came Dr. Martin Luther ... who struggled with the basic root problem of that day in the church — the doctrine of the meritoriousness of good works being the way to salvation. The Church could not provide Dr. Luther with an an-

swer to "How do I obtain a gracious God?" The final blow probably came when the church began selling indulgences as a false way of salvation in order to raise more money for the building of more structures in Rome.

On October 31, 1517 ... Dr. Luther protested the corruption in the church by nailing to the community bulletin board, located on the doors of the Castle Church in Wittenberg, a paper with 95 Theses (reasons) he wanted to debate on how the church should be reformed. ...

Action against Dr. Luther by papal authorities was swift, he was excluded from the Roman Church and declared an outlaw. (Excerpted from "The Reformation" by the Rev. Dr. David Eberhard, Historic Trinity Lutheran Church, Detroit, Michigan; www.historictrinity.org/reformation.html; accessed July 27, 2010).

Space does not allow me to dissect this entire statement, but here is just a sampling of how I could respond:

1. The Papacy and Magisterium were never against authentic reform.

2. The Church never taught that good works alone were the way to salvation.

3. The Church did in fact provide Luther an answer to the question "How do I obtain a gracious God?" but he either misunderstood it or outright rejected it.

4. The Church never endorsed the sale of indulgences as a means of salvation.

5. The Church's response to Luther's attack was not a swift declaration that he was an outlaw; Church leaders first engaged in attempts to reason with him and allow him to reconsider his position.

The danger of these kinds of simplified, slanted summaries of history is that they are easily passed along from professor to pastor to parent to child without examination. How many of us can testify to this process from personal experience? I can. From year to year, I dished out the Reformed campaign slogans without taking the time to check whether what I was saying was true.

Then, like Blessed John Henry Cardinal Newman, I discovered that "to become deep in history is to cease to be a Protestant." In becoming deeper in history, I discovered many truths that corrected my inadequate understanding of the Church and her history. I also became starkly aware of the differences between what Catholics are celebrating and emulating on their two feast days in November and those that Protestants celebrate and emulate on theirs.

The fall season can sharpen the edges of the ideologies that divide us, both religiously and politically, even as it calls us to prepare our hearts for the Advent of our Savior. Whenever we enter the Advent season, we should each express three *mea culpas* for whatever part we might have played in these divisions. And we should commit ourselves anew to being charitable agents of authentic Church renewal and unity.

CHAPTER 23

"Now Why Would You Want to Do That?"

"What did you say you do?"

"Oh, I work with an apostolate... er, a lay ministry that helps Protestant clergy, men and women, who are thinking about becoming Catholic."

"Do you help them change their minds?"

"We help them work through the many issues and hurdles they face as they go through the often difficult process of leaving their pastorates to become Catholic."

Silent stares with mixed looks of disdain and disbelief. "Now why would you want to do that? Does Rome still teach that non-Catholics are going to hell?"

"No, of course not ... I mean ..."

"Then why don't you just leave them alone?"

This is a caricature of a conversation I recently had on a flight to Birmingham to host my live *Journey Home* television program on EWTN. It includes a question that many of the CHNetwork staff and associates have been pressed to answer by phone, email, letter, or most uncomfortably, face-to-face with friends or family — non-Catholic and even sometimes Catholic.

"Doesn't the new Catechism teach that our separated brethren are innocent of the schism and that they can be saved just like us through their faith in Jesus Christ?"

"Sure, but ..."

"Then why mess up their lives? I mean hey, since Vatican II, Protestants don't even need to convert, right?"

Sound familiar? But if there is at least partial truth in the above statements — if sincere, non-Catholics can be saved through their faith in Christ — then why not leave them right where they are, especially if their conversions remove them from positions of ministry leadership where they are presently doing great work for the Lord?

The conversation might continue this way:

"One answer is that we want them to know and receive with joy the fullness of the Christian faith, as delivered by Jesus to His apostles, and which has consequently been preserved, protected, and proclaimed throughout the ages by the Catholic Church. What they presently have is a mixture of truth, partial truth, and untruth, depending upon which Christian tradition they belong to. We want them to embrace the fullness."

"Yes, that's true, but apparently the Church teaches that they can still follow Jesus, receive his blessings, and be saved without this fullness."

"Okay. Another reason is that we want them to experience all the avenues of grace provided by the Church through her sacraments, sacramentals, and devotions. We don't want to take the chance that without this grace they may not persevere (whether they believe they need to persevere or not)."

"But the Church teaches that, although we cannot be certain, God can pour forth His grace through any means He chooses, even through the limited sacraments and ordinances of non-Catholic traditions."

"Yes, that's true. But another significant reason we want to help them come home is that, as the Council of Florence taught in 1439, the level of the Beatific Vision we experience in heaven is directly proportional to the level of grace we attain in this life through our words, actions, and attitudes of the heart. They need to 'come home' so they will know they need to focus their lives on growing in grace. Too many of them are caught up in the presumption of the 'once-saved-always-saved' teaching, and they aren't aware of their need to grow in holiness."

"What council? Oh, never mind, but again, God can give them whatever grace He wills, and He will hardly hold them accountable for their ignorance. As Jesus said, whatever they do for the least of these they do for Him. They'll be rewarded in heaven for their works of charity, even if they know nothing about quantum levels in heaven."

Again, does any of this sound familiar?

On this same trip to EWTN, I began reading a newly revised version of Fr. Frederick William Faber's book *All for Jesus: The Easy Ways of Divine Love* (Richardson and Son, 1854). After all the twentieth century did to the thinking of most Catholics — good and bad — this book, from a highly respected nineteenth-century spiritual writer and convert, provides an inspiring, motivating, and practical standard of comparison about what it truly means to think, live, and love like a Catholic.

In the first chapter, Fr. Faber offers important answers to the questions we've noted:

> Now, let us look at the interests of Jesus. Let us take a view
> of the whole Church, which is His spouse. Look first into
> Heaven, the Church Triumphant. It is the interest of Jesus
> that the glory of the most Holy Trinity should be increased
> in every possible manner, and at every hour of night and
> day. And this glory, which is called God's accidental glory,
> is increased by every good work, word, and thought, every
> correspondence to grace, every resistance to temptation,
> every act of worship, every sacrament rightly administered
> or humbly received, every act of homage and love to Mary,
> every invocation of the saints, every bead of the rosary, ev-
> ery Sign of the Cross, every drop of holy water, every pain
> patiently endured, every harsh judgment meekly borne,
> every good wish … provided there be a devout intention
> along with all these things, and they are done in union with
> the merits of our sweet Lord (p.8).

The problem with the answers given in the dialogue I presented — which all contain some elements of truth — is that they are primarily self-focused, in the same subtle manner that the gospel itself can too often be expressed in solely personal, individualistic terms. "What must I do to be saved? What rewards will I get from this? How can I grow in grace?"

But as Fr. Faber so clearly states, the focus of our spiritual lives must be on increasing the glory of the Holy Trinity — in other words, on giving: "What can I do today, at this moment, in this place, in this situation, with this joy or this pain, to bring glory to God?"

A great case in point was mentioned by Fr. Faber: the rosary. Most non-Catholics, of course, do not understand Catholic devotions such as the rosary, and many converts have admitted that making the transition in prayer with the rosary is difficult. "How does it help me talk with God? How does it help me express my needs? How does it help me focus my mind?"

117

But as Fr. Faber suggests, the key reason for praying the rosary is that in doing so we increase God's glory. Each bead is a means of giving glory to God. In fact, Fr. Faber's thoughts have helped me understand more fully a repeated phrase of the rosary that too often merely stood as a closing "bookend" of each decade: "Glory be ..." That is precisely the point of the prayer. Glory be to God!

If increasing the glory of the Holy Trinity is to be our spiritual focus, then isn't this one of the main reasons non-Catholic Christians need to come home to the Catholic Church? What's important isn't only the amount of truth they know, or grace they receive, or heaven they experience, but how fully their heart is surrendered to giving all to the glory of God.

Yes, a great many Protestants know and preach this truth; just recall the hymn "To God Be the Glory." But I know that it wasn't until I was confronted by the truth of Catholic spirituality, and began to be purged by the power of sacramental grace, that I began to realize how self-centered my Christian faith had always been.

Our focus must not be on whether, as a result of our efforts — even our faith — we will be saved. That, in essence, is a self-centered request. Rather, our focus is to be, first, on giving glory to God; second, on growing by grace in holiness (the stages); and third, on trusting our eternal destiny, in hope, to the mercy of our heavenly Father.

Why should Protestant ministers and laity come home? Not primarily for what they can get, but for how they are called to love.

CHAPTER 24

What Does It Mean to Believe?

Recently two men from radically different spiritual backgrounds came to me privately and asked essentially the same question. The first was a Baptist minister on the journey towards the Catholic Church. He had already breached the walls of his former anti-Catholic prejudice, examined afresh the Church's teachings and found them convincing, accepted the authority and authenticity of the Catholic Church, and realized that he could no longer remain a Protestant, let alone a Baptist minister.

And yet there remained a question:

"I understand and accept the Church's teaching on the Eucharist, but I just can't seem to get myself to believe it. I kneel before the Blessed Sacrament, but all I do is argue within myself about what is there before me. How can I come to believe it to be real?"

The second man to ask the same question was a lifelong Catholic. He said:

"All my life I've known and accepted the Church's teaching; I've never intentionally missed Mass. Everyone who knows me presumes I am a faithful Catholic, and yet … I've never really been able to believe that Jesus is truly physically there, Body, Blood, Soul, and Divinity. I know all the arguments and can even defend the Church's teaching with the best of them. But down deep, in the privacy of my heart and mind, I just can't get myself to truly believe. What must I do to get beyond this impasse?"

Usually my knee-jerk suggestion to questions like this is to encourage them to pray the prayer offered by the father who wanted Jesus to heal his son: "I believe; help my unbelief" (Mk 9:24). Faith is a gift of grace, so if we are struggling with faith, we need to pray for more grace.

This encouragement may not help, though, if we have an inadequate understanding of what it means to believe. Too often, people wrongly think that believing in something requires emotional acceptance. They assume that we must eventually feel "in our gut" that something is true to *really* believe in it.

We sometimes make the same mistake about loving and forgiving. We may not believe that we really love someone or forgive someone unless we feel we love or forgive them. Yet this is not what Jesus means by loving, forgiving, or believing. These, all three, consist primarily of works of the conscience, intellect, and will, and only secondarily the emotions or even the understanding.

Our conscience is essentially our judgment of how and what we ought to believe, love, and forgive. Contrary to many modern views, however, our consciences are not infallible or ultimate voices of authority. Yes, God planted within everyone's conscience some innate sense of what is right and wrong (see Rom 2). But our consciences must be formed by infallible, authoritative voices so they can be deemed reliable. For this reason, Christ gave us the Church, guided by the Spirit, to preach, preserve, and pass on the truth.

With our intellect, we must examine our conscience — along with all the other voices in our lives — and decide what is true. Then with our will, we act: choose what and how to believe, to love, and to forgive.

Given all the data of our conscience and the decisions of our intellect, our emotions may not agree with what our will decides to do, nor may we yet fully understand, either. Nevertheless, we are still called to believe, for "this is the work of God."

I remember once while hiking in a national park coming upon a three-rope bridge traversing a deep, rocky, river gorge. It was the only way across. My emotions did not want to trust that precarious bridge! But the posted notice indicated that the bridge had recently been tested and approved as totally reliable by park management, with their stamp of authority.

What was I to do? Was I to believe? At last I willingly and safely traversed the gorge because my intellect chose to believe the park management and not my emotions.

Do you believe in the Trinity? Why? Don't say, "Because the Bible tells me so," because it doesn't "tell" this doctrine explicitly or clearly. The word "trinity" doesn't even appear in Scripture.

You believe this reality to be true (whether you realize it or not) because the bishops of the Church in an early council declared this doctrine and then explained the scriptural data accordingly. We personally believe this doctrine because, from a variety of sources, our intellect was faced with the data, and we chose to believe it.

I know personally that I didn't believe in the Trinity because I *felt* this to be true or because I claimed to understand it fully. Rather, I first believed, as an evangelical Protestant, because people I trusted convinced me that this is what the Bible taught. Then later, as a Catholic, I continued to believe because I recognized that it was originally the authority of the Church that had both determined these truths and confirmed the authority of Scripture.

The issue of the Eucharist, of course, is a bit more difficult. The physical data before us, as measured by our senses, contradicts what our conscience and intellect are being called to believe. Transubstantiation explains this contradiction, but this doesn't guarantee that our emotions will ever match our conviction or that, this side of heaven, we will ever fully understand.

Remember how, when Jesus taught about the Eucharistic reality, those who could not accept His teaching left Him. But when He asked whether the Twelve would also leave, Simon Peter responded with a profound expression of true belief: "Lord, to whom shall we go? You have the words of eternal life; and we have believed, and have come to know, that you are the holy One of God" (Jn 6:68–69).

Like St. Peter, outside of our Lord Jesus Christ and the Church He established in those first believing apostles, we have nowhere to go. The Church (the Body of Christ, the pillar and bulwark of the truth) has "the words of eternal life," and by grace "we have believed, and have come to know" that Jesus Christ is "the holy One of God."

Peter never fully explained what he meant by the phrase "have come to know." It may imply a deepening sense of believing. He may have had a resultant emotional assurance that what he had accepted intellectually was true, even against the witness of his senses or understanding.

Nevertheless, we must also recognize that when the going got tough, when faced with the arrest, trial, and execution of the one that St. Peter "had come to know" was the very "holy

One of God," the apostle denied him, and the rest (except John) abandoned him. Believing is never a one-time decision — especially, never a one-time *emotional* decision. It is a lifetime of obedience, by grace through faith, by means of the intellect and will.

Recently I heard about the experience of a particular Protestant pastor "revert": As a child, he had been baptized Catholic. But he eventually left the Church and was ordained a Protestant pastor. Even so, he had recently resigned from his pastorate and returned to the Catholic Church.

Unfortunately, this man was now looking backwards. He said he was shocked by what he had found. He had anticipated unity among Catholics but instead found as many divisions among individuals as he had left behind.

The staff and I, of course, were doing all we could to help him determine where God was calling him. But in the process, we came to realize that he may have come home to the Church for the wrong reasons, partly because he may have been poorly catechized. He had been led to convert less by an intellectual conviction and acceptance of the Church as the one, holy, Catholic, and apostolic Church founded by Christ, and more by feelings — feelings of disgust at the disunity among Protestants and the liberalism of his own denomination, and the expectation that none of this would be present among some Catholics.

In the end, our attitude towards the Church must be like that of St. Peter toward Christ: "Lord, to whom shall we go?" If, in the process, we experience feelings of warmth, satisfaction, and contentment in the Church — even with all her "warts" (and all of us are warts in one way or another) — then we have been blessed by God's mercy and grace.

On the other hand, if we overreact to what we find, we may become like those other disciples who exclaimed, "This is a hard saying; who can listen to it?" (Jn 6:60). And we could be destined for the same plight: "After this many of his disciples drew back and no longer went about with him" (Jn 6:66).

CHAPTER 25

Guarding the Deposit of Faith

Pope John Paul II stated in the opening sentence of his introduction to the *Catechism of the Catholic Church:* "Guarding the deposit of faith is the mission which the Lord entrusted to His Church and which she fulfills in every age."

This deposit of faith (in Latin, *depositum fidei)*, or the apostolic tradition, is defined in the new *Compendium of the Catechism* as "the transmission of the message of Christ, brought about from the very beginnings of Christianity by means of preaching, bearing witness, institutions, worship, and inspired writings" (12).

From the very beginnings of the Church, the Devil has relentlessly tried to stop, destroy, ridicule, and especially water down this deposit of faith by "flooding the market" with counterfeits. Understanding both the Church's efforts to preserve this truth and the Enemy's efforts to destroy it helps us understand how this deposit of faith has passed through the generations from Jesus to you and me.

To describe this process in detail would require, of course, far more space than we have here. But the following is a summary of how I have come to understand the history of this transmission of the deposit of faith.

Jesus said to those who had chosen to follow Him, both at His direct request and in response to His preaching: "If you continue in my word, you are truly my disciples, and you will know the truth, and the truth will make you free" (Jn 8:31–32).

But how were future generations to know "his word" so that they could "continue in" it? For this He chose twelve apostles, with one, Simon Peter, appointed as their head (see Mt 10:1–4; 16:18–19). He then promised to send them the Counselor, the Holy Spirit.

To the Apostles specifically He said that the Holy Spirit would teach them all things; bring to their remembrance all that He had said to them; guide them into all the truth; and declare to them the things that were to come. Finally, He told them that with this inspired information, they were to be His witnesses (see Jn 14:25–26; 25:26–27; 16:13–14).

With the promise of His continual presence and authority, Jesus charged them: "Go therefore and make disciples of all nations, baptizing them in the name of the Father and of the Son and of the Holy Spirit, teaching them to observe all that I have commanded you; and lo, I am with you always, to the close of the age" (Mt 28:19–20).

The Apostles and their disciples, eventually joined by St. Paul and others, then went forth preaching and witnessing to the death and resurrection of Jesus, and the truth about Him as they were instructed by the Holy Spirit. This oral preaching was the primary source and means of the spread of the gospel message. It was the passing along of the very words of Jesus and stories about Jesus, during the earliest years of the Church.

This oral preaching was also how St. Paul himself received the truth: "Now I would remind you, brethren, in what terms I preached to you the gospel, which you received, in which you stand, by which you are saved, if you hold it fast — unless you believed in vain. For I delivered to you as of first importance what I also received" (1 Cor 15:1–3).

This is how Sacred Tradition was described in the Second Vatican Council document *Dei Verbum:* "Sacred Tradition takes the word of God entrusted by Christ the Lord and the Holy Spirit to the Apostles, and hands it on to their successors in its full purity, so that, led by the light of the Spirit of truth, they may in proclaiming it preserve this word of God faithfully, explain it, and make it more widely known" (9).

Very quickly, however, the Devil began attacking the Truth by spreading confusion through the rise of false teachers offering counterfeit gospels. We see this development, for example, in the presence of the "Judaizers" in the Book of Acts and the references to other false teachers in Galatians, 1 and 2 Timothy, and other books.

The rising influence of these false teachers made it imperative that the faithful leaders and bishops no longer wait until they were physically present to challenge these counterfeits, especially leaders such as Paul and John, who were at times either in chains or exile. Instead they resorted to warning and exhorting as well as affirming their young Christian congregations by letter. These texts became the initial portion of what we call the New Testament, and St. Paul strongly instructed his readers to hold firmly to the traditions they had been taught "either by word of mouth or by letter" (2 Thes 2:15).

In instructions to his assistant, St. Timothy, St. Paul gives us an example of how the Apostles ensured that this oral and written tradition was to pass to future generations: "What you have heard from me before many witnesses entrust to faithful men who will be able to teach others also" (2 Tim 2:1–2).

This entire process was summarized by St. Clement, bishop of Rome, in his late-first-century pastoral letter to the Christians in Corinth:

> The apostles have preached the gospel to us from the Lord Jesus Christ and Jesus Christ was sent forth from God. Christ therefore was sent forth by God, and the apostles by Christ. Both these appointments, then, were made in an orderly way, according to the will of God. Having therefore received their orders, and being fully assured by the resurrection of our Lord Jesus Christ, and established in the word of God, with full assurance of the Holy Spirit, they went forth proclaiming that the kingdom of God was at hand, and thus preaching through countries and cities, they appointed the first fruits [of their labors], having first proved them by the Spirit, to be bishops and deacons of those who should afterwards believe. Nor was this any new thing, since indeed many ages before it was written concerning bishops and deacons. For thus says the Scripture in a certain place, "I will appoint their bishops in righteousness, and their deacons in faith." (42)

The Devil, of course, was not done trying to prevent the Truth from being received and believed. During the first centuries of the Church, besides trying to destroy the Church through a series of persecutions, he continued to flood the market with hundreds of counterfeit gospels and writings. Some of these were very believable and even convinced some Christian leaders as well as laity of their authenticity.

Nevertheless, as the impact of false teachings attempted to derail the deposit of faith through the rise and spread of the Arian heresy, the Church took definitive steps to ensure that future generations would be able to "continue" and "know" the word of Christ. Over a period of several centuries, several important ecumenical councils, such as those at Nicaea and Constantinople, clarified the Church's teaching about the Trinity and about Jesus Christ. Meanwhile, the regional councils of Rome, Carthage, and Hippo in the last decades of the fourth century defined the canon of Scripture.

As a result, through the constant protection, preservation, and proclamation of the Apostolic Tradition, written and oral, throughout the centuries by the Magisterium of the Church in union with the Bishop of Rome, we can today be confident that, aided by grace, we can "continue" in the word of Christ. Abandon the authoritative teaching of the Church, and we have no way of knowing whether we are correctly hearing or following Christ. Thank you, Lord, for the blessing of your Church.

CHAPTER 26

Where's the Power?

In the Year of St. Paul (June 2008–June 2009), Pope Benedict XVI asked us to reflect on the biblical writings and personal witness of this great pioneer apostolic missionary. One particular Pauline passage of Scripture has occupied my attention lately. In the second letter to St. Timothy, we find the following strong warning:

> But understand this, that in the last days there will come times of stress. For men will be lovers of self, lovers of money, proud, arrogant, abusive, disobedient to their parents, ungrateful, unholy, inhuman, implacable, slanderers, profligates, fierce, haters of good, treacherous, reckless, swollen with conceit, lovers of pleasure rather than lovers of God, holding the form of religion but denying the power of it. Avoid such people. (2 Tm 3:1–5)

More than once in the past two thousand years, these verses have been cited as a sign that we live in "the last days." Such a speculation is especially understandable in America of the twenty-first-century; after all, which of these ominous signs *isn't* descriptive of most cultures today? This is one reason why the Church has clearly taught, since the Day of Pentecost, that we are truly living in the "last days" (see Acts 2:15–21). As St. Paul emphasizes, then, we must always be ready for our Lord's return!

One particular "sign" on this list has strongly impressed me in recent days: *"holding the form of religion but denying the power of it."*

Not long ago, when my wife and I had the unexpected privilege of visiting Norway, we took a bus tour of the city of Bergen. Along our route, we passed several stone churches that were more than eight hundred years old. The guide described each church without emotion as "originally Catholic, but now of course Lutheran."

As I listened, I remembered that this was the same matter-of-fact description I'd heard given for the "once-Catholic-but-now-Lutheran" churches in Sweden, Germany, and Austria, the "once-Catholic-but-now-Reformed" churches in Holland, and the "once-Catholic-but-now-Anglican" churches in Great Britain.

I realized that this description mirrored my own way of thinking, back when I was receiving former Catholics as new members into the Protestant congregations I once served as pastor. Though these new members had been Catholic, I explained how they were now becoming Presbyterian.

In all these cases, what had changed? As I listened to the tour guide and reflected on my own experience, it struck me that we had thought of this transition simply as a change of beliefs, from one set of facts, doctrines, and practices (that is, one "form") to another. But as I considered what had actually changed in these circumstances, I came to realize afresh that the change had involved not a mere change of *form*, but a denial and rejection of the supernatural sacramental *power* of the Catholic faith.

When a group of Christians — or an individual — jettisons the connection to the Catholic Church to become part of a Protestant denomination, not only Catholic beliefs are given up, but also sacramental life and power, especially the real presence of Jesus Christ in the Eucharist. The denomination may retain a practice of valid baptism, but otherwise it has lost valid sacraments.

As I walked through dozens of former Catholic churches, these words of St. Paul began ringing in my ears, especially with his warning to "avoid such people." To modern ears, that may sound like an unloving attitude, contrary to the ecumenical spirit. But is it possible that the Apostle is wisely warning us, in these "last days," that unless we're careful, such denial of the power of religion can be contagious?

Is it any wonder that so many Christians today — non-Catholics as well as so many poorly catechized Catholics — no longer believe in the powerful and necessary life-changing graces that are received in the Sacraments? Is there any wonder that so many see the differences among the thousands of Christian traditions as mere differences of opinion or appearance?

If so, how can we recover the power of the sacraments in these "latter days"? For a start, I believe, following Pope Benedict's encouragement, we need to reread St. Paul's letters. We must listen humbly to what he says, perhaps for the first time. And I would strongly encourage us all to do so in the light of the writings of the early Church Fathers, particularly the Apostolic Fathers, with gratitude for the strong, inspired words of this man who gave his life so that we might have a faith, not merely in words, but in power.

PART TWO

The Difficulties of the Journey Home

CHAPTER 27

From Listening, Through Following, to Receiving

In *The Catholic Church and Conversion* (MacMillan, 1926), G. K. Chesterton described three stages or states of mind through which a convert commonly passes. He entitled these stages (1) patronizing the Church, (2) discovering the Church, and (3) running away from the Church. Though he claimed that he was never so anti-Catholic as to consider the Church "inhuman," yet as soon as he allowed the Church to be at least "human" — to admit that there was some "good" in it, so that he began giving the Church some benefit of the doubt — it was only a short road to recognizing that it was "divine."

He wrote: "It is one thing to conclude that Catholicism is good and another to conclude that it is right. It is one thing to conclude that it is right and another to conclude that it is always right" (p. 84).

This is indeed our typical journey into the Church. First, we allow that the Catholic Church is at least Christian, that she may have some shades of truth, while before we may not have considered that possible (patronizing the Church).

Next, we become startled by the beauty, the goodness, the truth we find (discovering the Church). We examine the fullness of the faith, doctrine by doctrine, article by article, devotion by devotion, while at the same time examining all the baggage we bring along with us: bad habits, inaccurate teachings, ill-conceived myths, and ingrained prejudices. All of this process, along with meeting Catholics who don't know or live their faith very well, can make the journey home quite difficult, even to the point of wondering whether we want to continue on.

Finally, we come to realize what conversion to the Catholic faith will mean, personally, practically, even vocationally. And we may find ourselves "running away from the Church."

Many on the journey toward the Catholic Church, especially pastors and their families, sometimes wonder with fear and trembling whether God is as faithful on the Catholic side of the Tiber River as He was on the other. I can assure you without hesitation, from my own experience as well as that of hundreds of others we have assisted over the years, that no matter how desperate things may appear, you need never doubt that God is always willing to guide if you follow. I will admit, though, that there have been times when I've doubted.

Two years after leaving my Protestant ministry to become Catholic, I was alone on retreat at a local state park lodge, trying to discern peacefully and patiently God's direction for my long-term future. Fortunately, soon after my conversion an international Catholic evangelistic outreach to teenagers had hired me as their North American director. I had landed on the Catholic side of the Tiber into a job where I could use my gifts for ministry and support my family. Praise be to God!

But now the news had come that due to lack of funding, the program would soon cease, as too would my job. So what now? Should I go back to school to earn a Ph.D. so I could teach? Should I try writing for a living? Should I seek another position in ministry management? Did I still have the riffs and vocal pipes to try a musical career? Or should I return to my pre-seminary secular career in engineering?

It seemed that as the door reopened for occupational choices, all the previous dreams I had considered over the years began to resurface. I swung emotionally from wondering whether there was anything at all open to me (anything at all that I could even do) to whether there was anything closed to me (anything at all that I could not do if I bravely tried). Somewhere in my forty-two-year-old adolescent brain, I still envisioned myself a folk-singing balladeer, strumming my faithful guitar to the standing applause of weeping, melancholy baby-boomers.

I spent an entire day trying to get myself focused, but my mind and body kept finding distractions. Another book I "needed" to read. A jaunt down to the book table at a Nazarene pastors' convention that was also meeting in the lodge. (Boy, if *they* only knew what kind of "infidel" was living among them!) A quick jog around the park in freezing rain followed by a welcome dip in the Jacuzzi, some catch-up tasks from work, and a few games of Solitaire on my laptop.

By evening I was much more relaxed, but no closer to reflecting on the reason for my retreat. I considered at that late hour diving into it, glancing at my untouched journal over on the table. But instead I chose to escape back into a Dorothy L. Sayers mystery.

In the morning, I found myself afraid to begin, afraid that I might not hear a "still small voice" or discern the "dew on the fleece." (Like many evangelicals, I spoke of personal signs from God in terms of the biblical accounts of Elijah in 1 Kings 19:1–18 and Gideon in Judges 6:36–40.) Nevertheless, at the least I had to start the morning with devotions, so I turned to the Daily Missal and read the following verse:

> Thus says the Lord: These were my orders: Listen to my voice, then I will be your God and you shall be my people. Follow right to the end the way that I mark out for you, and you will prosper. But they did not listen, they did not pay attention; they followed the dictates of their own evil hearts, refused to face me, and turned their backs on me. (Jer 7:23–24)

On that particular morning, the above text unexpectedly shook me with conviction. A pillar of fire and smoke seemed to rise from the pages, enveloping me, carrying me away from my self-centered confusion and finally bringing me, with eyes now free of scales, to a new-yet-old understanding of God's call for my life.

These prophetic words from Jeremiah spoke of the spiritual journey we all must take: *From listening … through following … to receiving.*

God promises us a close covenantal relationship, both corporate and personal, if only we will listen to His voice: "I will be your God; you will be my people. I will be your Father; you will be my child." He promises that if we "follow right to the end" what we have heard, He will bless us, if we keep His commandments and abide in His love (see Jn 15:10).

Normally, I tend to focus more on the "if" side of "if-then" propositions. I tend to focus, for example, on how well I have or have not been listening and following. And in this case, I did begin this way. I recorded in my journal, speaking to God:

> I've spent a lot of time and mental energy over the years, maybe most of my life, trying to nail down what I will do once I "grow up." I must admit that I have failed to be

faithful in the obvious — I have not always "listened" and "followed" in the way You have clearly marked out for me in Your Word. Therefore, it is understandable that I may be less than sure about my vocational direction. Why should I prosper? Why should You help me? Why should You direct my paths? (Remember Prv 3:5–6)

But then the pillar of fire seemed to flare up, and through the din of my self-absorption, I heard the still, small voice. I wrote:

Yet, You have done so; You have always directed my paths! You have been so good to my family and to me over the years. No matter how much I have failed you, You have never failed me! Maybe sometime long ago You delegated my case to a very patient yet persistent guardian angel!

It became very clear that my future was really not my concern. I was in fact living in the future I had once fretted over; at the present, I had a wonderful ministry which I could have neither imagined nor planned! As a Protestant seminarian or pastor, I never dreamed I would one day be the North American director of an international Catholic evangelistic outreach to teenagers. Nor that this ministry would bring me into contact with deeply committed Catholic Christians from all over the world!

Even as I sat in the silence of that retreat lodge, I had no inkling that the fledgling Network would become the Coming Home Network International with more than forty-four thousand members; that I would one day be hosting weekly live programs on EWTN television and radio; that my wife and I and our three sons would travel to Europe to visit with other Catholic ministries; or that my family and a collection of animals would be living on a small, peaceful farm in central Ohio. And I received all this spiritual "prosperity" not because of insightful career planning on my part, but solely because of God's faithfulness.

As I sat in the stillness of that lodge, there was no question in my mind — no doubt in my heart — that God would be faithful. If He had indeed called Marilyn and me, as He had called Abraham, to leave all that was familiar (for us, the Protestant ministry) and follow Him by faith into a strange land (the Catholic Church), He would have something for me to do. And he certainly did!

What He expects of us now is to *listen* and *follow* faithfully: *"Follow right to the end of the way that I mark out for you."* And this, of course, is true for every one of you who have heard and are following the still, small voice of God. Remember: God promises that He will never leave you or forsake you.

As the pillar of fire burned down to an ember and the smoke cleared within my heart, I sat in stillness in my lodge room, motionless. My mind began to wander. Once again I found myself dreaming. I was singing ballads before a crowd of attentive, reflective groupies. And as I strummed my guitar, allowing "Amazing Grace" to explain the truth of my self-insufficiency, I saw before me seated at a coffee table, right up front, Jesus, smiling.

CHAPTER 28

Faith Alone, Faith and Works, or Something Else?

One day as Jesus "was setting out on his journey, a man [in fact, a very rich man we learn later] ran up and knelt before him, and asked him, 'Good teacher, what must I do to inherit eternal life?' And Jesus said to him, 'Why do you call me good?'" (Mk 10:17–18).

This familiar opening question and response between a sincere inquirer and Our Lord illustrates one of the most important yet confusing and divisive issues in Christianity. What more important question is there in our faith and ministries than "What must I do to be saved?" Whether people ask boldly and directly as did the rich young man, or whether they seek it subtly or even subliminally, isn't this the core question of the gospel: Lost in sin, blindness, and rebellion, how can we be made acceptable to God?

But what salvation actually means or is, or who needs it, or what we must do to get it, or whether or not we can lose it, are all highly debated issues among Christians of different traditions. As a result, often in today's ecumenical discussions, where the emphasis is more often on "speaking in love" rather than "speaking *the truth* in love" (see Eph 4:15), the answer to these questions can be as seemingly evasive as Jesus' initial response.

Jesus, however, completed His response to the inquiring young man very concisely. First Jesus reminded him, whom Scripture says He loved, to keep "the commandments." Then He instructed him: "Go, sell what you have, and give to the poor, and you will have treasure in heaven, and come, follow me" (Mk 10:18–21).

Seems clear enough. But how have the many divergent Christian traditions interpreted this invitation and implemented this response in their doctrine, dogma, mission, and practice?

A poignant personal experience once brought this difficulty home to me. As a senior minister of a large Presbyterian congregation, one day I was seated beside the hospital bed of an elderly man who was certainly only days, maybe hours, from meeting his Maker. As I sat there wondering what words were appropriate, his soon-to-be widow broke the silence and asked, "Pastor, is my husband going to heaven?"

Normally, I might have merely grasped her hand and passed along a pastoral yet packaged Presbyterian response. But I was already becoming concerned about the cacophony of conflicting Christian voices on this and other issues, so I sat paralyzed in silence. I realized that if I were instead a minister in a Methodist or Lutheran or Baptist or Episcopalian or Church of God or Assemblies of God congregation, I would be giving different, even conflicting reasons why this man might or might not be saved.

141

I can't remember how I finally replied. But I do know that my recognition of the confusion existing over this centrally important issue convinced me that I could not remain a Protestant pastor.

Later, when I was "on the journey," studying more seriously the teachings of the Catholic Church, and contrasting them with what I had always believed, the issues of salvation and justification kept rising to the top. Before my journey, I essentially only saw things from a "faith *alone*" perspective, and ridiculed those who emphasized "faith *and works*" as promoters of "works righteousness." Once I was on the journey, I began to hear what Catholics truly believe, but this didn't quickly solve things. I would compare and contrast apologetic arguments from both sides, and though I was coming to see the wisdom and truth in what the Church had always taught and defended, I often would walk away feeling dissatisfied, empty.

As I considered this dilemma, an old story came to mind. I'm sure most of you have already heard this tale, and admittedly I'm a bit stale on the details. But it's the best story I know to illustrate a point I believe needs to be made in the midst of any apologetic discussion of the issues of salvation and justification. The story goes something like this.

Years ago along the northern coast of New England stood a small village. Directly off the coast within sight of land was a treacherous shoal of rocks. During one particularly devastating nor'easter, a sailing ship with over a hundred passengers struck the rocks and sank. People watched helplessly from shore as the ship and her passengers were smashed again and again against the rocks. Shocked by what they had witnessed, they immediately swore never to let this happen again.

The Life Saving Society was established with rescue boats, life preservers, blankets, and emergency rations. It trained villagers how to use the boats, maintain their equipment, and administer medical assistance when necessary. Everyone in this small town was involved and deeply committed to the Society's goals.

A year went by, and again during the stormy season, another ship faced similar peril. But this time the Society was ready, and almost all on the ship were saved. Great rejoicing followed, with new plans to insure that next time all would be saved.

More years went by, and although the stormy seasons came as usual, no ships came near the rocks. Yet the Society continued. New generations of recruits were sworn in, and since no ships were imminently in peril, they eventually felt the need to add other activities to help fight boredom. There were athletic teams, nature clubs, fellowships for all ages, as well as debating societies.

New facilities were needed to accommodate all these new activities, and the attractive and spacious grounds became a bragging point for this small community. Sometimes large crowds would come from miles around to hear respected debaters engage in great controversies. They argued about the optimum number of rowers per boat versus the number of people needed on shore; who had the authority to organize a Society; or even the legalities involved in rescuing versus not rescuing people.

As years went by and no ships crumbled on the rocks, attendance and membership began to dwindle. Additional programs were instituted to encourage the recruitment of new blood. Colorful uniforms were awarded to those of higher rank, and trophies were given to those with the highest attendance or recruitment statistics.

Being a high-ranking member of the Society became a mark of prestige in the community and an expected item on the resume of anyone who intended to run for public office.

Often at political rallies candidates would debate over the future needs and goals of the Society, sometimes even boldly questioning whether, given the growing financial needs of the struggling community, the Society had long since outlived its purpose.

Was it truly their responsibility to save these souls? Hadn't these foolish seafaring people accepted the perils they faced when they set sail? Wasn't it simply God's will whether they lived or died, a part of His greater plan?

Then one day during the annual storm season, the worst nor'easter in years hit, and a large sailing vessel carrying 138 immigrants bore down on the rocks. The few remaining members of the Society watched with terror from shore. They wrung their hands and gnashed their teeth, for not only had the lifesaving boats and equipment long since disintegrated through neglect, but the members no longer knew how to use them.

In addition, they were divided over whether they should or should not make any valiant efforts to save these people. Some asked, Isn't the predestined fate of those on the ship solely in the hands of God? Isn't the primary responsibility of the Society to pray for those in peril, hoping that God in His infinite mercy might choose to save their lives and souls?

Others responded: Isn't it up to us to rescue these dying people? God has placed us here at this moment with the freedom to respond to their desperate need, and how we respond will determine not only the fate of the people on the ship, but also our own eternal destinies. God will judge us by how we treat "the least of these."

The Life Saving Society remnant stood arguing and debating, impotent to do anything out of neglect, while all 138 passengers perished.

This story, of course, can be used to illustrate all kinds of aspects of the Church's mission — or failure to engage in mission. But I think it particularly applies to the issues of salvation and justification. As I wrestled in those days to understand the role of the Church, I remembered debates I had heard (and taken part in) especially during my seminary days over what is necessary for salvation. Not just Catholics and Protestants had debated each other, but also different Protestant denominations had debated among themselves.

In all these deliberations, I sensed the need for an important caution: We must not miss the central, most critical, issue — an issue that is too often missing in our polemics.

Those arguing for the necessity of both faith and works of charity through grace can be just as wrong as those arguing for faith alone if they forget this most central, essential element. And I believe that if this central element is not only remembered and emphasized, but also experienced through humble surrender, then people will be saved by faith through grace in Jesus Christ and in and through His Church.

What is this most critical element? Simply the necessity for changed hearts.

We can believe all the correct doctrines, even profess them with our lips. We can have the faith to move mountains. But as St. Paul emphasized in Romans 10:9–10, we must believe them in our hearts. Faith *alone* without a changed heart cannot save us.

Saying a quick prayer during an emotional moment at a crusade, camp meeting, or altar call can't save anyone without a heart touched and changed by the Holy Spirit. With a changed heart, however, faith will lead to the recognition of the need for repentance and surrender of self to Christ; for forgiveness of self and others; for charity towards God and others; for prayer for self, others, and even enemies; for a constant increase of Christ and decrease of self; for a life of obedience, holiness, and growth in grace.

Any sincere evangelical Protestant knows this to be true, as witnessed by the thousands of sermons calling for changed hearts preached from pulpits all over America. But sometimes this truth is lost in theological debates.

We can also do all the kinds of good works and rituals expected of us by our Church. We can faithfully fulfill every rite of passage and regularly practice every sacrament and sacramental. We can staunchly defend every doctrine, dogma, or legislation of our Church, fighting even against those in our own Church who might desire to water down the requirements or the rubrics.

But without changed hearts, all of this is meaningless grandstanding. A rosary said without a changed heart, without a heart in surrender to Christ, is just what Jesus warned about in Matthew 6 — an attempt to "babble like the pagans, who think they will be heard because of their many words." Again, any sincere Catholic knows this to be true, evidenced by the thousands of homilies calling for changed hearts preached from Catholic pulpits all over America.

St. Paul seems to be the source most often quoted for both sides of the salvation debate. But even he strongly emphasizes the necessity of a changed heart. For example, in 1 Corinthians 13 we hear him argue with great conviction that love is greater than anything else, including faith. But when we look at how he describes the kind of love that is greater than all, isn't it obvious that what he is really talking about is a changed heart? He speaks of love that springs from a heart that is patient, kind, not jealous, not pompous, not inflated, not rude, not self-seeking, not quick-tempered.

St. James is another witness often brought into the debate, but what does he say?

> If anyone thinks he is religious, and does not bridle his
> tongue but deceives his heart, this man's religion is vain.

> Religion that is pure and undefiled before God and the
> Father is this: to visit orphans and widows in their afflic-
> tion, and to keep oneself unstained by the world. … Who
> is wise and understanding among you? By his good life let
> him show his works in the meekness of wisdom. But if you
> have bitter jealousy and selfish ambition in your hearts,
> do not boast and be false to the truth. This wisdom is not
> such as comes down from above, but is earthly, unspiritual,
> devilish. (Jas 1:26–27; 3:13–15)

I could easily make a longer, more detailed scriptural defense of this insight. But the best way to recognize the necessity of a changed heart as a requirement for salvation and justification is to listen to what Jesus taught about how we are
saved. I don't mean reading Jesus through "the eyes of Paul"
or through any particular interpretation of Paul, but merely
reading the words of Jesus and listening to what He told his
followers was necessary for their salvation.

Recently I read through the Gospel of St. Matthew listening for Jesus' instructions on this matter. I ended up with over
ten pages of notes. Nearly everything He said challenges us
to have hearts surrendered to the Father as the foundation
for our faith and our works. Apart from changed hearts, both
faith and works are powerless to bring us to the Father.

I challenge you to engage in a similar project. Unless we
seek this reality for ourselves, nothing anyone else summarizes
for us can truly change our hearts. But to get you started, here
are a few snippets from Matthew: "Repent, for the kingdom of
heaven is at hand" (Mt 4:17).

Jesus' proclamation was the same as that of His precursor,
St. John the Baptist. To what were they both calling their followers but changed hearts?

Earlier, when the scribes and Pharisees came forward to
be baptized (see Mt 3:7–12), why was John so angry that they

came? Why wasn't he elated to see them? Weren't these the same teachers of truth Jesus would later tell His disciples to follow though not imitate (see Mt 23:1–12)? Wasn't the problem in both places that the Pharisees had hard hearts? (See also Mk 3:5.)

> Blessed are the poor in spirit ... those who mourn ... the
> meek ... those who hunger and thirst for righteousness ...
> the merciful ... the pure in heart, for they shall see God.
> (Mt 5:3–8)

I remember that the Beatitudes were a bit of a bugaboo for us "faith *alone*" folks, some of us relegating them to "Plan A," which had then been replaced by Paul's "Plan B" (see chapter 6). But aren't these in fact the most clear statements showing how Jesus understood the necessity of changed hearts if we are to "see God" (Mt 5:3–12)?

> Love your enemies and pray for those who persecute you,
> *so that* you may be sons of your Father who is in heaven. ...
> You, therefore, must be perfect, as your heavenly Father is
> perfect. (Mt 5:44–45, 48, emphasis added)

Being a "child of God" is a common scriptural description of those who are being saved (see Jn 1.12-13; 1 Jn 3.1-3). But here Jesus states that one criterion for becoming a son of the Father is a changed heart — not the mere act of loving or praying for an enemy, but a heart sincerely and sufficiently open to doing this.

After urging us to almsgiving, prayer, fasting, and other actions, Jesus concludes: "Your Father who sees in secret will reward you" (Mt 6:18).

What is it about our prayers, our almsgiving, our fasting, our actions, and our beliefs that the Father is looking for in secret? Isn't it the sincerity of our hearts?

> Lay up for yourselves treasures in heaven. … For where
> your treasure is, there will your heart be also. (Mt 6:20-21)

Where our heart is will be the key to which rewards in heaven we will receive from the Father. Are these only those rewards we receive after salvation, or isn't this also the reward of salvation itself?

> Not every one who says to me, "Lord, Lord," shall enter the
> kingdom of heaven, but he who does the will of my Father
> who is in heaven. (Mt 7:21)

These are strong words from our Savior. In this reference, what's missing from someone's inadequate profession is not merely good works, but all the things Jesus has been teaching up to this point, which involves hearts that are surrendered to the will of God.

> "Lord, I am not worthy to have you come under my roof;
> but only say the word, and my servant will be healed." …
> "Truly, I say to you, not even in Israel have I found such
> faith." (Mt 8:8, 10)

Was it merely this centurion's belief in Jesus' miraculous powers that impressed Jesus? Or wasn't it his humble, malleable heart, which caused him to set aside his Roman attitude of superiority to recognize his true unworthiness?

> Go and learn what this means, "I desire mercy, and not
> sacrifice." For I came not to call the righteous, but sinners.
> (Mt 9:13)

The "righteous" were those who may have believed and claimed the right things or who did the right things, but who did so from self-centered hearts. What Jesus wanted instead were those who had humbly faced up to their sinfulness — those with changed hearts.

149

> You brood of vipers! how can you speak good things, when
> you are evil? For out of the abundance of the heart the
> mouth speaks. … I tell you, on the day of judgment men
> will render account for every careless word they utter; for
> by your words you will be justified, and by your words you
> will be condemned. (Mt 12:34, 36–37; see also 15:18)

Seems like our words are *very* important, both to eternity and to our justification. Yet *not* merely our words (see also Mt 10:32–33), but the source of these words: our heart.

> You hypocrites! Well did Isaiah prophesy of you, when
> he said:
> "This people honors me with their lips,
> but their heart is far from me;
> in vain do they worship me,
> teaching as doctrines the precepts of men." (Mt 15:7–9)

Both sides of the salvation debate can be equally guilty in this regard. If our teaching of either "faith *alone*" or "faith *and works of charity*" neglects to emphasize that a changed heart is crucial for salvation, then our teachings can become merely "precepts of men."

So much more in Matthew and the other Gospels, as well as the other New Testament Epistles, clearly emphasizes the central importance of a changed heart as the underlying criterion for salvation. My guess is that most of you reading this are saying, "Duh, who said otherwise?"

Well, consider that Christians are so uncharitably divided over these very issues: men and women; scholars, clerics, and laity; churches, movements, denominations; taking sides and casting vengeful, hateful, prideful, and boastful epithets at one another. All of this and more proves to me that these polemics, as important as these distinctions are, too often blind us to what is most important: "You shall love the Lord your God with all your heart, and with all your soul, and with all your mind. ... You shall love your neighbor as yourself" (Mt 22:37, 39).

One last quote from Jesus. In the following statement, which is perhaps His clearest on what it truly takes to be a disciple, He doesn't emphasize "faith *alone*," though faith is certainly presumed, nor does He emphasize "faith *and works*," though again works are clearly mentioned. What He requires are hearts changed and surrendered and submissive to the will of God.

> If any man would come after me, let him deny himself and take up his cross and follow me. For whoever would save his life will lose it, and whoever loses his life for my sake will find it. ... For the Son of Man is to come with his angels in the glory of his Father, and then he will repay every man for what he has done. (Mt 16:24–27)

My wife, Marilyn, and I had the privilege of making a pilgrimage to the Holy Land. It was truly a blessed experience, but one incident during that visit clearly emphasizes this point.

We were at the Church of the Nativity in Bethlehem. It's an ancient Byzantine structure, the oldest surviving church in Israel, built over the cave where, from antiquity, it has been believed that Jesus was born. To get down to the exact spot where it's believed Jesus was born, marked now with a silver star on the floor, pilgrims must walk, bent over, through a stone tunnel, one at a time, into the ancient cave.

Before we could enter this blessed spot, we had to wait in a long line. Waiting with us were more than two hundred other Christian pilgrims from all over the world, representing many languages, cultures, customs, and sects, all trying anxiously to get into the tunnel. People became so excited about touching the very place where Christ was supposedly born that they began shoving and cutting into line. Some began shouting back and forth — maybe even cursing, though I couldn't understand their languages.

At one point a priest of another Christian tradition became so angry that his particular pilgrims weren't able to "cut in line" that he began pushing through the crowd ordering everyone to make way for his people. But he was quickly shouted down by those in front until he gave up and his group was ordered by the guards to go to the end of the line.

All of this just to see the site where our Savior — the gift of God's love — was born! Had we forgotten why Jesus had come? Where were our hearts?

When I listen to two Christians arguing over whether we our saved by "faith *alone*" or by "faith *and works*," I also wonder whether we have forgotten: "By this all men will know that you are my disciples, if you have love for one another" (Jn 13:35).

And what does Jesus mean by *having love* except loving one another from hearts truly changed by His love?

CHAPTER 29
Make Straight Your Paths

The words "make straight your paths" come from my favorite biblical Proverb:

> Trust in the Lord with all your heart,
> and do not rely on your own insight;
> In all your ways acknowledge him,
> and he will make straight your paths. (Prv 3:5–6)

All my adult Christian life, from my reconversion at age twenty-one, on through seminary, into the pastorate, eventually into the Catholic Church, and now as I try by grace to live as a faithful Catholic, I have found this promise from the Old Testament to be amazingly true. If by grace we turn our lives in His direction — heart, mind, soul, and strength — focusing not on ourselves but on Him, He promises not just to guide us but also to make straight our paths.

Do you believe this to be true? Has it been true in your own life? And particularly those of you who once heard and followed the call from God to become Protestant ministers, who went to seminary, were ordained, and then served as pastors — all because you believed he was making your paths straight: How do you feel now as you hear Him calling you home to the Catholic Church? as you see Him leading you along a path that seems to contradict if not negate everything you once thought He was calling you to do?

Do you wonder now whether in the past you may have misheard Him? By faith in Jesus Christ, you trusted Him with your whole heart, you did not rely on your own insight, you sought to acknowledge Him in all you did, and you pressed on into seminary, into the pastorate, banking your whole life on the ministry, believing He was making straight your paths.

Yet now, as you consider the Catholic Church and what this may mean for your future, your vocation, your career, and your family, you may ask whether He was indeed making your path straight? Is it possible that you had been misled, or rather that you had misheard? I believe that neither is the case, but let me explain.

I was thinking of this proverb last week while out seeding my farm pastures with clover seed using a hand-cranked spreader, the old-fashioned way. As I began, the question arose how I would make sure that my paths were straight enough to spread the seeds evenly.

I first learned what I thought was an adequate answer long ago as a young boy when my father handed over the keys to the push mower. After watching me make a few wavy, haphazard rows, he set down his iced tea, ran out, and said, "Son, don't focus downward at the mower at your feet. Look straight ahead to the end of the row. Avoid glancing down any more than necessary. Just focus ahead on your destination and trust."

At first, I found this approach quite awkward. I was certain I would leave lines of uncut grass. But eventually I became brave enough to do an entire row without looking down, and lo and behold, the path was straight with no missed grass. As I grew in courage, my anxieties waned, and soon I could cut the entire yard with hardly a glance of doubt downward.

This personal experience became a common preaching image in my sermons, with obvious analogies, for the fifteen years I served in Protestant ministry. I backed up the illustration with a scriptural text:

"We need to keep our eyes fixed firmly on Jesus; 'let us also lay aside every weight [distraction], and sin which clings so closely, and let us run with perseverance the race that is set before us, looking to Jesus the pioneer and perfecter of our faith' (Heb 12:1–2). We must not be like Peter who took his eyes off Jesus and sank into the water. We need to ignore the distractions and fears of life, and focus directly on Him and trust!"

This is a good analogy, as far as it goes, as was my father's advice, as far as it went. But then, in time, I became aware of its flaws.

You see, when my dad passed on to me the baton of lawn maintenance, we were living in northwestern Ohio, where our half-acre backyard was as flat as a pool table. Focusing straight ahead was just that — straight ahead. Since then, however, I've never had a yard that wasn't hilly, and now the entire Appalachian foothills farm we live on doesn't have a single flat spot.

I glanced ahead, holding my hand-cranked seed spreader, across ten rolling acres toward my destination. I saw trees and thorn bushes I would have to maneuver around, hundreds of cow and horse pies I would need to avoid. All the while, I would mostly be trudging through ankle-deep mud.

Life is very much like this hilly farm. God's promise to make straight our paths does not necessarily mean that we can plot a clearly discernible path of how our life in Jesus — past, present, and future — all makes sense.

How often have I said, "Now I see what He was doing and why He led me to do that!" This statement is certainly true sometimes. But I have come to see that the "straightness" of our paths, by grace, is not so much a matter of *direction* as it is of *holiness*.

The proverb we cited speaks of the partnership we have with God in our salvation: His sovereignty and our freedom of will to choose. We willingly and freely turn from ourselves into His direction, and in the process realize that somehow in the mystery of His mercy, He is the one who graced our action. While we are fully responsible for trusting in Him with our whole hearts, it is He who makes us straight — not just with regard to the trajectory toward which we are aiming, but right now, wherever we are currently standing in life.

It isn't that before we entered the Catholic Church He was misguiding or we were mishearing. Rather, in the mystery of His loving plan for each of us, He was making us holy in each of the many "hills" in our desire to follow His calling. Making straight our paths does not mean that He rids our lives of suffering, sadness, frustration, discouragement, radical changes in course, or even failure. It is in fact in the midst of these things that we are most called to trust fully in Him, to rely not on our own insight but to acknowledge Him in everything, and proceed in believing that He is making our lives straight — in other words, holy. That's why He allows them to happen.

Last week I sat back at the end of the day, sore and soggy from six hours of traversing our ten muddy acres in abnormally hot seventy-degree March weather. I felt a noble sense of accomplishment, certain that this was exactly what God had called me to do in this timely manner in the last weeks of winter. Now, however, after two days of continuous drenching rain, and with our county under a flood warning, I wondered whether any of the clover seed were left. I could have ended up with thick clover patches along the drainage ditches.

Was it all a waste? Had I misheard? I suppose in a material sense some might consider it a waste. But ultimately what is important is the condition, the attitude, of my heart: then as I was seeding, now as I look back, and tomorrow as I once again seek to live out this wise proverb.

CHAPTER 30

On the Meaning of Human Suffering

Any of you who have contemplated or made the journey from the Protestant pastorate into the Catholic Church, or who have prayerfully stood by those who have, know that packaged with all the joys are varying levels of suffering. I need not enumerate all of these, but only emphasize that sometimes the pressure from potential ramifications stops inquirers dead in their tracks and prevents converts from enjoying all the benefits of the fullness of the faith.

Given the continual flow of converts, regardless of the struggles, why is God calling so many Protestant clergy home to the Catholic Church specifically at this time in history? There may be as many answers to this question as there are converts, but usually the answers center on what converts bring to the Church because of their training, skills, and experience, as well as their zeal.

Pope John Paul II confirmed this reality when he wrote:

> Certainly, every convert is a gift to the Church and repre-
> sents a serious responsibility for her … especially in the
> case of adults, such converts bring with them a kind of new
> energy, an enthusiasm for the faith, and a desire to see the
> gospel lived out in the Church. (*Redemptoris Missio*, 47)

However, it was in reading this pope's apostolic letter, *Salvi-fici Doloris*, "On the Christian Meaning of Human Suffering," that I was struck by the significance of another major reason for today's flow of Protestant converts. God has been bring-ing home clergy converts, like myself and hundreds more, not only because of what we have to give to the Church, but be-cause the nature of our journeys adds a uniquely important element of suffering to the overall redemptive suffering of the Church. It's not that we ourselves are particularly important, for we are only branches (maybe just twigs). But the particular fruit we have to offer as a result of our individual and collective abiding journeys with Christ is the suffering we experience as we bridge the gap of schism and return home. This is our call-ing, our vocation.

Salvifici Doloris remains one of Pope John Paul's most powerful letters, examining a topic very real and imminent to nearly every person. In the sections called "Sharers in the Suf-fering of Christ," "The Gospel of Suffering," and "The Good Samaritan," he developed a strong biblical and philosophical argument for the redemptive meaning of suffering, addressing the deep mysteries expressed in Colossians 1:24 — a text that, as a Protestant, I did not understand: "In my flesh I complete what is lacking in Christ's afflictions for the sake of his body, that is, the Church."

It was the following passage that particularly caught my at-tention in relation to the issue of why God is calling Protestant ministers home to the Catholic Church:

> The answer which comes through this sharing, by way of the interior encounter with the Master, is in itself something more than the mere abstract answer to the question about the meaning of suffering. For it is above all a call. It is a vocation. Christ does not explain in the abstract the reasons for suffering, but before all else he says: "Follow me! Come! Take part through your suffering in this work of saving the world, a salvation achieved through my suffering! Through my cross!" Gradually, as the individual takes up his cross, spiritually uniting himself to the cross of Christ, the salvific meaning of suffering is revealed before him. (*Salvifici Doloris*, 26)

Yes, clergy converts, as well as anyone else who comes home to the Church with training, gifts, experience, and zeal for the gospel, have much to give. But I encourage you to reflect seriously on the possibility that the main reason Jesus has called any of us home is to share with Him the suffering of His Church, torn by schism, by dissent, and most importantly by a nearly universal lack of love.

Sometimes we whine, "Okay, Lord, what do you want me to do now?" (I am guilty of such whining a hundredfold.) Sometimes we anxiously ponder, "How will I support my family if I give up this pulpit?" When such questions and concerns come to mind, we must not miss the special grace of the moment: Jesus is giving us a great gift, an opportunity to grow.

> Down through the centuries and generations it has been seen that in suffering there is concealed a particular power that draws a person interiorly closer to Christ, a special grace. To this grace many saints, such as St. Francis of Assisi, St. Ignatius of Loyola, and others, owe their profound conversion. A result of such a conversion is not only that the individual discovers the salvific meaning of suffering, but above all that he becomes a completely new person. (*Salvifici Doloris*, 26)

The ultimate reason that Jesus brings us from the often comfortable spirituality of our Protestant lives and service into the fullness of the Catholic Church is so that we can even more fully give ourselves "as a living sacrifice" for the sake of His Church. He isn't done working with us yet, we have not arrived. He still wants us to become "a completely new person."

It may even be possible in this journey — according to the mysterious wisdom of His will — that He may decide that we never again use any of the gifts or training He once led us to receive. He may want us to detach ourselves completely from everything in our past, so that He can lead us more freely into the future He has for us. Of course, after our detachment, He may surprise us, as He has done for many of us! But we must first let go.

Jesus challenged the rich young man in the Gospel: "Go, sell all you have, give to the poor, and follow me" (Mk 10:21). For many years I taught that this young man's riches were the primary idol preventing him from reaching the kingdom of God. John Paul II, however, helped me realize that what Jesus also wanted this comfortable man to do was accept suffering — for his own sake, in empathy with and active service to the suffering poor, and ultimately for the sake of the kingdom.

In what ways is Jesus calling you to suffer? In what ways is this call to suffering too daunting, too demanding, too radical, as it was for the rich young man who turned away? Remember the many words of encouragement in Scripture: "Have no anxiety about anything ... fear not ... take my yoke upon you ... rejoice in the Lord always!" (Phil 4:6; Mt 10:31, 11:29; Phil 4:4).

At the end of his letter, Pope John Paul II offers this plea:

> And we ask all you who suffer to support us. We ask precisely you who are weak to become a source of strength for the Church and humanity. In the terrible battle between the

> forces of good and evil, revealed to our eyes by our modern
> world, may your suffering in union with the cross of Christ
> be victorious! (*Salvifici Doloris*, 26)

Compared to the gruesome suffering, persecution, and cruelty experienced by so many in our world, the suffering we undergo in leaving our pastorates and pasts to become Catholic is truly minor. By grace we must accept it without complaint, and "offer it up" in reparation for the myriad divisions we and others have brought upon the Body of Christ. "Lord Jesus Christ, Lamb of God who takes away the sins of the world, have mercy on me, a sinner."

CHAPTER 31

Conversion Means Sacrifice

Conversion to Jesus Christ and His Church always requires sacrifice. This process of course includes conversion to His Church, because true conversion to Jesus requires acceptance of *all* that He taught (see Mt 28:19), not just those teachings that make life comfortable. In the Gospel of Mark we're told that after Jesus had described the suffering He must go through for His disciples, He turned the tables:

> If any man would come after me, let him deny himself and
> take up his cross and follow me. For whoever would save
> his life will lose it; and whoever loses his life for my sake
> and the gospel's will save it. (Mark 8:34–35)

Following Jesus requires sacrifice. This is a requirement not just for the few, but for all.

When St. Paul strongly asserted in Romans 8:16–17 that "we are children of God, and if children, then heirs, heirs of God and fellow heirs with Christ," he said this conditionally. He wasn't offering some trump card we now can flash whenever our sins put us in danger of "going to jail." Rather, our status as God's children and fellow heirs with Christ is true, the Apostle added, only *"provided we suffer with him in order that we may also be glorified with him"* (emphasis added). Conversion from being a child of the world to being a child of God requires sacrifice.

Mother Teresa: Come Be My Light (Image, 2009) is a collection of the private correspondence of Blessed Teresa of Calcutta. In one letter, she relates a vow made soon after her final profession to become a nun: "I made a vow to God, binding under [pain of] mortal sin, to give to God anything that He may ask, 'Not to refuse Him anything'" (p. 28).

The book's author treats this vow as if it is extraordinary. But isn't this vow precisely what every single Christian is expected to make? What was extraordinary about Mother Teresa was not that she made such a vow, but how by grace she was able to live it out in obedience under such extraordinary circumstances: serving Jesus selflessly by caring for the poorest of the poor.

You and I, if we say we desire to follow Jesus as one of His disciples, are called "to give to God anything that He may ask, 'not to refuse Him anything.'" Thanks be to Jesus that He fully recognizes that apart from Him we can do nothing (see Jn 15:5) and gives us the necessary graces. We just need to abide in Him.

This is one of the primary reasons we work towards visible unity in the Church, calling all to come home: Everyone needs, for salvation, the graces that can be received *with certainty* only through the sacraments of the Catholic Church.

Conversion to Jesus Christ and His Church always requires sacrifice. This has been true since the very first Christian conversion.

Imagine yourself the "man lame from birth" in Acts 3. Every day, for as long as you can remember, a family member has carried you out to the gate called Beautiful, where you have begged for alms from those passing to enter the temple. Your infirmity has prevented you from any education or from learning anything else except begging, so this is how you support yourself and your family.

Then one morning, as on every morning, you are begging those who walk by for alms. When you ask two men from Galilee for money, one of them unexpectedly says, "I have no silver and gold." You are about to turn your gaze away to beg from others passing by, but the man continues speaking: "But I give you what I have; in the name of Jesus Christ of Nazareth, walk."

You are about to utter an expletive when he takes you by the right hand and raises you up. Suddenly your feet and ankles feel strong for the first time in your life. Before you know it, you are leaping up and walking around, praising God. You then enter into the temple with the two strangers, where everyone from whom you have been begging alms for years sees you and becomes filled with wonder and amazement!

You cling to these two strangers in amazement. With everyone gathered around, they preach a sermon about this man Jesus in whose name you were healed. Your life has been changed radically forever!

When the crowd thins out and the two men leave, you do something you've never done before: You walk home on your own two feet. You wave at everyone along the way as the wonder and amazement continue — until sometime in the night, when you begin considering what you will do in the morning.

How will you now get money to support yourself and your family? Sure, you can walk, but now you no longer can beg, and you have no skills for anything else! Maybe a friend will have pity on you and give you some kind of work. But in the end this healing and conversion, which you did not seek, have radically changed your life forever.

The report of another interesting episode in Acts includes few details, yet has important similarities to the sacrifices required of today's clergy converts: "And the word of God increased, and the number of the disciples multiplied greatly in Jerusalem, *and a great many of the priests were obedient to the faith*" (Acts 6:7, emphasis added).

We never again hear of the plight of these early clergy converts to Christianity, but we can imagine their sacrifices. They probably were disowned by their non-converted Jewish friends and family. Moreover, in abandoning their positions as priests of the temple, they lost their livelihood, their shares of the sacrifices. They became "unemployed" and had to subsist through the merciful benevolence of the growing Christian community.

Today's clergy converts must face the same sacrifices whenever they contemplate leaving the Christian community in which they were nurtured, educated, ordained, and employed. Entering into the Catholic Church, they receive no guarantees that they will have opportunities within the Church to use their training, gifts, and experiences to support themselves and their families. Many of them feel a bit like the healed beggar must have felt: grateful to be home, but now what?

Today's clergy converts also face difficulties that the clergy converts of yesteryear never faced. We live in a much more complicated economy that requires, besides room and board, the funding of expensive health care plans and provisions for the future.

It's one thing to quote Jesus' words: "Do not be anxious about your life, what you shall eat or what you shall drink. ... do not be anxious about tomorrow. ... Let the day's own trouble be sufficient for the day" (Mt 6:25, 34). But it is quite another thing to *live* these words when you're in your fifties or sixties, a husband and a father, contemplating abandoning your pastoral ministry, your salary, and your denomination's health and pension plan — especially if this ministry is all you have ever done.

Some may consider these concerns "worldly." They may judge as "weak in faith" those who delay or even decide against "coming home" because of these concerns. They may even believe that such people are in danger of damnation since the Church still teaches: "They could not be saved who, knowing that the Catholic Church was founded as necessary by God through Christ, refuse either to enter it or to remain in it" (CCC, 846; *Lumen Gentium,* 14; cf. Mk 16:16, Jn 3:5).

Yet the Church very carefully and charitably qualifies this statement without lessening its meaning. The Catechism continues (CCC 847–848):

> This affirmation is not aimed at those who, through no fault of their own, do not know Christ and his Church:

> Those who, through no fault of their own, do not know the gospel of Christ or his Church, but who nevertheless seek God with a sincere heart, and, moved by grace, try in their actions to do his will as they know it through the dictates of their conscience — those too may achieve eternal salvation. (*Lumen Gentium,* 16; cf. DS 3866–3872)

> "Although in ways known to himself God can lead those who, through no fault of their own, are ignorant of the gospel, to that faith without which it is impossible to please him, the Church still has the obligation and also the sacred right to evangelize all men." (*Ad gentes* 7; cf. Heb 11:6; 1 Cor 9:16)

For these reasons, we must not stand in judgment, nor push, pull, or prod anyone into making such a drastic, life-altering decision to enter into the fullness of the Catholic faith. Of course, we prayerfully hope that anyone on the journey will complete it, following the teaching of the Church. Yet conversion to the Catholic faith must always be a decision freely made. We who have already come home, or have always been home, will continue to offer our patient and understanding prayers and support for those still on the journey.

CHAPTER 32

Drooping Hands and Weak Knees

Several years ago my oldest son, Jon Marc, and I had the privilege of visiting sites associated with the lives of the English martyrs. We stood in the halls of Oxford where St. Edmund Campion and others had studied while they were discerning God's call for their lives. (Blessed John Henry Cardinal Newman had studied there as well.) We stood outside Lyford Grange, the house where Campion was celebrating a secret Mass when he was betrayed, arrested, and taken to the Tower of London.

We toured the Tower of London and saw the prison cells with the inscriptions of St. Philip Howard, St. Thomas More, and St. John Fisher. We also saw the block upon which they were beheaded. We visited Arundel Castle, a center for recusant Catholics in the years after the Reformation. (The *recusants* were the English Catholics of the sixteenth through eighteenth centuries who refused to attend the services of the Church of England or to recognize its authority.)

All these sites stood as a sobering reminder to me. I sometimes tell myself that I sacrificed a great deal in giving up my pastorate to enter the Catholic Church. But then I consider what other men and women gave up, martyrs such as Edmund Campion, John Southworth, Margaret Clitherow, Margaret Ward, Thomas Becket, Thomas More, and John Fisher. I realize that my own sacrifices and worries pale in comparison. These men and women were driven to sacrifice all in defense of the Church they loved.

I stood on the coast near the place where Edmund Campion and others secretly came back into England, knowing what would face them there. The words of Hebrews 12 became clear to me in a new way:

> Therefore, since we are surrounded by so great a cloud of witnesses, let us also lay aside every weight, and sin which clings so closely, and let us run with perseverance the race that is set before us, looking to Jesus the pioneer and perfecter of our faith, who for the joy that was set before him endured the cross, despising the shame, and is seated at the right hand of the throne of God.

> Consider Him who endured from sinners such hostility against himself, so that you may not grow weary or fainthearted. In your struggle against sin you have not yet resisted to the point of shedding your blood.

> And have you forgotten the exhortation which addresses you as sons? "My son, do not regard lightly the discipline of the Lord, nor lose courage when you are punished by him. For the Lord disciplines him whom He loves, and chastises every son whom he receives."

> It is for discipline that you have to endure. God is treating you as sons; for what son is there whom his father does not discipline? ...
>
> For the moment all discipline seems painful rather than pleasant; later it yields the peaceful fruit of righteousness to those who have been trained by it. ...
>
> Therefore lift your drooping hands and strengthen your weak knees, and make straight paths for your feet, so that what is lame may not be put out of joint but rather be healed. (Heb 12:1–7, 11–13)

That line about "drooping hands" and "weak knees" really hit home, considering that for forty years I hardly bent a knee in worship. And then once again that line "make straight paths for your feet" reminded me of those encouraging words from Proverbs 3:5–6, which we noted in an earlier chapter: "Trust in the Lord with all your heart, and do not rely on your own insight. In all your ways acknowledge him, and he will make straight your paths."

After being a Catholic now for several years, I have encountered many surprises along the path. Through my readings and discussions, and particularly my experiences taking part in the Mass and other sacraments, I have encountered countless truths that over and over again confirm: The Catholic Church is indeed the Church that Jesus Christ planted, with all its warts, with all its weaknesses, and especially with all its sinners, people like me. What a privilege of grace to share in its joy!

CHAPTER 33

Believe That You May Understand

He who created all things from nothing
   Would not remake his ruined creation without Mary.
For God begot the Son,
   Through whom all things were made,
And Mary gave birth to Him
   As the Savior of the world.
Without God's Son, nothing could exist;
   Without Mary's Son, nothing could be redeemed.
St. Anselm, Archbishop of Canterbury (1033–1109)

Catholic dogma about the Immaculate Conception of Mary is a consistent bugaboo for Protestants considering the Catholic Church. A part of me, responding to those residual Protestant attitudes still haunting my subconscious, would like to leave this doctrine up on the "nice shelf," out of the normal day-in, day-out circuits of my Christian walk. I sometimes still hear that nagging voice, that demanding criterion: "Show it to me in Scripture!"

But then the rejoinder comes immediately: "Show me where in Scripture it says that I've got to show you in Scripture!"

I find yet another quote from St. Anselm, the great medieval philosopher and theologian, enlightening on this and many other subjects: "I do not seek to understand that I may believe, but I believe that I may understand: for this I also believe, that unless I believe I will not understand."

Isn't this statement true of all that we understand in our Christian faith? What little I truly understand about the Trinity or the divinity of Christ comes basically from my belief that the Holy Spirit can be trusted to lead the Church into all truth and, therefore, to interpret Scripture and Tradition correctly. Apart from this belief, we are left only with some form of reductionist "Christianity" such as Unitarianism or "Jesus-only" fundamentalism, or the modern forms of Arianism, Modalism, and even polytheism.

When we honestly consider God's choice of Mary, we are faced with the reality that God's plan was dependent upon Mary's choice of God. In God's unfathomable wisdom, He chose to make His plan subject to the will of a young Palestinian peasant girl. He didn't send Gabriel to command Mary to submit. Instead, He sent the angel to announce His plan in order to elicit her response.

The mystery we encounter here is summarized in the exchange between Gabriel and Mary:

> And the angel said to her ... "For with God nothing will be impossible." And Mary said, "Behold, I am the handmaid of the Lord; let it be to me according to your word." (Lk 1:35, 37–38)

This exchange is important to those who struggle in their journey home to the Catholic Church, particularly as they look to the future — as they wonder not only how they will support their families if they resign from pastoral ministry, but how exactly they will continue to serve the Lord in the Catholic Church. These words give both a promise and a premise.

The promise is one we fully believe as Christians, but must also be willing to act on: that all things are possible with God. He can do a whole lot more for us, and better than we can ever imagine: I certainly never dreamed, when I left my Presbyterian pastorate, that I would one day be the host of a Catholic television program interviewing converts to the Catholic Church!

The premise is that in Mary, God has given us a perfect example of how we should respond to God's grace. All that she was and ever would be was a gift of God's grace. The response that was necessary to receive all that He might give and accomplish through her was total trust and surrender. Her words, "Let it be to me according to your word," are to be our unfettered answer to God's call.

Even Mary had questions about how the impossible becomes possible. But when reminded that God is greater than any impossibility, she responded in the same way we must respond to God's infinite greatness: obedient surrender. Only then can He freely work in and through and for us.

As you prayerfully discern how and where God is calling you to follow, let Mary's words be like the hound of heaven, pursuing you, beckoning you to step out in faith, trusting the Holy Spirit as he calls you home.

CHAPTER 34

Now What, Lord?

About two thousand years ago Joseph, betrothed to Mary, received some information that shattered whatever expectations, plans, and dreams he had for his future. I think of him sometimes when I recall how discovering the fullness of the Catholic faith has had a similarly jarring impact on many of our lives.

The burden St. Joseph carried, of course, was much greater than ours could ever be. If he had been a different sort of man, he might have belittled the worries that so many of us expressed when we discovered that we might lose our jobs and vocations. Scripture tells us, however, that Joseph was a righteous man. So we can be sure that he has great empathy for clergy converts and their families today as they face the uncertainties that confront them.

Let's take a closer look at St. Joseph's situation. We know few of the details, but let's imagine.

He was betrothed to the woman of his dreams. She was beautiful, pure, and surprisingly holy, compared to the rest of the girls he knew. He could find no fault or flaw in her. And she was his betrothed! What a blessing. What a future!

I picture him to be much like the young tailor in the Broadway musical *Fiddler on the Roof* who courted and finally won the hand of Tevye's first daughter. The tailor was planning for their future and had his eyes set on a new, modern sewing machine. Did Joseph perhaps envision the enlarged carpentry shop he would need to support his future family?

All this was shattered, however, when he found his betrothed "with child." Imagine the questions that went through his mind as she stood with distended stomach before him. We don't know the order of the events, but shouldn't we presume that at this point Mary had already accepted her marching orders from the angel and visited her cousin Elizabeth? Now she stood before her beloved, several months with child.

We've all heard speculations about what went through Joseph's mind and eventually motivated his response. Please allow me, if you would, to add another thought to this mix.

In Genesis 3 we read how Eve, "the mother of all living" (Gn 3:20), explained to the Lord God what had led to her "changed situation." Though often described as an instance of "passing the buck," Eve's words merely explained truthfully what happened: "The serpent beguiled me, and I ate" (Gn 3:12).

The Church Fathers called Mary "the second Eve" because she is "the mother of all living" in Christ, who has redeemed our fallen race. She too had to explain, to Joseph, her "changed situation." So how did she do it?

Though movies have interpreted this scene with theatrical flair, Scripture does not relate her explanation to Joseph. Shouldn't we presume from Matthew's account (see chapter 1) that, like the first Eve, she described exactly what happened? If she believed that "with God nothing will be impossible," then she could surely trust that Joseph's response would also be in God's hands.

And how did Joseph respond to Mary's explanation that the child in her womb was "of the Holy Spirit" (Mt 1:20)? How would you or I have responded? Was he heartbroken that all his dreams and plans were shattered? Was he fearful of what his friends and family might think? Was he afraid that this development would offend his customers and destroy his business?

Scripture tells us that "being a just man and unwilling to put her to shame, [he] resolved to divorce her quietly" (Mt 1:19). Again, many explanations abound for why he would have this intention: It would prevent Mary from being stoned, or even allow her to marry "the true father."

Again, please allow me to suggest another possibility. It's probably safe to assume that at first Joseph, being a just man and believing Mary at her word, may not have known what to do. The angel who had startled Mary with what would happen to her had not included instructions for Joseph. If the child to be born was not of his seed, but of the very seed of God Almighty, what should he have done? What would *you* have done?

We could also presume from what is written that Joseph had only her welfare and the larger plans of God in mind. In his righteousness, he wanted to be obedient to the Lord. Isn't it also possible, then, that Joseph, without instructions to the contrary, resolved as he did because he felt he was far too unworthy to remain betrothed to the woman God had chosen to be the mother of the Messiah?

Joseph was much in the same boat as the Old Testament patriarch Abraham, dreaming large dreams but faced with a difficult decision. Kneeling over his only son, with the knife poised, Abraham had been willing to do whatever God commanded — even if it seemed pointless!

In the case of Joseph, with only Mary's information and no instructions, he made the best decision he could. Then the angel appeared, confirming Mary's story and giving Joseph his marching orders. Scripture tells us that Joseph "did as the angel of the Lord commanded him" (Mt 1:24).

Joseph is a wonderful model to emulate, as well as a powerful intercessor upon whom we can rely. I encourage those of you who are on the journey — whose dreams, plans, vocations, and self-understanding have been shattered by discovering the fullness of the Catholic faith — to draw comfort and wisdom from the experiences of this righteous man of God. Isn't it significant that the angel didn't give Joseph his instructions for the future until after Joseph had resolved how he would respond to the truth of God's plan?

All of us in the CHNetwork can vouch for the constant and more-than-generous care our Lord has given us after we followed through on our resolutions. Yes, for some this has involved hardships like those faced by Joseph: flights into Egypt and then to Nazareth, no place to stay, less-than-ideal living situations, dependence upon gifts for sustenance, and even taking a back seat to the more visible purposes of God.

But like Joseph, we must never forget or doubt that God is good. He always has for you what is best. Remember St. Paul's promise: "In everything God works for good with those who love Him, who are called according to His purpose" (Rom 8:28). If you have an awareness of His love for you, a "hunger and thirst for righteousness" (Mt 5:6), then you can be certain you have been called. Now your only task is to follow Joseph's example, loving and trusting God.

CHAPTER 35

Do I Have To?

During a recent *Journey Home* episode, my guests and I received the following email. Since it expresses many of the issues that CHNetwork staff and volunteers confront every day, I thought it was important for us all to ponder. As you read it, think about all the questions and concerns facing this sincere Christian couple:

> My wife and I are Lutheran, but she is feeling a strong attraction to the Catholic Church. She feels that this is the true Church that Jesus founded. I have no real problem with this, but she also feels that the only path to heaven is in the Catholic Church. She is torn between honoring the husband-wife relationship by worshiping with me in my Lutheran church or becoming Catholic. Do I have to be Catholic to get to heaven? I don't question the authority of the Catholic Church and its origin. I don't question the disciplines practiced by the Catholic faith. But must I be Catholic to receive God's grace of eternal life?

Though most likely written by a Lutheran layman, this email certainly expresses the concerns of many, especially those whose spouses are being drawn to the Catholic Church. His central concern focuses on the age-old question: "Is there salvation outside the Catholic Church?"

The quick answer is found in the Catechism, 846–848:

"Outside the Church there is no salvation."

846 How are we to understand this affirmation, often repeated by the Church Fathers? (Cf. Cyprian, *Epistle* 73.21: *Patrologia Latina 3, 1169*; *De unit.*: *Patrologia Latina 4, 509–536*). Reformulated positively, it means that all salvation comes from Christ the Head through the Church, which is his Body:

> Basing itself on Scripture and Tradition, the Council teaches that the Church, a pilgrim now on earth, is necessary for salvation: the one Christ is the mediator and the way of salvation; he is present to us in his body which is the Church. He himself explicitly asserted the necessity of faith and Baptism, and thereby affirmed at the same time the necessity of the Church which men enter through Baptism as through a door. Hence they could not be saved who, knowing that the Catholic Church was founded as necessary by God through Christ, would refuse either to enter it or to remain in it. (*Lumen gentium* 14; cf. Mk 16:16; Jn 3:5)

847 This affirmation is not aimed at those who, through no fault of their own, do not know Christ and his Church:

> Those who, through no fault of their own, do not know the gospel of Christ or his Church, but who neverthe-less seek God with a sincere heart, and, moved by grace, try in their actions to do his will as they know it through the dictates of their conscience — those too

> may achieve eternal salvation. (*Lumen gentium* 16; cf.
> Enchiridion symbolorum, 3866–3872)

In other words, Jesus intended there to be a Church as the means of receiving the necessary graces for salvation. Through conversion to Jesus Christ — through baptism and by faith — we become children of God and members of the Body of Christ, His Church. He did not intend that there would be thousands of disconnected churches, or that salvation was merely an individualistic experience: "me and Jesus." No, the normal way to receive the graces necessary for salvation is to be a member of the Church.

This does not mean, however, that God holds anyone guilty and punishes him or her eternally for not knowing about the truth of the Church. We believe in the merciful love of God and therefore pass no judgment on anyone outside the bounds of the Catholic Church.

Yet, because we believe Jesus' words when He said, "Apart from me you can do nothing," we must never take anyone's salvation for granted. We cannot assume that anyone is so "invincibly ignorant" that it is not necessary for them to become a member of the Church and receive the necessary sacraments. (In Catholic teaching, "invincible ignorance" is ignorance that is impossible for a person to overcome.)

No, we recognize that God, through the work of the Holy Spirit, can put within the consciences of those who have never heard the gospel the truth about moral and immoral living; and that He can, in the final judgment, hold them accountable for how they lived according to this light. This is what the apostle Paul was teaching when he wrote in Romans:

> For he will render to every man according to his works:
> to those who by patience in well-doing seek for glory and
> honor and immortality, he will give eternal life; but for
> those who are factious and do not obey the truth, but obey

wickedness, there will be wrath and fury. There will be
tribulation and distress for every human being who does
evil ... but glory and honor and peace for every one who
does good. ... For God shows no partiality. All who have
sinned without the law will also perish without the law, and
all who have sinned under the law will be judged by the law.
For it is not the hearers of the law who are righteous before
God, but the doers of the law who will be justified.

When Gentiles who have not the law do by nature what the
law requires, they are a law to themselves, even though they
do not have the law. They show that what the law requires
is written on their hearts, while their conscience also bears
witness and their conflicting thoughts accuse or perhaps
excuse them on that day when, according to my gospel,
God judges the secrets of men by Christ Jesus.
(Rom 2:6–16)

Being a member of the Church is no guarantee of salvation.
Nor does walking down the aisle for an altar call and saying a
"Sinner's Prayer" guarantee a "once saved, always saved" form
of "eternal security." We are called to live by faith, which entails
an entirely changed life directed by grace towards holiness.

Nevertheless, this new way of life is nearly impossible
without the graces of the sacraments. For this reason, our separated brethren need to come home, and if we love them, we
must not merely presume on the supposed graces and blessing
of various non-Catholic substitutes for the sacraments. To do
so is essentially gambling with someone's eternal life.

As it says in the Catechism:

848 "Although in ways known to himself God can lead
those who, through no fault of their own, are ignorant of
the gospel, to that faith without which it is impossible to
please him, the Church still has the obligation and also the

> sacred right to evangelize all men." (*Ad gentes* 7; cf. Heb
> 11:6; 1 Cor 9:16)

We should note other interesting facets of our Lutheran friend's inquiry. First, notice that he describes his wife's leanings as based on feelings. This reference may merely be his accommodation to modern modes of expression, but it also might indicate that he's not taking her leanings seriously: "They're nothing but *feelings*, or just the remnants of a bad sandwich. She only *feels* the Catholic Church is true, so 'this too will pass.'"

Here's a question: When your non-Catholic family members or friends consider your leanings toward, or conversion to, or membership in, the Catholic Church, do they merely write it off as *feelings*? Or have you given them "a reason for your hope" (1 Pt 3:15 NAB)?

A second element to notice in our Lutheran friend's letter is the number of things he "has no problem with." He has no problem with the Catholic Church's authority, practices, or origin as the one Church founded by Jesus Christ. Can you imagine having no problem with these critical issues, yet not feeling compelled to take the Catholic Church seriously? If these things are true of the Catholic Church, then what could be true of Lutheranism or any other non-Catholic Christian tradition?

Think about it: When our friends and family express opinions like this (in relation to our leanings toward, or conversion to, or membership in the Catholic Church), what are they actually saying? Are they serious, or are they just avoiding the inevitable conflict between where they are and where we might be heading or have already arrived?

But isn't this Lutheran's true concern most clearly revealed in his question, "Do I have to?" What is the mandate? Do I have to be a Catholic to be saved? If not, then why convert, especially if conversion will only wreck my vocation, my occupation, my family, my friends, and especially my marriage?

We can point him to the basic answers in the Catechism, but the "letter of the law" doesn't always address the complicated ramifications of conversion, as many converts can attest. One of the most important tasks of evangelization is the patient willingness to stand beside men and women on the journey, like the Lutheran couple in this email. We must help them hear the fullness of the truth of Jesus Christ and His Church, and to help them work though all the implications of their conversions. And if they decide for whatever reason not to convert, we must never abandon them, but remain with them, always willing to answer their questions "with gentleness and reverence" (1 Pt 3:15).

Let's continue together to help seekers like this man and his wife, especially through our prayers, to come home to the fullness and sacramental graces of the Catholic Church.

CHAPTER 36

This Deaf, Dumb, and Blind Kid

Some of the best things about becoming Catholic I didn't discover until after coming home. Beforehand, I might not have understood and appreciated them anyway. I particularly mean Catholic mystical theology. Because of what spiritual writers such as St. John of the Cross, St. Teresa of Avila, Fr. Reginald Garrigou-Lagrange, Fr. Thomas Dubay, and others have taught me ("deaf, dumb, and blind kid" that I am spiritually), I am particularly driven to help those outside the Catholic Church come home to taste the sweetness of the fullness of faith.

We might say that God will not hold them accountable for what they never heard or understood, and this is true (to the extent that they were truly invincibly ignorant). However, when I look back at my own Protestant journey, especially my responsibilities as a Protestant pastor and leader, I become concerned about the blindness that prevents them from experiencing all that God would want them to have, both in this life and in the next.

For example, the Apostle John wrote in his first letter: "Do not love the world, or the things that are in the world. If anyone loves the world, the love of the Father is not in him" (1 Jn 2:15).

So what exactly did he mean by this? From a Protestant pastoral perspective, what exactly should a pastor preach that his people should or should not do, avoid or not avoid? And does it really make a difference? If a person is "once saved, always saved" by "faith alone," then so what if he gets lost in the love of the world? But can a "once saved, always saved" person who has failed in loving the world still be saved if "the love of the Father is not in him"? Did the Apostle John mean complete and total detachment from all things in the world?

This matter hits home with me because as a Protestant pastor I often taught from First John, my favorite New Testament book, and even helped write a commentary on it. I considered myself an expert on that book. But then I became a Catholic, and read books by Fathers Dubay and Garrigou-Lagrange, and Sts. John of the Cross and Teresa of Avila, and discovered what a "deaf, dumb, and blind kid" I was.

Just to scratch the surface, in *Ascent of Mount Carmel*, St. John of the Cross writes of two purgations or nights we must go through to grow in union with Christ. He describes the first dark night as "a privation and purgation of all sensible appetites for the external things of the world, the delights of the flesh, and the gratifications of the will" (*The Collected Works of St. John of the Cross*, trans. Kieran Kavanaugh, O.C.D. and Otilio Rodriguez, O.C.D., ICS Publications, 1991, p. 119).

Here he is obviously alluding to what the Apostle John meant by not loving the things of the world: "the lust of the flesh and the lust of the eyes and the pride of life" (1 Jn 2:16).

St. John of the Cross further explains:

> We are not discussing the mere lack of things; this lack
> will not divest the soul if it craves for all these objects. We
> are dealing with the denudation of the soul's appetites and
> gratifications. ... Since the things of the world cannot enter
> the soul, they are not in themselves an encumbrance or
> harm to it; rather, it is the will and appetite dwelling within
> that cause the damage when set on these things. (p. 123)

I obviously don't intend to attempt here a thorough reflection on St. John's mystical theology. I just want to point
out how damaging "faith alone" theology can be. St. John
further warned:

> The road and ascent to God ... necessarily demands an
> habitual effort to renounce and mortify the appetites; the
> sooner this mortification is achieved, the sooner the soul
> reaches the top. But until the appetites are eliminated, one
> will not arrive no matter how much virtue is practiced. For
> one will be failing to acquire perfect virtue, which lies in
> keeping the soul empty, naked, and purified of every ap-
> petite. (p. 129)

As the following suggests, St. John of the Cross was fully
aware of the post-Reformation "new theologies" touting salvation by "faith alone":

> A person enters the second night by living in faith alone,
> not in a faith that is exclusive of charity but a faith that
> excludes other intellectual knowledge ... for faith does not
> fall into the province of the senses. (p. 120)

But how do these appetites cause harm if they remain un-
checked even in those who have surrendered heart, mind,
body, and soul to Jesus? "They deprive them of God's Spirit;
and they weary, torment, darken, defile, and weaken them"
(p. 130).

187

I wish I had understood then what I am beginning to understand more fully now. In any case, I just want to point out that what St. Paul once said of some of his contemporaries was also true of me: "Claiming to be wise, they became fools" (Rom 1:22). Could this be true of you, too, and perhaps of many thousands of otherwise sincere Christians who still differ from one another on essential aspects of faith and spirituality?

Let's keep each other constantly in our prayers as together by God's grace we seek to "mortify our appetites" in our journeys to Him: "He must increase, but I must decrease" (Jn 3:30).

CHAPTER 37

St. Paul's Vocational Conversion

We're all familiar with the details of St. Paul's faith conversion on the road to Damascus. But have you ever considered his vocational conversion — from Saul, Pharisee and persecutor of the Church, to St. Paul, apostle to the Gentiles? How and when did he discover this new vocation?

New clergy converts to the Church often feel they must relinquish their vocational calling, accepting reluctantly St. Paul's otherwise joyous admission in Philippians: "Forgetting what lies behind and straining forward to what lies ahead, I press on toward the goal for the prize of the upward call of God in Christ Jesus" (Phil 3:13–14). The context of this passage, however, does not refer to St. Paul's vocational change. He notes only that the prerogatives and privileges he had as a Pharisaic Jew, which he previously considered so important, were useless for attaining salvation and righteousness before God.

So how was St. Paul's vocation after his conversion connected to his pre-conversion vocation? Let's examine his testimony, distributed throughout his letters.

First, what was his spiritual and vocational background?

> I am a Jew, born at Tarsus in Cilicia, but brought up in this
> city at the feet of Gamaliel, educated according to the strict
> manner of the law of our fathers, being zealous for God as
> you all are this day. ... My manner of life from my youth,
> spent from the beginning among my own nation and at
> Jerusalem, is known by all the Jews. They have known for a
> long time, if they are willing to testify, that according to the
> strictest party of our religion I have lived as a Pharisee. ...
> I advanced in Judaism beyond many of my own age among
> my people, so extremely zealous was I for the traditions of
> my fathers. (Acts 22:3; 26:4–5; Gal 1:14)

St. Paul obviously was more than just a very religious, observant Jew. He must have discerned a religious vocation to spiritual leadership as a Pharisee, and then obeyed this calling by receiving the best training. Essentially he went to seminary.

But things were changing in his world: "And the word of God increased; and the number of the disciples multiplied greatly in Jerusalem, and a great many of the priests were obedient to the faith" (Acts 6:7). The new "heretical" sect, called the Way, was not going away quietly. The Way was ordaining its own hierarchy of leadership, and, worst of all, Jewish priests were converting! Something had to be done!

> Then they cast [Stephen] out of the city and stoned him;
> and the witnesses laid down their garments at the feet of a
> young man named Saul. ... And Saul was consenting to his
> death. And on that day a great persecution arose against the
> church in Jerusalem. (Acts 7:58, 8:1)

Though it isn't stated directly, it's fair to conclude that in this incident, Saul sensed a more specific calling from God.

First let's hear of this in the words of St. Luke (the author of Acts) and then in those of St. Paul himself:

> But Saul laid waste the church, and entering house after house, he dragged off men and women and committed them to prison. ... Saul, still breathing threats and murder against the disciples of the Lord, went to the high priest and asked him for letters to the synagogues at Damascus, so that if he found any belonging to the Way, men or women, he might bring them bound to Jerusalem. (Acts 8:3; 9:1–2)

> I myself was convinced that I ought to do many things in opposing the name of Jesus of Nazareth. And I did so in Jerusalem; I not only shut up many of the saints in prison, by authority from the chief priests, but when they were put to death I cast my vote against them. And I punished them often in all the synagogues and tried to make them blaspheme; and in raging fury against them, I persecuted them even to foreign cities. Thus I journeyed to Damascus with the authority and commission of the chief priests. (Acts 26:9–12)

In the process of carrying out this "vocation," Saul experienced his conversion to Jesus Christ, a conversion with which we are all familiar (see Acts 9; 26:12–18).

Saul's conversion also meant a redirection of his vocation, from persecutor to proclaimer. Nevertheless, this new vocation was not immediately appreciated — neither by his new brothers and sisters, whom he previously had persecuted, nor by his old Jewish friends:

> For several days he was with the disciples at Damascus. And in the synagogues immediately he proclaimed Jesus, saying, "He is the Son of God." And all who heard him were amazed, and said, "Is not this the man who made havoc in Jerusalem of those who called on this name? And he has come here for this purpose, to bring them bound before the

chief priests." But Saul increased all the more in strength, and confounded the Jews who lived in Damascus by proving that Jesus was the Christ.

When many days had passed, the Jews plotted to kill him, but their plot became known to Saul. They were watching the gates day and night, to kill him; but his disciples took him by night and let him down over the wall, lowering him in a basket. And when he had come to Jerusalem he attempted to join the disciples; and they were all afraid of him, for they did not believe that he was a disciple. But Barnabas took him, and brought him to the apostles, and declared to them how on the road he had seen the Lord, who spoke to him, and how at Damascus he had preached boldly in the name of Jesus. So he went in and out among them at Jerusalem, preaching boldly in the name of the Lord. And he spoke and disputed against the Hellenists; but they were seeking to kill him. And when the brethren knew it, they brought him down to Caesarea, and sent him off to Tarsus. (Acts 9:19–30)

In his letter to the Galatians, St. Paul reported that he had remained separated in Tarsus (Cilicia), away from the growing church, for nearly fourteen years (see Gal 2:1). He gave no explanation why, nor did he tell what he was doing. But isn't it possible that he was taking these years to rethink his Jewish background and Pharisaical education in relationship to Jesus the Messiah, the Son of God?

Those fourteen years may have been difficult and lonely. He may have struggled with separation and rejection by his family and friends. All this is not unlike what clergy converts today experience during the time after their conversions, when they are forced to rethink their lives, their training, and their vocations.

Eventually, however, through the intercession of St. Barnabas (since the CHNetwork did not yet exist!), Saul was retrieved from obscurity and encouraged to continue in his religious vocation:

> So Barnabas went to Tarsus to look for Saul; and when he had found him, he brought him to Antioch. For a whole year they met with the Church, and taught a large company of people. ... Now in the church at Antioch there were prophets and teachers, Barnabas, Symeon who was called Niger ... and Saul. While they were worshiping the Lord and fasting, the Holy Spirit said, "Set apart for me Barnabas and Saul for the work to which I have called them." Then after fasting and praying they laid their hands on them and sent them off. (Acts 11:25–26; 13:1–3)

In time, after Saul, now Paul, had been confirmed as the apostle to the Gentiles and was serving as a bishop, he wrote and spoke of his new vocation on several occasions:

> [H]e who had set me apart before I was born, and had called me through His grace, was pleased to reveal His Son to me, in order that I might preach Him among the Gentiles. ... But I do not account my life of any value nor as precious to myself, if only I may accomplish my course and the ministry which I received from the Lord Jesus, to testify to the gospel of the grace of God. ... Of this gospel I was made a minister according to the gift of God's grace which was given me by the working of His power. To me, though I am the very least of all the saints, this grace was given, to preach to the Gentiles the unsearchable riches of Christ. (Gal 1:15–17; Acts 20:24; Eph 3:7–8)

In essence, St. Paul, the convert, became a helper to others on the journey. In the following passage we see that he was a helper to St. Timothy, encouraging and empowering him to use his apostolic gifts:

> I thank Him who has given me strength for this, Christ Jesus our Lord, because He judged me faithful by appoint-

> ing me to His service, though I formerly blasphemed and
> persecuted and insulted Him; but I received mercy because
> I had acted ignorantly in unbelief, and the grace of our
> Lord overflowed for me with the faith and love that are in
> Christ Jesus. … You then, my son, be strong in the grace
> that is in Christ Jesus, and what you have heard from me
> before many witnesses entrust to faithful men who will be
> able to teach others also. (1 Tm 1:12–14; 2 Tm 2:1–2)

Every one of us has a calling from God to use our gifts for extending the kingdom. St. Paul's previous religious training and vocational experiences actually prepared him in certain ways for what God was calling him to do after his conversion. (For example, as a Pharisee he already believed in the resurrection — unlike the Sadducees — which prepared him to become the great proclaimer of the fullness of the resurrection in Jesus Christ.)

Our work of evangelization *must* not end once a convert enters the Church. Like St. Barnabas and St. Paul, we must help all converts (as well as Catholic laity) discover how best to utilize their gifts, training, and experiences for announcing the Good News of Jesus Christ and His Church.

If you haven't done so already, you must read the important encyclical of Pope John Paul II on "The Lay Members of Christ's Faithful People" (*Christifideles Laici*, 1988). In it, the Holy Father explained clearly — as St. Barnabas probably did to St. Paul, and then St. Paul to St. Timothy, and then on and on down to us — how we each, clergy and laity, "have an essential and irreplaceable role in this announcement and in this testimony; through them the Church of Christ [you and me!] is made present in the various sectors of the world as a sign and source of hope and of love" (7).

CHAPTER 38

Go, Sell, Give, and Follow

I recall how, not long after I had resigned from the pastorate and had been received into the Catholic Church, I was sitting in a beautiful chapel one day during Mass, awaiting the proclamation of the Gospel. I must admit that at the time I was not feeling the joy that Jesus had promised would accompany my walk with him. Instead, I was overwhelmed by anxiety over decisions and situations piling up in my life.

Drastic changes had occurred in the direction of projects and programs for which I was responsible. New plans made new demands for my moving ahead into new areas and projects for which I had no previous personal experience to prepare me. Countless details and red tape were involved in moving out of our home and into a new one. Through all this, I felt frustrated because I missed being actively involved in the pastoral ministry.

As I watched the priest lead us in worship, I felt strangely disconnected and isolated. In my dreamlike distraction, as I reflected on my past experiences leading worship, I began focusing on things the priest was doing that I thought could be done differently or better.

Awaiting the Gospel reading, I heard in my mind the cry of the psalmist: "Why are you cast down, O my soul?" (Ps 42:5) or even more strongly, to God, "Why have you forgotten me?" (Ps 42:9). Then I stood for the Gospel, blessed myself with the triple signs of the cross, and heard, not coincidentally but providentially, my favorite story from the life of Christ: that powerful incident when Jesus is confronted by the rich young man (see Mk 10:17–27).

This account has always spoken to me, challenging me to reexamine what is the center of my life. At different places along the journey of faith, this story has confronted me to cast off various spiritual impediments. When I was an engineer considering a fulltime ministry, this passage encouraged me to lean not on the financial security of my engineering career, but to be willing to let it go to follow Christ.

Years later, this story challenged me to be willing to let go of the security and familiarity of my Protestant ministry so I could again follow the words of Jesus: "You lack one thing; go, sell what you have, and give it to the poor, and you will have treasures in heaven and come, follow me" (Mk 10:21).

As I heard those words again, I asked, "What is the thing that I lack this time? What is it, besides Christ, that I'm tightly clinging to, that I must be willing to let go, sell, give away, in order to follow with abandon my Lord Jesus?" As I considered this question, it struck me that maybe it was time for me to quit being a Catholic convert, and instead be just a Catholic.

In those days, I still tended to view and portray myself primarily as a convert, an ex-Protestant pastor, rather than moving on and accepting the fact that I was now a Catholic. Yes, I will always be a convert, and I may never lose the perspective that my forty years as a Protestant, including nine years as a

Protestant pastor, have given me. But I must not forget that every Catholic is a convert from sin to a new creation in Christ.

As I sat there repeating the words from the Mass, "Lord, I am not worthy to receive you," I sensed Christ challenging me to embrace that place, where He had me at that time, at that moment, as the place exactly where He wanted me to be. He wanted me to be doing those projects, emphasizing those priorities, drafting and implementing those plans, that He had given me, even though they may have had little connection whatsoever with the Protestant pastoral ministry I had been doing five years before.

The Lord had merely, by his wisdom, placed me in a new place with a new assignment in the ministry of His kingdom. I might have brought to that assignment more than forty years of a great variety of experiences from the past. Nevertheless, it was to that assignment, at that point in my life, in that place in my life, in those relationships, and in this wonderful Church that He had called me to "go, sell, give, and follow."

The stress I was feeling was mostly worry about tomorrow. But He had called me to "go, sell, give, and follow" today. My wife, Marilyn, and I had recently moved into a beautiful new home. If I allowed myself to become anxious about how I would finance it and support my family in the future, I would again find my soul growing weary.

But Jesus' words reminded me that all the resources, even the very job I had found, were gifts of God's grace that only a few years before I could never have dreamed of having. Once again I needed to remember that the future rests completely in His hands.

Many clergy on the journey, for whom conversion will mean resignation from their pastoral positions, and thus the loss of their means of supporting their families, express their concern over such matters. How will they handle the financial needs of the future? How will they fulfill the ministerial calling they once heard and followed? How will they faithfully fulfill Paul's exhortation to Timothy?

> Do not neglect the gift you have, which was conferred on you through the prophetic word with the imposition of hands of the presbyterate. Be diligent in these matters, be absorbed in them, so that your progress may be evident to everyone. (1 Tm 4:14–15 NAB)

From my own family experience, all I can say is to "go, sell, give, and follow." Where you are right now, and all that you have accomplished up to this point, have come through the grace of Jesus Christ. Where you will be tomorrow and all that you will accomplish then will come from the same source. To follow Jesus means being willing to carry whatever cross He gives.

I suppose Jesus could have told that rich young man, "You have done a superb job in your diligence at keeping the commandments; keep up the good work," and then let him go. The young man had probably been more faithful than most.

But Jesus wanted more for him, and of him. Our Lord probably saw that through this young man's personal sacrifice not only he, but many others as well, would be drawn to the kingdom. So Jesus placed before him a demanding choice, and then let the young man choose freely. I sense that God is challenging many of you with the same kind of choice.

When we think of the incarnation of Jesus Christ, our Lord and Savior, we are reminded of other difficult decisions that involved great sacrifice: the decision of Mary to be willing to do whatever God called her to do, and the willingness of the very Son of God, who, as St. Paul says in Philippians, "though he was in the form of God, did not count equality with God a thing to be grasped, but emptied himself, taking the form of a servant, being born in the likeness of men" (Phil 2:6–7).

My prayer is that these models of surrender will be an encouragement to those of you who are still struggling in your decisions along your pilgrimage toward the Catholic Church. Great joy is to be found here, and a reassuring sense of freedom when you stand on the rock foundation of Catholic truth.

I pray that the Spirit of Christ will empower you boldly to take the step to "go, sell, give, and follow" Jesus Christ into the Church He established in His apostles, centered on Peter.

CHAPTER 39

How Do We Discern How Fast God Is Calling Us to Step Out in Faith?

Sometimes Scripture calls us to wait: "Wait for the Lord; be strong, and let your heart take courage; yes, wait for the Lord!" (Ps 27:14). At other times it seems to encourage acting without hesitation: "Jesus said to them, 'Follow me...' And they immediately left their nets and followed Him" (Mk 1:17–18).

Often it's difficult to discern which of these approaches God is calling us to take. How do we discern how fast or how soon God wants us to move in ministry? What criteria should we use? What if our spouse or family isn't in agreement? What if the "fleece" isn't wet on either side, and the "still, small voice" is inaudible?

I'm drawn back again to the difficult issue of making the courageous jump out of Protestant ministry into the Catholic Church, because every week the CHNetwork staff and I continue to encounter men and women struggling somewhere along this journey. I've talked with many who are convinced that the Catholic Church is the true Church of Jesus Christ, but the juxtaposition of the difficult knowns and unknowns in their lives causes them to stand poised with their hand on the plow wondering which way to proceed and when.

Of course, I must be careful not to push too strongly. We each must discern God's call for ourselves. However, I have no hesitation whatsoever in affirming the faithfulness and providence of God for my family and me.

Within a month of joining the Church, I realized that the income I thought I could depend upon to support my family through the transition was gone. Once I let our needs be known, however, God continued to open doors both to use my gifts and training in ministry and to support my family. Our experience has proven to us as a family that trusting God means being boldly obedient to whatever God is calling us to do right now, while leaving the needs and responsibilities of tomorrow to Him.

Such a response has required us to be flexible, to accept a different standard of living, to leave friends and familiar places. But God has always given back to us much more than we have ever given up for Him! Our cup now overflows, especially with new friends who are loving and supportive.

God's faithfulness has been proven over and over again in the lives of others who have made this difficult yet joyful journey home. Consider this letter I received from a Protestant minister in Canada who had been a cradle Catholic:

> Some good news. Today I have finally been able to resign my position as associate pastor at my church. I will finish up there on May 31st, and then on June 1st I will start my new job as Director of Adult Faith Formation at our local Catholic parish.

This parish is just a five-minute walk from where we live, and that part of my double life has kept me sane over the last several months. I'm grateful for the director of the catechumenate, who trusted me and invited me to be part of the RCIA team so that I could get my feet wet again in ministry in a Catholic setting. It led to invitations to teach the charismatic group, and they believe I'm the answer to their two-year-long prayer for someone to teach them. To oversee the group is part of my job description.

Truly the Lord is wonderful! I feel like I am home at last. There is such a sense of comfort for us in this parish community that my ministry is a pleasure rather than labor as it so often was.

The task before me is not an easy one, and I will need much wisdom and grace. There are twenty-eight hundred families in the parish with only about twenty percent who have a meaningful relationship with the Lord. The staff has defined my task to be evangelizing the sacramentalized.

May the Lord make me equal to the task. As sojourners in a strange land our circumstances have been different from most, but the Lord has shown that He himself does what He commanded Israel to do in the First Testament — show kindness to the stranger. Blessed be His name. Thank you so much for your prayerful support.

A month ago, another pastor paid us a visit from out West. After many years in the Presbyterian ministry, he was finally ready to consider following his convictions into the Catholic Church. Yet over dinner he shared his concerns and his many unanswered questions. Then, a week later I received a note that said he was making the move; he was ready to accept whatever God had in store for him.

Two days ago I sat across from a Lutheran pastor who after thirty-two years of ministry desires with great joy to enter the Catholic Church. Yet he faces the difficult question that so many face: What will he do now? Does he wait three more years until retirement? Does he remain in a situation where he must keep his inner convictions private — where he questions whether the sacramental ministry he now performs is even valid?

His local Catholic bishop may offer him a position as pastoral administrator, but he is not sure. He first must face a difficult hip replacement in two weeks, and then he will decide when to make his move.

I know of many others whose experiences have been very difficult, who have gone long periods without employment or income, whose marriages have suffered or even disintegrated.

The decision is not easy. As St. Paul states, "Let each man be fully convinced in his own mind" (Rom 14:5).

But this is why we must hold each other up in prayer. We must encourage one another, sharing our blessings, our victories, and our resources with one another. Together we must pray for the Church and its leaders, that they might be continually more open to the gifts and experiences Protestant converts bring and desire to share in the ministry of the gospel.

CHAPTER 40

The Steady Stream Home

For the first forty years of my life, I never considered the possibility of becoming a Catholic. No Catholic had ever talked to me about the faith, and it never crossed my mind that there was any reason whatsoever even to consider the Catholic Church. In those forty years, I had freely progressed from the Lutheran church of my youth, to the Congregational church of my adult "born again" reawakening, and on into the Presbyterian church of my pastoral ministry.

We even considered moving on to other Protestant denominations as my wife and I struggled with the "problems of Protestantism." But the Catholic Church was never an option.

One lack of information that reinforced my lack of interest was that I had never heard of a Protestant minister becoming Catholic. I was very aware of Catholics becoming Protestant — a third of the people in my congregations were ex-Catholics — and I had heard of priests and nuns as well as laity being "rescued from the whore of Babylon." I was also aware of Protestant laypeople becoming Catholic through marriage, but I assumed they could do this only because they either had not understood their Protestant faith or merely lacked convictions.

In any case, the idea that a well-informed, sincerely convinced evangelical Protestant minister could become Catholic was for me far beyond the pale. Absurd! (Since then, I have found that this ignorance of clergy converts to the Catholic faith was shared by most of my convert friends before they entered the Church.)

One day, however, through the grapevine I heard a rumor about an old seminary classmate, who upon graduation had also become a Presbyterian minister. According to the rumor, he had "poped." Because this development didn't fit into any of my mental categories, and ran across the grain of my personal knowledge of his staunch Calvinist convictions, I gave the rumor no heed. I waved it off and moved on.

Later I discovered not only that he and his wife had become Catholic, but also that many others, a steady stream of men and women clergy, had converted or were presently on the journey. Is this stream of highly informed, non-Catholic intellectuals into the Church only a contemporary phenomenon? Is it merely the result of a recent crisis within Protestantism teamed with the increased accessibility of truth about the Catholic Church through technical media?

Many of us became aware of conversions to the Catholic Church only through contemporary conversion stories: Scott and Kimberly Hahns' *Rome Sweet Home* or Stephen K. Ray's *Crossing the Tiber*; collections of stories such as Patrick Madrid's *Surprised by Truth* or our own *Journeys Home*. Even so, a continual stream of these books had actually been published throughout the twentieth century, such as John A. O'Brien's *The Road to Damascus*, which appeared in 1949. Moreover, books such as Patrick Allitt's *Catholic Converts* and Joseph Pearce's *Literary Converts* remind us that our generation is not the only one to have seen numerous clergy and lay converts to the Catholic Church.

A recent find, however, really opened our eyes! In 1907, D.J. Scannell-O'Neill published *Distinguished Converts to Rome in America* (Herder). This 180-page book contains nothing less than a stunning annotated list of three thousand American converts since the discovery of America! The author writes:

> The list of converts contained in this book, while as full as the compiler has been able to make it, is by no means exhaustive. Of the revisers who have looked it over, [all were] able to add from personal knowledge the names of several converts of prominence. No doubt many hundreds of others are still [lacking]. Perhaps they will be supplied some day. Until then we are sure the present list will prove quite serviceable. (n.p.)

What was particularly amazing about this list is that the religious backgrounds of these converts were not limited to the "usual suspects" (Anglican, Episcopal, or Lutheran), but included more than fifteen Protestant denominations. Among the converts were a bishop, 372 clergymen, 3 rabbis, 115 doctors, 126 lawyers, 45 U.S. Senators and Congressmen, 12 governors, and 180 military officers! Many of these names are well known in history, though most histories ignore their Catholic convictions.

If you are considering the Catholic Church, you can be reassured that you are a part of a long stream of men and women who by grace have been called home by God to His one, holy, Catholic, and apostolic Church.

PART THREE

The Journey Onward

CHAPTER 41

Still Moving Closer to Christ?

So those who received [Peter's] word were baptized, and
there were added that day about three thousand souls.
And they devoted themselves to the apostles' teaching and
fellowship, to the breaking of the bread and to the prayers.
And fear came upon every soul; and many wonders and
signs were done through the apostles. (Acts 2:41–43)

Few classes in the RCIA (Rite of Christian Initiation of
Adults) can boast three thousand in a single season. Yet the
annual combined numbers for new Catholics every year is
quite impressive. When all the rites and celebrations of Easter
are over, and our newly baptized and confirmed brothers and
sisters have taken their seats beside the more seasoned parish-
ioners, what then? Where will they be next Easter or in five
years? Where will they be next month?

More importantly, what will be the condition of their souls?

The Rite of Christian Initiation of Adults includes this instruction: "Before the rite of election is celebrated, the cate-

chumens are expected to have undergone a *conversion in mind and in action* and to have developed a sufficient acquaintance with Christian teaching as well as a spirit of faith and charity" (120, emphasis added). This is the ideal set by the Church for every RCIA program and catechumen.

Nevertheless, conversion is a gift, a work of God's efficacious grace. A good RCIA program can provide the necessary environment and instruction, can plant the seeds and nurture the growth. But it cannot ensure that this conversion happens.

We must never presume that what was attained and confessed by a new Catholic at the Easter Vigil is guaranteed to remain afterward, without continual nurture, encouragement, prayer, and, of course, sacramental grace. For this reason, the Church stresses that RCIA must never end at Easter, but must continue on with the post-baptismal mystagogy. The instructions in the Rite continue:

> This is a time for the community and the [new members of the Church] together to grow in deepening their grasp of the paschal mystery and in making it part of their lives through meditation on the Gospel, sharing in the Eucharist, and doing the works of charity. ... *For [the new members of the Church] have truly been renewed in mind, tasted more deeply the sweetness of God's Word, received the fellowship of the Holy Spirit, and grown to know the goodness of the Lord* (244, 245, emphasis added).

These words echo a passage in the Epistle to the Hebrews, which offers this caution:

> For it is impossible to restore again to repentance those who have once been *enlightened, who have tasted the heavenly gift, and have become partakers of the Holy Spirit, and have tasted the goodness of the word of God and the powers of the age to come, if they then commit apostasy,* since they

> crucify the Son of God on their own account and hold him
> up to contempt. (Heb 6:4–6, emphasis added)

Have you ever known people who went all the way through the process — baptism, catechesis, CCD, retreats, Confirmation — only to fall away into nominal faith, inactivity, or schism? Hard to bring them back, isn't it?

This biblical warning is important — not just for RCIA directors, new Catholics, and their sponsors, but for every one of us. We must never presume we have arrived spiritually. We must keep on growing.

As Pope John Paul II emphasized in his 1979 apostolic exhortation on catechesis, *Catechesis Tradendae:* "The definitive aim of catechesis is to put people not only in *touch* but in *communion*, in *intimacy*, with Jesus Christ" (no. 5, emphasis added).

Are you merely "in touch" with Jesus? Or are you growing in intimate communion with Him? As many of the saints have reminded us, in the ways of God, whoever does not progress, loses ground.

Are you progressing, or are you losing ground? All it takes to progress is to turn regularly to God in prayer, away from sin and temptation, to one another in charity, and all this through the powerful graces of the sacraments.

After conversion and entrance into the Church, many joys and blessings come. But the journey has not ended. Conversion is a continual process of growing in grace. As T.S. Eliot once wrote, quoting the ancient Greek philosopher Heraclitus, "The way up and the way down are one and the same" (Epigraph of the "Four Quartets").

The journey involves both ups and downs, joys and sacrifices, blessings and sufferings. But through the aid of grace, both the ups and the downs can lead to spiritual growth.

CHAPTER 42

Of Faith and Football

Our favorite team had gone undefeated and was ranked number one all year. Our quarterback had received the Heisman trophy, and he and several others on the squad had become household names across America. Nearly every poll and every commentator had projected our team to be the clear winner of the national championship.

After our star receiver took the opening kickoff ninety-three yards for a touchdown, my family and I did back flips, lost in our joyous presumption that surely we were on the road to a blowout! Well, the game did indeed prove to be a blowout, but with our team in the loser's column.

I think we should note something about that game that few commentators admitted. Television, radio, and newsprint pundits posed dozens of excuses for this unexpected debacle, all of which have merit. Yes, our Heisman-trophy quarterback and other award-winning players did not live up to their expectations, and the other team's offense and defense performed much better than expected. But I think the pundits missed the most obvious reason for the outcome: The game was simply won and lost in the trenches.

Basically, their offensive and defensive lines defeated our offensive and defensive lines. If our offensive line had kept their defensive line out, our Heisman-winning quarterback would have had the time to run his game and be his old self. Instead, from the opening play our quarterback was scrambling for his life.

Meanwhile, if our defensive line had broken through their offensive line, we would have prevented their quarterback from carrying out their coach's superior game plan. Instead, from their opening drive, they ran over us like the proverbial hot knife through butter.

For all my sorrow about the loss, I still love football, in part because, like no other sport, it offers so many insightful analogies to life in general and specifically to our life together in the Church. That painful loss clearly illustrates that every single player on a team is important, not just those who are most visible. Our quarterback would never have been nominated for the Heisman if the nationally known receivers had dropped his passes, the nationally known running backs had fumbled his handoffs, and especially if the lesser-known, even unknown, center, tackles, guards, and others had failed their assignments in each play.

The more that each player on a squad fulfills his assignments, the more successful a team becomes. Some players become famous, some remain unknown, but every player is important. And so it is with the Church.

The Catechism states in its prologue:

> Those who with God's help have welcomed Christ's call
> and freely responded to it are urged on by love of Christ
> to proclaim the Good News everywhere in the world. This
> treasure, received from the apostles, has been faithfully

guarded by their successors. All Christ's faithful are called
to hand it on from generation to generation, by professing
the faith, by living it in fraternal sharing, and by celebrating
it in liturgy and prayer.

I can see at least two lessons for us in this statement. First, it
has become a lifestyle for many to complain about the present
state of things in the Church, and especially to point fingers at
the more visible candidates for blame — the "quarterbacks" —
charging that they aren't doing their jobs! "They're failing to
fulfill their callings; they're letting us down."

Yet as this statement from the Catechism insists, though
the treasure of the apostolic deposit of faith "has been faithfully guarded by their successors, *all Christ's faithful* are called
to hand it on" (emphasis added). And like a Heisman-trophy
quarterback, our bishops and priests cannot do their jobs well
unless we lesser-knowns do ours.

Over the past seventeen-plus years, more than eighteen
hundred ministers have contacted the CHNetwork for help or
encouragement in their journeys toward the Catholic Church.
Many, if not most, of these formerly ordained clergymen presume that God is calling them to continue at the same level of
ministry once they become Catholics: from "quarterbacks" to
"quarterbacks" — from ministers to priests.

For some, of course, this is true, and we want to do all we
can to help them in the discerning process. For most of us,
however, God has called us home to use our gifts, training,
and experience as active laymen and women in the Church.
Let's pray for all those on the journey, lay or clergy, that they
may clearly discern how and where God is calling them to use
their gifts, training, and experience. Ask the Lord to help them
humbly accept this calling, whatever it is: quarterback, receiver, lineman — even water boy!

CHAPTER 43

A Boat, a Branch, and a Helicopter

I'm sure you've all heard the joke about a boat, a branch, and a helicopter many times. I heard it first in a sermon many years ago, and like all sincere, well-intentioned speakers, I promptly stole it and used it myself. Just in case you can't recall it, let me refresh your memory.

A man was caught in his home in a flash flood, and the waters were rising around him. The streets and yards were covered, and the water had reached the base of the window-sills. Seeing his neighbors scurrying for safety, he nevertheless stood firm and prayed confidently, "Dear Father in heaven, please save me from this coming retribution."

Immediately the man heard a voice from outside. He looked out and saw his neighbors floating by in a boat, calling out to him, "Hurry, jump in before the waters overtake you!"

Seeing how crowded and uncomfortable the boat was, the man answered, "Thanks, but I know my God will save me."

"Have it your way," the neighbors said as they rowed to safety.

The waters kept rising, overflowing the windowsills and filling the first floor. The man fled to the second floor and prayed once more, with a little less conviction, "Dear Father in heaven, please save me from this coming retribution."

Immediately he noticed, outside the second-floor window, a large branch floating by with several other neighbors clinging to it. They cried out, "Hurry, jump on before the waters overtake you!"

Seeing how wet and uncomfortable they were, the man answered, "Thanks, but I know my God will save me."

"Have it your way," they cried as the current carried them off.

The waters continued to rise, flooding the second floor, forcing the man out onto the roof. As the available surface area slowly dwindled, he cried out in panic, "Dear Father in heaven, please save me from this coming retribution!"

Immediately down out of the clouds swooped a helicopter dangling a long rescue rope. Struggling to control the copter, the pilot yelled, "Quick, grab hold and I'll take you to safety!"

Seeing the roughness of the rope and imagining himself trying to hold on through the rain and wind, the man yelled back, "Thanks, but I know my God will save me."

Blown by the wind, the pilot called back as the copter banked off into the distance, "Have it your way!"

And the waters continued to rise until the roof was covered, the man was overcome, and he drowned.

The next instant he found himself standing in the clouds face to face with his Creator. He complained in desperation, "Didn't you see me down there? Didn't you hear me? Three times I pleaded with you to save me, but you let me drown. Didn't you care?"

God the Father looked with pity upon the man and responded, "I sent you a boat, a branch, and a helicopter. What more did you want?"

I thought of this story recently when I received a phone call from a priest friend and member of the CHNetwork. He was about to attend a deanery meeting with his bishop. They were to discuss what drastic measures they would implement to meet the growing spiritual needs of their diocese, given the worsening shortage of priests and seminarians.

The priest wanted detailed information about the many clergy converts we have on our rolls to determine whether any of them could help. I told him that across the country clergy converts were serving as priests, deacons, directors of religious education, diocesan directors of evangelization and retreat centers, and parish administrators. I also told him, however, that for the most part the dioceses in which they lived have not been tapping their gifts, training, and experience. More often than not clergy converts tell me that they feel put off by the local diocesan structure — they sense that they've been given the message, "Don't call us; we'll call you."

As the priest took the information and prepared to hang up, it was he who reminded me of this joke. "A boat, a branch, and a helicopter" were his words, which he planned to pass along tactfully to his bishop.

We must continue to pray that those who are on the journey home to the Catholic Church, especially ministers and educators, will find that doors open for them in the Church to use their gifts for ministry. After all, isn't the present influx into the Church of highly trained and skilled men and women, from denominations all across America, truly providential?

CHAPTER 44

Thoughts Around a Bonfire

My family and I love to make bonfires. Our small farm, far from efficiently developed (that's why we call it "Weed 'Em & Reap Farm"), is strewn with dead trees and brush. The boys and I could make a bonfire a month for the rest of our lives and still not conquer the chaos.

During one such conflagration, it struck me how little humankind has progressed in being a faithful steward of one of the greatest gifts God has given us: fire. All our amazing technologies come ultimately from God; none are purely of our creation. We have merely developed what grace has revealed to us, and we still utilize this most primitive of gifts only inefficiently.

As I reflected, there before me was a spectacular thermal reaction: Worthless, dead, natural wood and leaves were being transformed into brilliant light and intense heat. On this particular occasion, the heat was so unbearable that we had to whittle extra-long hot dog skewers from ten-foot sapling spicebush branches.

With our dog Bungie at my side, I wondered: We live in a modern age of previously unimaginable technologies, where many of the world's conflicts concern how to provide energy to power these technologies. Yet here, right before me, was the most primitive of technologies — fire — and we had not yet discovered how to save and utilize this energy efficiently, particularly here in my own backyard.

Sure, on a larger scale we can put a closed pot of water over fire to produce steam to turn a fan to drive a turbine to produce electricity to power a light bulb or a furnace. But think of how inefficient this process is. Many indirect steps are necessary to turn heat and light into heat and light, and in fact the original light produced by the fire isn't even used.

Scientists are presently working with silicon nanowire technology in an attempt to shorten the energy transference. But with all we have accomplished and are discovering, we are still a long way from conserving and utilizing directly the heat and light energy of a basic backyard bonfire.

There's a spiritual analogy here: We (the Church) are not always efficient stewards of the fires of religious conversion.

Nothing in the universe is so powerful as a soul that has been changed by grace, from a lackluster, cold, self-absorbed sinner into an enthusiastic, enlightened, on-fire-yet-humble servant of God. When this conversion takes place, either as a long, slow, grace-filled process or a grace-sparked explosion, God has given His Church the gift of this on-fire convert for the work of the gospel. Yet with all our modern means of communication, transportation, and organization, and after two thousand years of R&D (*Revivificare et Dissipare*), individual bishops and parish priests are still too often inefficient at implementing, engaging, and utilizing these gifts.

In America especially, at least since the Catholic faith became a legal and tolerated religion after the Revolution, the primary emphasis of much Church leadership has too often seemed to be on squelching "enthusiasm" and preventing the production of "waves." This situation is particularly true with regard to the conservation of the energy (that is, gifts, training, experience, convictions, and enthusiasm) of clergy converts. Several of the bishops with whom I have talked admit that as a group, the American bishops just don't seem to know how best to engage and use the gifts of clergy converts for the good of the gospel and the Church.

On the morning after that bonfire, when I walked out to the site of the previous evening's fun, only a large gray circle of ashes was left. We had enjoyed the light and the heat for a brief time, but now only the spent coals remained. I felt a letdown.

Sometimes I feel the same way when I consider how many enthusiastic clergy converts are unutilized and unappreciated by individual bishops and parish priests. Before "coming home," they were actively serving Jesus Christ, preaching, teaching, counseling, inspiring, consoling, bringing lost souls to Jesus and salvation. They were respected and appreciated leaders who were basically interested in one thing: spreading the gospel of Jesus Christ.

Now, as Catholics, their flames are often doused. Many church leaders struggle to utilize the gifts of clergy converts and to inspire and engage laity in general for the work of the gospel.

After two thousand years, only seventeen percent of the world's population claims to be Catholic, and what part of this seventeen percent is truly converted? Yet how many American dioceses spend the majority of their efforts focused inward, struggling to meet the perceived needs of membership, with little emphasis placed on reaching the unevangelized folks next door? This arrangement is only to be expected, given the low emphasis on evangelization in our Catholic colleges and seminaries.

I believe that every convert is a gift of fire to the Church, and I'm certainly not the first to say this. As we noted in an earlier chapter, Pope John Paul II said the same in *Redemptoris Missio*. It bears repeating here:

> Certainly, every convert is a gift to the Church and represents a serious responsibility for her ... especially in the case of adults, such converts bring with them a kind of new energy, an enthusiasm for the faith, and a desire to see the gospel lived out in the Church. They would be greatly disappointed if, having entered the ecclesial community, they were to find a life lacking fervor and without signs of renewal! We cannot preach conversion unless we ourselves are converted anew every day (47).

Certainly there are matters in which a Smokey Bear mentality (focused on putting out fires) makes sense. But not with regard to fulfilling Christ's Great Commission. In fact, Jesus wanted far more than a forest fire of evangelization. He asked for the entire world to be set on fire: "I came to cast fire upon the earth; and would that it were already kindled!" (Lk 12:49).

I believe that one reason God inspires so many Protestants to abandon any dreams for a regular secular career and instead to go to seminary, to get ordained, and to serve as pastors and teachers — and *then* to call them home to the Church — is so they can become needed sparks of renewal in the Church.

So what can we do to ensure that the heat and light of their conversions is not squandered? How can we prevent buckets of quenching discouragement from dousing their enthusiasm? I wish I could give the easy answer, just as I wish I could invent the technology to power my home from my backyard bonfires.

Part of the challenge is that the answer must come from the top down, and it indeed has: All our most recent popes have called for a reemphasis on evangelization, renewal, and especially the encouragement of the lay apostolate. The problem is that their messages have had a hard time permeating downward, through the national, diocesan, and parochial filters. In the Catholic Church as elsewhere, it's difficult to break free from TWWADT ("The Way We've Always Done Things").

As a lowly individual outside the powerful technological industrial stream, I can't expect to solve the big energy questions, nor can I waste my life waiting for the opportunity to do so. In the meantime, however, I can enjoy the heat and light of my backyard bonfires, share this energy with my family and friends, and look for other ways to utilize this God-given free source of heat and light. (In the deep cold winter, in fact, we are able to bring that bonfire into our wood-burning stove, heat our entire home, and enjoy popcorn by the firelight.)

In an analogous way, each one of us, recognizing God's call and the gifts He has given us, can begin right now to look for ways to share the heat and light of our conversions with those around us — not from above, as if our conversions make us somehow superior, but from beside. We can also look for ways to work at the local level, from the bottom up, to open doors for others who have felt frustrated by the "system."

Let's ask God to help us see how we can help others "rekindle the gift of God that is within" each of us, through our baptisms, through our confirmations, and through "the laying on of ... hands." As St. Paul told St. Timothy, "God did not give us a spirit of timidity but a spirit of power and love and self-control" (2 Tm 1:6–7).

Power ... love ... self-control. These are forms of God-given energy, and we certainly can look for more ways to help each other conserve and implement them! Lord, help us! Living all around each of us are people in need of the heat and light of the gospel; may they not go without because we haven't taken the time to share.

CHAPTER 45

Which Direction Are You Spinning?

A humbling experience last Christmas put me in my place.

I grew up an only child, so my mother developed a special annual holiday tradition. After all the other more mundane presents were opened, she brought out from hiding for my father and me "the annual game." No matter how exhilarating and valuable the other gifts may have been, it was that game — a different one each year — that captured our attention for the rest of the day and for days to come.

The most memorable of those annual games was the mechanical hockey game we received when I was eight or so. You know the kind: a three-foot-long, elevated cardboard rink with molded players that moved and spun in response to geared rods from underneath.

My dad and I played that game every day and night, as dedicated as any modern youth with a computer game, until the players were bent and mangled and the gears were stripped.

We went through another, more advanced hockey game beginning the Christmas of my twelfth year, and I knew that one day when I had children of my own, one Christmas morning we would awake to find just such a game waiting for us.

Well, this was the year. All the packages had been opened. It seemed the festivities were complete. Then Marilyn, my wife, brought out another gift.

Sure enough, when the wrappings were ripped away, the beautiful, more up-to-date, yet nostalgically identical game was erected front and center. All three of my sons took turns, while I patiently sat back and waited.

You see, I was sure that for me, playing this game would be like riding a bike. From my many years of training, I would certainly have too much of an advantage. I would too quickly whup them all. So I waited.

Then on the third day of Christmas, my middle son, Peter, challenged me.

Why not? I took my place, willing to hold back at first, and only later letting my well-honed skills reveal themselves.

But then, suddenly, I was struck with dismay! This new, "improved" rendition of the old game was geared differently! In the good old days, you see, a clockwise spin of the controls caused a direct counter-clockwise spin of the players. But this newfangled version of the game had been redesigned to operate "correctly": a clockwise spin made the player spin clockwise.

The problem? I was so accustomed to doing it the old way that I could not, no matter how hard I concentrated, relearn the skill. Consistently my players were always spinning the wrong way, sometimes sending the puck into my own goal!

I tried over and over, and in the end I just had to give up. It was like trying to ride a bicycle whose gears worked backwards; you would have to peddle backwards to make it go, and forward to set the brake. Having grown up doing it the old way, I found it nearly impossible to change.

As I sat watching my boys play on, unhindered by old, in-grained habits, I pondered the difficulties we face when we seek to follow Jesus. Faith involves more than mere mental assent. It requires that we realign every aspect of our lives into His direction according to His will and truth.

The problem is that most of us for far too long have been spinning the controls of our lives in the opposite direction. Change doesn't come easily, especially when a large part of our mind, heart, and conscience doesn't want to change!

Conversion — which is a continual process, not a one-time event — challenges the way we talk, the things we choose to look at, listen to, or touch, and the way we treat one another. So if the spin of our lives has been to greet everyone in the morning with a Scrooge-like grouchiness, for example, conversion requires that in charity we change our ways.

Even so, it's hard to change gears after we've been spinning our lives one particular way for so long. Yet we need not give up in frustration every time we fail. I may not have received any divine assistance in defending my lifelong hockey prowess. But in the process of conversion, God promises to give us all the grace we need.

He does more than demand that we turn our lives around. He helps us turn in the right direction, into His direction. All we need to do is ask.

CHAPTER 46

What Kind of Soil Does Your Heart Hold?

The Parable of the Sower (Mt 13:1–23) is one of Jesus' most familiar stories. In it, as you'll recall, a farmer scatters seed on four types of soil, with differing results.

Traditionally, the parable has been understood to describe four ways in which people receive, or fail to receive, the gospel message. Three of the soils (one rocky, one thorny, one lying in the path where birds feed) represent people who receive the gospel inadequately and thus fail to bear fruit. But the fourth, the "good soil," represents the person who hears the word, understands it, and consequently "bears fruit and yields a hundred or sixty or thirtyfold" (Mt 13:23).

Over the years I've met people representing all different qualities of spiritual "soil." I've known some at every point along the spectrum, from those who are completely alienated from God to those who are in near-rapturous union with Him.

With the desire to help the alienated ones come closer to God, I've often noted this parable and asked: "Which kind of soil are you? What 'rocks' or 'thorns' or 'birds' keep you from bearing the fruit of God's word?"

I heard the parable once again recently. It caused me to reflect especially on the many converts to the Catholic faith, and the many "reverts" who left the Church but later returned, that I've interviewed on the *Journey Home* television program. It struck me that Jesus was referring not only to four different kinds of people, but also to four *stages* of the spiritual journey that many of us go through in our walk with Christ.

In His explanation of the parable, Jesus first notes: "The seed sown on the path is the one who hears the word of the kingdom without understanding it, and the evil one comes and steals away what was sown in his heart" (Mt 13:19).

Doesn't this sound like what happened to so many of us when we were children? We heard the faith taught when we were very young, perhaps in religious education classes, but we never came to "understand" it. It was planted in our hearts by faithful teachers and preachers. Yet over time the Evil One snatched it away, or at least turned our attention completely away from what remained planted deep within us. As a result, we walked away from the Church and our faith. Does this sound familiar to you or someone close to you?

Jesus then explains: "The seed sown on rocky ground is the one who hears the word and receives it at once with joy. But he has no root and lasts only for a time. When some tribulation or persecution comes because of the word, he immediately falls away" (Mt 13:20–21).

Doesn't this sound like what has happened to so many of us during our youth and young adult years? Still rather naïve, we responded with enthusiastic joy to some charismatic preacher or winsome Bible teacher, carried away by a "born again" conversion experience. With great emotions we came back to Jesus, often bewailing our childhood teachers who "failed" to teach us the true gospel! In time, though, as our lives became more complicated and challenges rose to our newfound faith, we drifted back into spiritual inactivity. Does that also sound familiar?

In the parable, Jesus continues: "The seed sown among thorns is the one who hears the word, but then worldly anxiety and the lure of riches choke the word and it bears no fruit" (Mt 13:22).

Doesn't this sound like what has happened to so many of us later in our adult years? Establishing a family and pursuing a career, we became distracted by the concerns of work and home life, and God's word was silenced within us.

Yet Jesus also speaks of the fourth soil (see Mt 13:23). He talks about that point in our lives when, by the grace of God, we not only heard but understood the gospel. When we finally recognized that whatever in our lives has choked the faith out of us did so only with our own consent. When by grace we humbly recommitted our life to Him, and returned in obedience as an active member of His Church.

At what stage are you in your soil's development?

CHAPTER 47

Changed But Still Changing?

In his first letter to St. Timothy, St. Paul warned that when Timothy appointed new bishops in the churches under his charge, he must not appoint "a recent convert" (1 Tm 3:6). The primary reason St. Paul gave for this caution was that a new convert raised to the level of leadership too quickly may become "puffed up with conceit and fall into the condemnation of the devil." But why is this temptation a particular danger for new converts? Isn't this also true for anyone raised to leadership?

Yes, of course it's a danger for all leaders. But converts are a special case because it takes time for them to recognize, appreciate, and deal with the differences between their previous beliefs and their new Catholic beliefs. Converts can be blind to many of these important differences, not just while on their journey, but also months, even years after their conversion. I know this to be true, for there are many things that I myself am still wrestling with years after my conversion.

It has taken me years, for example, to appreciate the difference between the Protestant and Catholic understanding of baptism. In none of my former Lutheran, Congregationalist, or Presbyterian traditions did I believe that baptism — whether a sacrament, an ordinance, or merely a symbolic act — was essential to salvation. I considered only belief in Jesus Christ as my Lord and Savior to be essential to salvation. Whether or not a person was baptized, or whether or not a person was in a church, was to me inconsequential.

In time, by God's mercy, I've come to understand and appreciate more fully the Catholic understanding of the essential nature of baptism, especially as expressed in St. Paul's letter to the Ephesians.

In the Sacrament of Baptism, then later in the Sacrament of Confirmation, the Holy Spirit came to dwell within us. St. Paul described this reality in his letter to the Ephesian Christians:

> In him you also, who have heard the word of truth, the gospel of your salvation, and have believed in him, were sealed with the promised Holy Spirit, which is the guarantee of our inheritance until we acquire possession of it, to the praise of his glory. (Eph 1:13–14)

In 2 Corinthians, the Apostle described the radical change that happens through this indwelling of the Holy Spirit:

> Therefore, if anyone is in Christ, he is a new creation; the old has passed away, behold, the new has come. All this is from God, who through Christ reconciled us to himself and gave us the ministry of reconciliation. (2 Cor 5:17–18)

Through these powerful sacraments, we were changed. As St. Paul explained in Ephesians, as a result we were "no longer strangers and sojourners, but ... fellow citizens with the saints and members of the household of God, built upon the foundation of the apostles and prophets, Christ Jesus himself being the cornerstone" (Eph 2:19–20).

This transformation took place whether or not we felt any different after these sacraments. And this change has taken place in three dimensions for all who have been baptized, again as explained in Ephesians: We have been reconciled to God, to others, and to ourselves.

Yes, through the sacraments, we have been changed — but this is only the beginning! It's no guarantee that the process of salvation has been completed. From the moment of that change, we have moved either forward toward intimacy with God or backward away from Him, depending upon how we have responded and continue to respond to Him in grace.

We don't merely remain the same. We have immediately been changed within by the sacraments, yet we are left with the same habits, attitudes, passions, and lusts. We must act on the graces we've been given to resist the downward slide away from His love.

In Ephesians, St. Paul described this active journey of faith when he begged the newly baptized: "Walk in a manner worthy of the calling to which you have been called, with all lowliness and meekness, with patience, forbearing one another in love, eager to maintain the unity of the Spirit in the bond of peace" (Eph 4:1–3).

The Apostle also prayed:

> According to the riches of his glory [may he] grant you to be strengthened with might through his Spirit in the inner man … that Christ may dwell in your hearts through faith; that you, being rooted and grounded in love, may have power to comprehend with all the saints what is the breadth and length and height and depth, and to know the love of Christ which surpasses knowledge, that you may be filled with all the fullness of God. (Eph 3:16–19)

This journey begins with choosing to lead a life worthy of Him, by grace and obedience, and then by getting back up again whenever we fall by going to the Sacrament of Reconciliation (Confession). We aim toward being filled with His fullness.

Later in Ephesians, however, St. Paul also described people who have taken the journey in the opposite direction.

> They are darkened in their understanding, alienated from the life of God because of the ignorance that is in them, due to their hardness of heart; they have become callous and have given themselves up to licentiousness, greedy to practice every kind of uncleanness. (Eph 4:18–19)

This list is significant because St. Paul is describing the former lives of his Christian audience — what they were like before they were baptized.

But weren't they changed? Why do they need to worry about returning to their old ways of life? Because, sadly, this is exactly what far too many baptized and catechized Christians do: They fail to act on the graces they have received, out of ignorance, discouragement, or sloth.

The truth is that there's not one of us who hasn't failed. Even as St. Paul himself admitted:

> Not that I have already obtained this or am already perfect; but I press on to make it my own, because Christ Jesus has made me his own. Brethren, I do not consider that I have made it my own; but one thing I do, forgetting what lies behind and straining forward to what lies ahead, I press on toward the goal for the prize of the upward call of God in Christ Jesus. (Phil 3:12–14)

So how do we effectively forget what lies behind and strain forward to what lies ahead? How do we start all over again, when we have fallen so many times? In Ephesians, St. Paul gives a clear challenge that I think every one of us ought to memorize, and repeat every day, hearing it as God's merciful words to each of us:

> Put off the old man that belongs to your former manner of life and is corrupt through deceitful lusts, and be renewed in the spirit of your minds, and put on the new man, created after the likeness of God in true righteousness and holiness. (Eph 4:22–24)

In our baptisms, we were changed. Yet we are called to keep on changing, all the way to the end, when by grace we are given the privilege of standing before Him in the Beatific Vision. Every day, when we cross ourselves in remembrance of our baptisms and what He did for us in love on the Cross, we are called to remember that "we are his workmanship, created in Christ Jesus for good works, which God prepared beforehand, that we should walk in them" (Eph 2:10).

I encourage you to take this challenge every morning in prayer, every time during the day you feel the temptation to fall backwards, and every night as you pause to examine how successfully you have followed Him that day. In time, by grace, this habit will help you fulfill your baptismal calling so you can "press on toward the goal for the prize of the upward call of God in Christ Jesus" (Phil 3:14).

CHAPTER 48

Is Something Missing?

Through hosting the *Journey Home* program on EWTN and working with the CHNetwork, I've met hundreds who have "come home" from Protestant backgrounds to the Catholic Church. What's the most common reason they give for becoming Catholic? At some point many of them came to realize that "something was missing."

They may have been quite content with the preaching, teaching, worship, and fellowship of their former religious traditions. But they sensed that they lacked something essential, though they didn't know for sure what it was. Thus began a search. And after an unlimited variety of paths, the majority eventually figured out what they were missing.

It was the Eucharist.

Many of these Christians once considered the "Lord's Supper" a mere commemorative meal, of passing significance compared to preaching the Word. Its elements were but symbols. Yet they came, by grace, to accept Jesus at His word: the "Supper" He intends is no mere meal, but a Sacrifice. Through the words of consecration, the bread and wine truly become the Body and Blood, Soul and Divinity of our Lord Jesus Christ, delivering grace — the divine life of Christ — to all who partake, believing.

But here's a puzzle. When I was a Protestant minister, more than a third of each congregation I led was composed of ex-Catholics. Why had they left behind the treasures of this Church and her sacraments? I also noted that many former Catholics drift from place to place spiritually, remaining members of one congregation or denomination for only two to three years before passing on to another.

When asked why they drift, they typically respond that even when they're satisfied with the preaching, teaching, worship, and fellowship, "something is missing." And so it is, even though they may not realize what it is.

Now it's understandable that those outside the Church, lacking sufficient catechesis, wouldn't know about the blessings conveyed through the reception of the Eucharist. But what about Catholics? Do even faithful Catholics, who regularly receive the sacraments, sometimes wonder whether "something is missing"?

Apparently, they sometimes do. And if they lack sufficient spiritual formation, that "something" they're missing may well be an understanding and appreciation of the Eucharistic mystery. Its beauty, truth, and power may be largely hidden from them.

So how can we make sure we don't miss the infinite blessings of the Eucharist? Here are four suggestions.

First, remember that the primary reason to attend Mass is to give, not to get. We go to Mass to worship God, to lift up our hearts to Him who in love and mercy has given us "every spiritual blessing in the heavenly places" (Eph 1:3). Though we receive great gifts there, if we go primarily for what we can get, sooner or later we'll be disappointed, because our focus will be self-directed.

Second, we must believe that what Jesus said and the Church teaches about the Eucharist is true. Believing is not based on feelings or even understanding. It involves an intellectual, willing choice. We must trust the authority of the word Christ has given us: That Host *is* Jesus, and we *do* receive grace when we receive Him, regardless of what our senses or feelings tell us.

At the same time, we must beware of a prideful presumption that shouts, "I know better than the Church!" about what is true or real or moral. We must resist the assumption that the Church really doesn't understand "my condition" or "my situation" or even "my insight." Those attitudes make the Devil laugh; they rob us of grace at Mass.

The last two suggestions come from the teaching of St. Ignatius Loyola: "Work as if everything depends on you. Pray as if everything depends on God." What work is this? In Ephesians, St. Paul tells us, "He chose us in Him ... that we should be holy and blameless before Him" (Eph 1:4). You have received the graces of the Eucharist. Now act upon them. Do all you can, in deed and word, to become holy.

Meanwhile, each time you receive Communion, humbly recognize that everything you have and have done, or will ever have or do, is a gift of God's grace.

CHAPTER 49

Sock Drawers and Spiritual Entropy

Many laws shape and guide our spiritual lives. Some are mere descriptions of reality. Others are instructions that require our willing initiative.

An example of the first type is found in 1 John: "God is light and in Him is no darkness at all. If we say we have fellowship with him while we walk in darkness, we lie and do not live according to the truth" (1 Jn 1:5–6). This statement describes a spiritual reality that we must accept as true and then heed.

An example of the second type of law is the Golden Rule: "Whatever you wish that men would do to you, do to them" (Mt 7:12). Here Jesus was teaching us how we need to live if we expect to reap the benefits of God's blessings.

The Scriptures are replete with both types of laws. One significant reason we must be ever vigilant in reading and meditating on Scripture is so we can know and live according to these spiritual laws. As the Apostle John reminds us:

> Let what you heard from the beginning abide in you. If
> what you heard from the beginning abides in you, then you
> will abide in the Son and in the Father. And this is what he
> has promised us, eternal life. (1 Jn 2:24–25)

Nevertheless, one particular spiritual law — a law of the first type, describing a reality that shapes all our lives — can best be learned from a parallel in the physical sciences. Technically called the "Second Law of Thermodynamics," or the "Law of Entropy," that law is stated this way: "The entropy of a closed system shall never decrease, and shall increase whenever possible."

At first glance you may wonder, "What has this to do with my walk with Christ? I don't even know what 'entropy' is!" But I guarantee that this law, rightly understood, has everything to do with your walk with Christ.

Entropy is most commonly described as a measure of the "disorder" in a system. Lots of disorder means high entropy, while lots of order means low entropy. A *closed system* is any system, such as our universe, that cannot receive any additional matter (atoms, molecules, and so on) or energy (especially heat) from an exterior source.

For entropy to decrease within a closed system (and for order to increase), energy must be added from an exterior source. Therefore, we must conclude that after God created the universe *ex nihilo* (out of nothing; see Gn 1), any increasing order we witness (such as the beginning of life) comes from God, who is outside the universe. The order He established in this closed system now operates by this law He initiated — unless intervention occurs, either supernaturally or by our operating in His image.

The operation of this law can be illustrated by filling a jar half full of black marbles and half with white marbles, and then shaking the jar. The marbles will become mixed — and further shaking will never separate the marbles back into groupings of black and white. For the same reason, a tablespoon of sugar will become evenly distributed in a recipe containing five cups of flour; it will distribute randomly. In both cases, additional energy or effort is needed from outside the system to bring order back to the marbles or to separate the original ingredients of the recipe.

The effects of this law can be seen all around us in nature, at all levels of creation. If you let ten acres of finely tilled farmland go for ten years without supplying any effort to manage or control the plant growth, you end up with a mess — in fact, the beginnings of a forest will emerge. Other biological laws are at work, of course, so many layers of order and disorder can be detected. But it's obvious that letting the land go without management would never produce a finely manicured golf course or an award-winning arboretum.

Much more could be said about the implications of the Second Law of Thermodynamics, which explains the direction we find in physical actions throughout the natural universe. But this brief description should be enough to uncover its dire implications for the direction of our everyday lives.

Fail to maintain vigilance in keeping your home straight, and entropy will win the day. If you're anything like me, the simplest example of this law is the common dresser drawer. I can spend an evening sorting out all the socks, underwear, tee shirts, loose coins, receipts, and other random trash according to genus and species, color and style, clean or unclean, whole or holey, shape or state of being. However, if I don't repeat this process regularly, the drawer will quickly regress into what I have now: a completely random collection of everything mentioned, plus.

A traditional law (of the second type already mentioned) was summed up in a quip by some astute mother, surely centuries ago, to combat this daily increase of entropy: "A place for everything, and everything in its place." If this law is heeded with regularity and discipline, the entropy of our lives decreases, and order reigns. (My sock drawer may remain a mess, but at least the overall entropy of our home will decrease, because there won't be underwear in the silverware tray.)

Obviously, the law of entropy pervasively influences our physical circumstances. But you may never have realized before how much it influences our spiritual circumstances as well — for our devotional lives are in many ways like a sock drawer. Unless we make constant and regular determined effort to keep our spiritual lives well ordered, entropy will increase in our souls.

As we noted in an earlier chapter: "In the ways of God, whoever does not progress loses ground."

In this life, we will *never* reach a point spiritually where we can presume we have somehow arrived, so we can kick back and wait for our heavenly rewards. We must continually fight the natural spiritual entropy of our souls by heeding St. Paul's example:

> Brethren, I do not consider that I have made it my own; but one thing I do, forgetting what lies behind and straining forward to what lies ahead, I press on toward the goal for the prize of the upward call of God in Christ Jesus. Let those of us who are mature be thus minded. (Phil 3:13–15)

Isn't "spiritual entropy" exactly what the Scriptures mean when they speak of spiritual darkness? As darkness increases in our soul, spiritual entropy increases, until, as John warned: "He … is in the darkness and walks in the darkness, and does not know where he is going, because the darkness has blinded his eyes" (1 Jn 2:11).

How can darkness blind the eyes? Entropy can so fill our lives (we can become so accustomed to disorder) that we no longer recognize it as disorder. (We learn to live with messy sock drawers — who cares?)

Why am I pontificating about all this? Because I believe one of the greatest reasons for coming home to the Catholic Church is to benefit from the powerful spiritual heritage she provides for combating spiritual entropy. The wealth of spiritual traditions, the advice of the great saints and spiritual writers, the sacramentals, and of course the sacraments have all been developed, preserved, and handed down for two thousand years to help us grow in grace so that our hearts, souls, minds, and strength can become ordered to the ways of God.

I believe that all the teachings and spiritual disciplines that the Catholic Church has preserved and promoted under the guidance of the Holy Spirit are to help us fulfill what the Apostle John said to those who would consider themselves children of God: "Abide in him, so that when he appears we may have confidence and not shrink from him in shame at his coming" (1 Jn 2:28).

What better reason to tell all our friends and family about the beauty and fullness of the truth of the Catholic Church: so that when they one day stand before Jesus, the spiritual condition of their souls won't display the same entropy as their sock drawers?

CHAPTER 50

Where Does the Water Come From?

Where's the water come from? Ask most children this question, and the usual answer will be "From the faucet, silly!"

You could press them on the matter. "You mean that's all there is to it?" you might ask. "Water just comes from the faucet?"

And they might well respond with conviction, "Of course not! You have to turn the knob first! See — let me show you."

You might get a similar response if you asked where electricity comes from or where television or radio programs come from. From the wall socket, or from the television set, or from the radio. Oh, and of course, you've got to turn them on first.

A better-informed child, however, might respond this way: "Actually, water comes from a river or a well filled by the rain. Electricity comes from the power plant. Television and radio programs are produced in studios all around the world."

Sounds better, and with these answers they may pass the quiz. But are these better-informed answers sufficient? Water comes from the ground and then out our faucet. Is that all there is to it? Electricity is generated at a plant and then comes out a wall socket. Is that the whole story? *The Journey Home* live television program is produced in the studio at EWTN and then seen or heard on your television, radio, or computer monitor. Is that it?

No. Between the rain and your faucet is an extremely complicated system of pumps, pipes, filters, joints, electronics, and hundreds of diligent people providing this service. And of course in our society it all costs money. Similar necessary middle stages, normally invisible in our daily lives, can be identified for the other services.

It's important for our children to understand the interconnectedness of the often invisible aspects of these services we too often take for granted. But there's an even more important spiritual analogy here.

An even better informed, spiritually aware child — the kind that makes us parents preen our proud feathers — might respond: "Actually, all these things come from God, and we owe Him gratitude and homage for every single thing we have, from large to small."

True, very true, and this answer should earn a gold star on the quiz! And yet, we must never forget the necessary, often invisible, middle stages through which the water, or power, or broadcast must pass.

All this reminds me of a story I once heard. A tourist was driving through Scotland and passed a very lovely, intricately managed and tended farm. It was so impressive that the tourist stopped to speak to the farmer as he toiled on a row of beans. The tourist exclaimed, "I'm overwhelmed at this beautiful farm God has blessed you with!"

The farmer responded: "Yes, but you should have seen it when He had it all to His lonesome!"

Between God's gift of everything and our reception of it all lie the countless middle people — philosophers would call them the "secondary causes" — that God has used to bless our lives. Yes, Jesus warned that apart from Him, we can do nothing (see Jn 15:5). But in that same passage of Scripture He tells us that although He is the life-producing vine, we are the branches through which the vine produces fruit (see Jn 15:4–5).

This analogy, of course, reminds us how important each one of us is as a secondary means of communicating to others the truth of God's love and salvation in Jesus Christ. Sure, the message comes ultimately from Jesus to them. But we are that indispensable middle voice without which they may never hear the truth.

At the same time, this analogy reminds us of the Church's essential role. She is the preeminent channel established by Christ through which He intends for us to receive His blessings and graces.

Too many people think, "All I need is Jesus. I don't need the Church!" But that's like saying, "The water from my faucet rains down from the sky. I don't need any of those things in between!"

CHAPTER 51

Time for a Heart Exam?

At every Mass we repeat words that are perhaps far more self-accusatory than we suspect. The priest beckons, "Lift up your hearts," and we obediently (or perhaps sometimes mindlessly) respond, "We lift them up to the Lord."

So what does it mean to "lift up our hearts" at Mass? In that act, aren't we offering up our hearts, our souls, our consciences for God's inspection?

Jesus warned, "For where your treasure is, there also will your heart be" (Mt 6:21). In the context of everything else He taught, the flip side is equally true: Look where your heart is, and there you'll find what you treasure.

So where is *your* heart? When you lift it up for God's examination, what does He find?

This provocative question came home to me, hard, several years ago. I was only five months a Catholic when a priest asked me to lead a day of recollection on the topic of "The Sacred Heart of Jesus in Scripture." My knee-jerk response was skeptical: "Hey, the Sacred Heart of Jesus ain't *in* Scripture!"

"Maybe it's not there in the way you expect," he replied, "but it's in there. Do the recollection anyway."

Half*heart*edly, I began. My strategy was this: Find out what Jesus taught about the human heart. Use this understanding to analyze His Most Sacred Heart. Then, since we are called to imitate Jesus, figure out what these insights teach us about living in a way that shows devotion to His Most Sacred Heart.

I found that Jesus' teachings about the heart may be summarized by three questions He wants us to answer honestly:

1. What is the *center* of my heart?

2. What is the *condition* of my heart?

3. What *comes forth* from my heart?

Applying these questions to Jesus, what do we discover?

1. The *center* of His heart was to do the will of the Father.

2. The *condition* of His heart was not hard and self-centered, but malleable and open to the needs of others.

3. What *came forth* from His heart was always love, but love shaped by the *conditions* of others' hearts. For example, Jesus loved the poor, the leper, the tax collector, the Pharisees, His disciples, and those who nailed Him to a cross. But each expression of His love was uniquely shaped by the needs of the *conditions* of their hearts.

Now we must apply these insights to ourselves. What does all this teach us about living in such a way that our heart becomes like Jesus' Most Sacred Heart — which is the best way to show our devotion to it?

I must admit that my first opportunity to put these reflections into practice came on the very morning I was to lead this day of recollection. My wife, Marilyn, and I were having one of our occasional "misunderstandings," and after she had said something that hurt, I was about to respond in kind.

But suddenly, all the "heart" questions came flooding into my mind and, like a "2-by-4" of God's grace, they got my attention.

What's at the center of your heart? "Right now," I had to confess, "to retaliate."

What should it be? "To do the will of the Father."

What's the condition of your heart? "At this moment," I answered, "hard, self-centered, vengeful."

What should it be? "Contrite, caring, Marilyn-centered."

So now you must choose: What will you allow to come forth from your heart?

Yikes!

What should come forth? Well, what is it that her heart truly needs? Why are we having this brouhaha? Could it be that I've been so busy lately that she feels unloved? Instead of words that merely feed the flames, maybe I should give her a hug, a kiss, some of my time and attention — the things she really needs.

By God's grace, that's what I did. And the brouhaha ended.

Maybe it's time that we all underwent a heart exam. Just ask yourself: When you lift up your heart at Mass, what is it that God finds?

Chapter 52

The Missing Ingredient

Ever eat a nice, hefty bowl of freshly popped popcorn ... without salt? Ever have your mouth set for an ice-cold glass of cherry Kool Aid® ... only to find that somebody left out the sugar? Yuck!

The best of recipes minus a single key ingredient falls far short on the palate. And the same is true in our walk with God.

So you say your spiritual life seems lacking. You try to maintain a healthy spiritual diet, following all the directions as best you can. It's not easy, but you're sure your mind and heart are in it!

Even so, something's wrong. You put on your best face, yet the anxieties, stresses, and strains of everyday life always seem to get the upper hand.

Jesus said, "Do not be anxious about your life!" (Mt 6:25). But you just can't seem to break the hold that worry has on your heart — for long periods or maybe even for a brief moment. You can't seem to experience the inner peace Jesus promised to all who would follow Him (see Jn 14:27).

In essence, your life with Christ just doesn't *taste* right, at least not in the way He seemed to promise. Is it possible that some essential ingredient, some necessary "spice," is missing from your spiritual life?

The Apostle Paul once passed on to his Christian friends a short, foolproof recipe for receiving this inner peace of God. He wrote to those whose spiritual progress was being impeded by concerns about the present and future:

> Rejoice in the Lord always; again I will say, Rejoice! Let all men know your forbearance. The Lord is at hand. Have no anxiety about anything, but in everything by prayer and supplication … let your requests be made known to God. And the peace of God, which passes all understanding, will keep your hearts and your minds in Christ Jesus.
> (Phil 4:4–7)

You may object: "But I do that! I rejoice already — I put on the good face of forbearance. As for 'prayer and petition,' a day doesn't go by when I'm not spilling my guts to God and asking for His help. So where is this 'peace'? Does it just 'surpass my understanding' so far that I don't even know I've got it?"

Well, the truth is that I left out a critical phrase in the biblical passage I just quoted. Now here's the full text with the missing words emphasized — the key ingredient in St. Paul's "recipe" for joy:

> Rejoice in the Lord always; again I will say, Rejoice! Let all men know your forbearance. The Lord is at hand. Have no anxiety about anything, but in everything by prayer and supplication *with thanksgiving* let your requests be made known to God. And the peace of God, which passes all understanding, will keep your hearts and your minds in Christ Jesus. (Phil 4:4–7)

Do you see it? St. Paul said, *"With thanksgiving!"* Do you see how absolutely essential this ingredient is? The only way our hearts can fully turn away from ourselves, from the false securities of this world, from the entangling, unavoidable anxieties of our infinite web of relationships — the only way to receive the gift of God's peace — is through the "spice" of thanksgiving.

In the necessary detachment of thanksgiving we humbly recognize God as the source of everything we have or have attained or will ever receive in this life or the life to come. And it is only through the habitual practice of thanksgiving that we can truly, authentically, rejoice, especially in the midst of spiritual dryness or physical and material need.

"But I don't *feel* thankful!" you may protest. If that's the case, you need to recall that thanksgiving involves an act of the will. Just as true love and forgiveness are not feelings but acts of the will, so we must *choose* to direct our thoughts to all the reasons God deserves our gratitude, then *choose* to thank Him. And when we make a habit of that choice, feelings of genuine gratitude eventually follow by God's grace.

"Give thanks," St. Paul urged, "in all circumstances" (1 Thes 5:18). Thanksgiving is much more than an annual holiday. It's a whole way of life.

CHAPTER 53

Staying in the Boundaries

A newspaper reporter once hit the streets of New York interviewing people at random about what they considered the most important invention of the modern era. He received a surprising variety of answers: the airplane, the telephone, the automobile, nuclear weapons, air conditioning, space travel, computers, antibiotics. The possibilities went on until one fellow gave an unexpected reply.

"Why, that's obvious," he said. "The thermos."

"The thermos?" responded the reporter, nonplussed.

"Of course. When things need to be hot, it keeps them hot. But when things need to be cold, it keeps them cold."

The newspaperman blinked. "So what?"

"Well — how does it *know*?"

As we seek renewal in the Church, some things need to be kept "hot," and some need to be kept "cold." But sometimes discerning the difference can be difficult. On numerous important issues and doctrines of our Catholic faith, people often take alternative, even contradictory, positions in their calls for renewal. So many of us may be left asking, "How does a faithful Catholic *know*?"

No doubt, from the beginning, the Church has always needed renewal. There was no pristine time in the near or distant past when everyone in the Church — made up of sinners like you and me — was perfect. Paul, James, John, and Peter had to write letters to shape up the first-generation churches. All historians agree that the Church needed renewal in the years leading up to the Protestant Reformation — and many Catholic leaders and eventual saints were actively involved in trying to bring it about.

Nevertheless, when faced with the need for authentic renewal, how do we know what can and must be done to bring it about?

As I've tried to sort through the wide array of opinions about what it means exactly to be a faithful Catholic in this post-Vatican II era, I've come up with three guidelines or, more accurately, boundary lines. They may represent a rather simplified formula, but I offer them for your consideration. They help set the perimeter within which faithful Catholics must stay as they discern what changes might be necessary, allowed, or avoided in promoting the renewal of the Church.

In my view, being a faithful Catholic, as we respond to the need for authentic renewal, means staying within the following three boundaries:

Boundary 1: Recognizing that renewal always builds on the past. It involves authentic development.

On the one hand, some step over this boundary line when they always prefer the *new* to the *old*. They run fast ahead in the name of progress while jettisoning the past, kicking the dust from their feet.

On the other hand, some step over the line when they hold too tightly and exclusively to the old — resisting, even rejecting, change simply because it is new. Jesus called us, however, to recognize that both the new wine and the old wineskins are important (see Mt 9:17). It's not as important what Catholics did one hundred years ago or might be able to do one hundred years in the future; Christ calls us to be faithful Catholics now.

Boundary 2: Recognizing that in renewal, some things can be changed, but others cannot. In general, both extremes transgress this boundary. Some lean toward viewing all things as open to change, while others resist any change at all. The right attitude lies in a famous quote often attributed to St. Augustine: "In essentials, unity; in nonessentials, diversity; in all things, charity."

Boundary 3: Recognizing that God has given us an authority that can be trusted to make the above distinctions: the Magisterium in union with the successors of St. Peter. Again, in general, both extremes transgress this boundary when they lift themselves up above the Church — because they think the Church is either too conservative or too liberal.

Many people try to entice us to step over the lines, especially political candidates who flaunt dissent for the sake of winning votes. But we must trust that the Church Jesus gave us is still being guided faithfully by His Spirit.

CHAPTER 54

Is It Really All About Me?

Maybe it's just me. But when life sneaks up from behind to pull out the proverbial rug or deliver a hefty whack to the backside, I tend to ask, "Why me, Lord? Why are you letting this happen, or causing this to happen, to me?"

It's not an unreasonable question. The belief that God is intimately involved in every incident, every moment of our lives, monumental or mundane, is firmly based on the teachings of Scripture and Sacred Tradition. Though beyond our human capacity to understand or perceive, God is mysteriously and lovingly concerned with every hair on our head. Not a sparrow falls without His knowing it (see Mt 10:29–30).

Sometimes it's tempting to imagine, then, that all the people in our lives have been carefully orchestrated by God for our personal benefit, either to provide aid when we need encouragement, or frustration when we need patience.

For example, you're looking forward to a quiet, relaxing plane flight on which to read a new novel. But then a harried mother and her screaming child sit down next to you. *Why me, Lord?*

You're driving in a hurry, due partly to your poor planning. But you discover that around the next corner is a bumper-to-bumper traffic jam caused by a farmer on a tractor "with no particular place to go" and no hurry to get there. *Oh, come on, Lord!*

You hired a cousin to handle the family business, and you thought she was trustworthy and ethical. But she turns out to be a devil in disguise! *Lord, why did you let this happen to me?*

Are such people placed in our lives almost like angels (or demons) to teach us patience, charity, self-control, and humility?

The first answer to this question, accepting the mystery of God's intimate involvement in our lives, is *yes*: We should recognize every relationship as somehow God-sent, as a gift from a loving Father to a son or daughter, to help us grow in holiness.

But there's another answer, equally true, that affirms the flip side of this reality: We ourselves have been placed by God in every one of our relationships for the sake of others. We're in their lives not for our benefit, but for theirs; we're the designated angels, or "demons," to help them grow in holiness.

I'm reminded of a line in the Broadway musical *My Fair Lady*. Professor Henry Higgins declares, disingenuously, "I'm talking about you, not me!" In reality, Higgins never got beyond himself, but our amusement at his self-absorption should awaken us to our own.

For a number of years I flew almost every week from Ohio to Alabama and back to host my live television program on EWTN. I presume that God is pleased with my efforts to provide this worldwide media witness to His Son and His Church. But it could well be possible that when I stand before my Lord one day, I'll discover that the primary reason He placed me on those long plane rides was not what I had thought.

What if His main objective was not to get me to the studios or to allow me to bury my face in my books — but rather to have me share His love and concern with the people sitting beside me?

What if the reason you're delayed in traffic is so you can demonstrate patience or offer up a prayer for someone whose life might be a little more demanding and a little less materially blessed than yours?

What if that less-than-trustworthy employee was placed alongside you so that she could learn from your patience and integrity, and with God's grace break from the unethical business practices that have always controlled her life? Was God using you and your company as an opportunity to draw this person's heart toward home?

Every one of us can start today, right now, to ask God to show us how He has planted us in the lives of others to help them grow closer to Him. It's not so much that our lives are not about us; it's that our lives are about us *in our role of helping others.* We must never forget our Lord's words: "As you did it to one of the least of these my brethren, you did it to me" (Mt 25:40).

CHAPTER 55

Lessons From the Berry Patch

St. Francis de Sales in his *Introduction to the Devout Life* exhorts us to listen for God's daily inspirations. But how do these come to us? Or have we given up even trying to listen because our experience has convinced us that He isn't speaking?

Maybe we need to remember what happened to the Old Testament prophet Elijah, who expected to hear God's voice as a powerful, clear, unmistakable message from above. Instead, it came as a "still small voice" in the wilderness (1 Kgs 19:12).

The Church and her saints teach that the number of ways God is trying to speak to us every day is almost infinite — He loves us that much. One version of His "still small voice" came to me while berry picking on my farm.

The nickname of our farm is *Weed' Em & Reap*. So true, right? The problem, though, is that so far we've reaped mostly weeds. I haven't erected an arched stone entrance sign telling our neighbors our farm's name, though, because to do so would imply that we're serious about being a farm. And I learned long ago that I am far from worthy to be called a farmer.

What is our main crop, you ask? Well, our only intentional crop was Marilyn's strawberry patch, which did extremely well. Our bumper crops were wild raspberries and blackberries, but our largest showings were in ironweed, spice berries, stinging nettles, and multiflora rose.

Some of you might be impressed, but any farmer who saw our land would know with a smirk that *Weed 'Em & Reap Farm* is being run by a disorganized, ignorant, displaced city dweller. I could easily fill a book with the mistakes I've made, such as not knowing our goat was pregnant, burying my tractor axle deep in muck, and being thrown ankles over armpits by an escaped pig. But there have also been many victories, and we're learning a lot and enjoying the process together.

Even so, take it from me: Gathering more than a dozen quarts of bramble berries doesn't come easily. And as I labor to harvest those berries, God speaks to me through the parallels I find between my farming efforts and my spiritual life.

First, I've learned that invariably the largest, most luscious berries are deep within the brambles, and those prickly picker branches hurt! The way they attack, you'd think there were little demons in those bushes. The minute I stretch deep into a bush to pluck two or three of the little fruits, two or three pickers literally wrap themselves around my back, locking me in until rescuers arrive. I'm no biblical scholar, but I'm sure that God must have added the prickly pickers *after* the fall of Adam and Eve.

Those little thorns remind me of St. Paul's teaching in Romans that, though we're heirs of Christ, this privilege comes "if only we suffer with Him so that we may also be glorified with Him" (Rom 8:17). As it is with harvesting bramble berries, so it is in our spiritual lives as well: The greatest blessings always come with suffering.

257

A second message from God's "still, small voice" also comes through berry picking. The greatest blessings always require patience as well, as it says in Psalm 37: "Be still before the Lord, and wait patiently for him; ... those who wait for the Lord shall possess the land" (Ps 37: 7, 9).

Those who pick berries in a hurry, who just want to get it done so they can move on to something else, will invariably have three times the number of picker pricks and a third the number of good berries. Or more likely, no berries at all, since they usually get spilled while running home. (Just ask my youngest son.)

If we relax and take the time to delight carefully in the God-given privilege and beauty found in picking each berry (or any other task He gives us), the overall experience is always more rewarding. This too is the advice of the psalmist: "Take delight in the Lord, and he will give you the desires of your heart" (Ps 37:4).

Finally, God provides yet one more lesson through the art of berry picking: We must never be so sure that we've picked the bushes clean.

When I begin picking, I pick the easy-to-reach berries. When I have all those collected, I could easily declare that my work's done. But I know there's more. So I fight the good fight into and through the shoulder-high bramble patch, then pause on the other side to gloat over a job well done.

But then I inevitably turn around and discover dozens of luscious berries taunting me in plain view. From the other direction, they were hidden behind leaves, but now from this new angle they are blatantly manifest.

So it is with sin and bad habits. We must not stop after we've cleansed ourselves of the easily obvious sins, nor gloat in self-contentment once we've attacked and conquered every other fault or vice of which we're aware. We need only look around at ourselves from a fresh angle — from the perspective of our suffering Savior as St. Paul did (see Phil 3:7–16) — and we'll see that none of us have yet reached perfection.

In all these ways, then, God speaks to me while I'm picking berries. In what ways, in the routine, everyday events of your life, is God trying to speak to you?

CHAPTER 56

Are Liturgical Rules a Straightjacket?

In the Sermon on the Mount, Jesus called His would-be disciples to a deeper, fuller conversion. To follow Christ is no merely external obedience, but a matching obedience of the heart.

Our external piety and the motives of our heart should be directly connected. As the Catechism explains:

> Jesus' call to conversion and penance, like that of the prophets before Him, does not aim first at outward works, "sackcloth and ashes," fasting, and mortification, but at the conversion of the heart, interior conversion. Without this, such penances remain sterile and false; however, interior conversion urges expression in visible signs, gestures, and works of penance. (CCC, 1430)

Jesus addressed this matter directly in His teaching on prayer, almsgiving, and fasting: "Beware of practicing your piety before men in order to be seen by them; for then you will have no reward from your Father who is in heaven" (Mt 6:1). For those who sincerely want to grow closer to Jesus, who are striving by grace to "be perfect, as [our] heavenly Father is perfect" (Mt 5:48), this can pose a sticky conundrum.

When we attend Mass — the most vivid occasion when we "practice our piety before men" — what do we do when the practices of people around us differ from what we believe is right? What should we do when few of the people around us are genuflecting, kneeling, bowing, crossing themselves, or showing reverence to Our Lord in the Tabernacle?

On the other hand, what should we do when the people around us seem to be going overboard in their piety, in ways that seem far too showy, extravagant, or self-promoting?

In either situation, when expressing our piety in public requires being different from those around us, how can we be sure we're doing it for God's sake rather than as a statement to others?

Some, in the name of "freedom," dismiss liturgical rules and rubrics as a straightjacket to spiritual expression. They protest: "It really doesn't matter how you pray or what you do with your body; all that matters is uniting your heart with God. We should be free, and that means being spontaneous!"

But the Devil laughs at such a notion. In our striving to be "free," we find it nearly impossible to focus on God when the overpowering motive is to be different and separate from those around us. Too often in these circumstances, the underlying motive is not to please others or even God, but to feed the ego.

How do we avoid this problem? Herein lies the beautiful freedom of the liturgy. In her wisdom, the Church insists that liturgical rules and rubrics free us from the tyranny of trying to please others or ourselves. She teaches in the *General Instruction of the Roman Missal* (GIRM):

> The gestures and posture of the priest, the deacon, and the ministers, as well as those of the people, ought to contribute to making the entire celebration resplendent with beauty and noble simplicity, so that the true and full meaning of the different parts of the celebration is evident and the participation of all is fostered. Therefore, attention should be paid to what is determined by this General Instruction and the traditional practice of the Roman Rite and to what serves the common spiritual good of the People of God, rather than private inclination or arbitrary choice. (GIRM, 42)

Consider: When is a railroad train the most "free"? When it remains on the tracks, where it can roam full-steam ahead within trustworthy limits.

And when are we most free to worship God without the inner conflict of mixed motives? When, in willing obedience, we simply worship within the guidelines of our loving Mother, the Church. For then we can be confident that our "Father who sees in secret will reward" us (Mt 6:4).

CHAPTER 57

A Staircase to Conversion

Each year, Lent seems to sneak up on us, challenging us to reexamine the genuineness of our faith. Of course, this isn't the first time we've reexamined our convictions, realigned our life, and started afresh.

So what happened to all those previous restarts? And how can we once again make the effort to get our spiritual life back on track when so many times before it has seemed fruitless?

Maybe the problem is that we don't fully realize the extent to which the way up is also the way down.

For our Lenten journey of self-examination, there's no better map to follow than that given to us by our Savior as the central foundation for all His teachings: the Beatitudes (see Mt 5:1–12). Too often we may have passed over these as a merely random selection of well-meaning affirmations addressing specifically the poor, the meek, the hungry, the peacemakers, the persecuted, and so on.

Great teachers of the early Church, however, recognized that the Beatitudes are not randomly arranged, nor are they addressed only to particular groups of Christians. Instead, they lay out carefully the progressive steps by which every believer can grow in union with Christ.

In the late fourth century, St. Chromatius, Bishop of Aquileia (died c. 407), described the Beatitudes as a kind of spiritual ladder or staircase. In them, he insisted, "our Savior establishes extremely solid steps of precious stones by which saintly souls and faithful can climb, can rise to this supreme good, which is the kingdom of heaven."

This insight was confirmed by Pope St. Leo the Great in his sermon on the Beatitudes: "Concerning the content of Christ's teaching, His own sacred words bear witness; thus whoever longs to attain eternal blessedness can now recognize the steps that lead to that high happiness."

The first step of the ladder towards intimacy or union with Jesus is poverty of spirit (see Mt 5:3). This is the virtue of detachment upon which Jesus reflects so often in His Sermon on the Mount.

We must recognize that everything we have is a gift of God. We must never be so attached to anything or any person in this world that we can't freely give of ourselves completely to Jesus. Jesus begins here because without this detachment, we really cannot progress any closer to Him, for our false attachments fight for our attention.

We make this first step by grace, and as a result, we receive more grace to move on. In the next step, we "mourn" for our sinfulness, for the myriad ways we have let Him down (Mt 5:4). This mourning requires remorse for our sinful habits and appetites, and again requires much grace.

Even so, it allows us to move one step closer to God: We learn to accept "meekness" or humility — essentially, detachment from self (Mt 5:5).

Notice how this ladder towards union with Jesus, though it ultimately takes us upward, begins with what certainly looks to be three steps down: poverty, mourning, and meekness. But recall our quote from T.S. Eliot in an earlier chapter: "The way up and the way down are one and the same." Or as St. John the Baptist put it: "He must increase, but I must decrease" (Jn 3:30).

Nevertheless, if by grace we have progressed through these first three downward steps, the road begins turning upward. By grace we gain a hunger and thirst for righteousness (Mt 5:6) and, as a result, we begin to show the kind of mercy we have each received from Him (Mt 5:7).

Then, if we continue to grow in grace, our heart experiences a purity only He can give (Mt 5:8), which leads us to reach out boldly in peace to others (Mt 5:9), even into situations where the peace of God isn't wanted — again, as He did for us (Rom 5:8: "While we were yet sinners Christ died for us").

The final steps of this progression in grace lead to a kind of glory the world cannot understand. If He was rejected, then we will be, too — persecuted for being righteous and for seeking to do so in His name (Mt 5:11–12).

Does this seem like too tall an order? If so, remember that Jesus never commanded us to do anything we can't do — with His help.

If you initiate a spiritual reawakening in your life, I encourage you to start each day praying through the Beatitudes. Ask God to grant you the grace to understand how each one applies to your life. Then ask Him for the grace to take the necessary steps for change, in His direction.

CHAPTER 58

Are You Talking to Yourself?

Do you ever talk to yourself? Yes, I know. People who talk to themselves are usually accused of being loony, or as my sons like to say, "a few sandwiches short of a picnic." But what if talking to yourself can sometimes be a good thing?

When we read the Psalms, we find that King David used to speak to himself. So did other psalmists, sometimes with great energy. They seemed to think the habit was not just acceptable but necessary for their spiritual health.

Since the Christian tradition has always encouraged the recitation and praying of the psalms, I guess this means that we, too, are encouraged to speak to ourselves.

In Psalm 43:5, for example, David says: "Why are you cast down, O my soul, and why are you disquieted within me? Hope in God; for I shall again praise him, my savior and my God."

Who is it that David confronts here? His own soul! In doing so, he's showing us how to deal with a common problem:

the difficulties we face when our inner feelings conflict with our convictions.

I'm not so much talking about those times when our inner convictions are different from what we profess. I mean those times when we recognize, though others perhaps don't, that our inner spiritual life seems less than what we're expecting or want it to be.

At one level, we all experience this dilemma every day when the inner voices of temptation and discouragement battle for control of our hearts. On a deeper level, we may sometimes experience longstanding inner struggles with elements of the Church's theology or practice that we just don't understand or even accept yet, although we've told no one about it. It might even be a festering bitterness toward those in the Church who insist on living contrary to the teachings and values of our faith.

At an even deeper level, this struggle might reflect what spiritual writers have sometimes called the "dark night of the soul." When what we hope to experience in our inner being runs contrary to the convictions of our faith, and we're certain no one we know could understand, how do we deal with it?

David's words suggest that he experienced this kind of dilemma. He had known times of great joy and confidence (see Ps 18), even times when he brimmed with glad songs (see Ps 40). But now in his inner being, he felt "cast down" and "disquieted within."

Had his faith left him? Was he no longer a believer? Was he lost in doubt?

Apparently not, given the course of his life as Scripture records it. Yet neither did he try merely to brush off his discomfort. Instead, he continued to act in faith, regardless of how he felt.

David first commanded his soul "to hope in God," to turn its attention away from the distractions of trials and temptations, to turn in God's direction instead. Then David chose to "praise God," for this is the correct attitude for all of life.

Isn't this one reason why the Church requires her members to attend Mass at least once a week — not just when we feel like it? For we need not only the sacramental graces and the Scripture readings to help us live in obedience, but also the opportunity to gather together as Christ's Body to praise Him, however we may feel.

In some of her private correspondence, now published, Blessed Teresa of Calcutta confessed that she felt downcast in her soul throughout much of her adult life. But did she wait until she no longer felt this way to live out her calling, to show the love of Jesus to the poorest of the poor?

Not at all. Instead, she persevered heroically in the practice of her faith, the fulfillment of her vocation. And I suspect that she was able to do that at least in part because she talked to herself.

I can just imagine how, even when her soul was "disquieted" within her, as David's soul had been, Teresa found ways to tell it to hope in God. Then she praised Him, not just with her lips, but with her entire life.

So should we. Starting now.

CHAPTER 59

Are You Watching Your Step?

As I write, the heat of summer is upon us. It's vacation time for a majority of working and studying humanity in this part of the world. For many it's a season to kick back, relax, take it easy, and not take life too seriously.

At a time like this, I recall the words of St. Paul in Philippians 3:13–14. (Given how many times I've already cited this biblical passage, you must know by now that it's one of my favorites.) These words are encouraging, and we receive them enthusiastically — but only in part. The Apostle writes: "Forgetting what lies behind and straining forward to what lies ahead, I press on toward the goal for the prize of the upward call of God in Christ Jesus" (Phil 3:13–14).

We're glad to hear him say, "forgetting what lies behind," because we're glad the pressures of the spring semester or the post-winter dregs of work are behind us. But we're not quite ready yet to be "straining forward to what lies ahead."

We want to enjoy the sun by the beach, or the popcorn in the stands, or the lazy breeze wafting through the trees. But while we're relaxing and defragging our mental hard drives, does this mean we've been given permission to put our spiritual lives on hold? Of course not.

When St. Paul tells the Thessalonians to "pray constantly" (1 Thes 5:17), he doesn't include the disclaimer, "except when you're on vacation." The context of this statement makes that abundantly clear: "Rejoice always, pray constantly, give thanks in all circumstances; for this is the will of God in Christ Jesus for you" (1 Thes 5:16–18).

So does this mean that St. Paul is against our having fun or taking time out to recharge our batteries? Hardly, though the conditions in which he lived out his own calling left little time for relaxation — except possibly for the time he spent in chains.

Instead, the Apostle gives clear instructions in Ephesians on how to use our time, whether we're working, studying, exercising, or relaxing: "Look carefully then how you walk, not as unwise men but as wise" (Eph 5:15).

When you live on a farm as I do, with critters everywhere, you take this verse seriously! It's never wise just to go stomping through the pasture in your Sunday best, throwing your cares to the wind. You never know what you might step in!

Nor is it wise during vacation to let down your guard in the spiritual battle. When you break free from the normal stresses of life, you may become complacent enough to think you're safe from the usual temptations. But you must "look carefully" — be attentive — no matter where you are.

Why? St. Peter tells us why: "Be sober, be watchful. Your adversary the devil prowls around like a roaring lion, seeking someone to devour. Resist him, firm in your faith" (1 Pt 5:8–9).

St. Paul, continuing his letter to the Ephesians, provides an additional reason to be careful: We must be "making the most of the time, because the days are evil" (Eph 5:16). If his times were evil, ours certainly are no less so.

We're always surrounded by voices trying to convince us to fill our time with wasteful, useless distractions. Again, this doesn't mean we can't relax, read a book, watch a movie, take a walk, or spend an afternoon fishing. But in all these activities, we must still be "sober and vigilant," looking for ways to make the most of this time by reading good books or watching appropriate movies or praying while we're relaxing, walking, or fishing.

Finally, St. Paul warns the Ephesians: "Therefore do not be foolish, but understand what the will of the Lord is" (Eph 5:17). With hindsight, from experience, it's easy to see how foolish we can be when we aren't vigilant in watching how we walk. So he calls us to "understand what the will of the Lord is."

And what exactly is God's will for our lives? The Apostle has already told us in the words we quoted: "Rejoice always, pray constantly, give thanks in all circumstances; for this is the will of God in Christ Jesus for you" (1 Th 5:16–18).

When we approach all of life, even our times of relaxation, with these attitudes, then we're wisely watching carefully how we walk.

CHAPTER 60

The Sin of Projection?

Have you ever heard of the sin of *projection*? It's not included in the traditional list of vices, but it's imperative, for the sake of your spiritual life, to avoid it.

Surely I'm not the only one in the world who struggles with this nagging vice.

"Projection" is actually a psychological term that describes something most of us do at some time or another, usually unconsciously: We project onto other people our own prejudices, impulses, and thoughts. We see them doing something, and then we read into their actions our own motives.

Even though we can't read other people's minds, we still think we know why they're doing what they do, and sometimes we judge them accordingly.

In everyday life, for example, do you ever find yourself thinking cynical thoughts when you observe other people? Someone's wearing a nice, spiffy suit and driving a new car. Do you judge him as too materialistic? Do you conclude that he's vain?

If *you* were wearing those clothes and driving that car, you insist, *you* would be doing it because of vain materialism. And since you know this is wrong, *you* would never wear those clothes or drive that car. But look at him! He must be a vain materialist!

Or how about in the spiritual realm? You're worshipping at Mass, and someone prays the liturgy with great emotion, perhaps using what you consider to be overly demonstrative body gestures. Do you presume that she's doing it all for show? That she's just trying to look holy?

You insist that *you* would do these things only for bad motives. Knowing this is wrong, then, you resist using demonstrative gestures when you're in public worship. And when you see others doing that, you presume that their motives are impure.

The list of examples could go on, but you get the picture. Behind each one is the slippery sin of projection.

The truth is that we cannot truly know other people's motives unless they choose to reveal them to us. And even if they tell us their motives, we can never be certain we've heard the "whole truth and nothing but the truth."

In fact, none of us are completely aware even of our *own* motives. We try to justify our actions not only to others, but also to ourselves. The bottom line is that only God really knows the depths of our own hearts.

When we project, we judge other people's actions through the lens of our own motives. We presume to know what our own motives would be if we were doing what they're doing, so we presume that their motives are the same as ours. And because we can be wrong even in identifying our own motives, we can certainly be way off base in guessing the motives of others.

This is precisely why Jesus warned us never to pass judgment on anyone (see Mt 7:1–2). And St. Paul added to that warning his own: "You have no excuse ... when you judge another; for in passing judgment upon him you condemn yourself, because you, the judge, are doing the very same things" (Rom 2:1).

We can't see inside a person's heart. We can only see their actions or hear their words. In the end, what's important is not what *we think* others are doing and why, or what *others think* about what we're doing and why, but what *God knows* about what we're doing and why.

Jesus warned us:

> Beware of practicing your piety before men in order to be seen by them; for then you will have no reward from your Father who is in heaven. ... But when you pray, go into your room and shut the door and pray to your Father who is in secret; and your Father who sees in secret will reward you. (Mt 6:1, 6)

Obviously, our Lord didn't mean by this statement that the only true form of prayer is performed in complete solitude. Rather, He was saying that our attitude in prayer is to be singularly focused: without concern about what others are thinking about us, and without concern about why others are praying the way they are.

In one sense, it should be as if, even in the midst of a crowded church, we're alone speaking to our God. In fact, we form one great body of believers together talking with one united voice, yet to God alone.

The sin of projection distracts us from the one thing that's important: If there's anything we're to project onto people we meet, it's the awareness that they are made in the image of God. We must see in them His children — those for whom Christ died.

CHAPTER 61

Are You Singing?

Sacred Scripture is so rich that sometimes the seemingly simplest verse can carry the deepest meaning. Such is the case with Psalm 95:1.

Before we consider this short verse — which, by long tradition, all bishops, priests, and religious are to pray nearly every morning of their lives as they open the day with the Liturgy of the Hours — let me remind you: As Catholics, we believe that our life in Christ involves not one conversion experience, which then sets some guaranteed direction for our life. Rather, we recognize that Christians need a lifetime of conversions by grace in God's direction.

We don't merely turn once from sin and into God's direction for eternity. Instead, we must do so daily, sometimes hourly, and, for some of us, every minute. We must intentionally, by the aid of grace, turn away from the enticing voices of the world, the flesh, and the Devil, and toward Jesus our Lord.

This is essentially what Psalm 95:1 says in its simplicity. The psalmist wrote: "O come, let us sing to the Lord."

At first, these words may seem like so many other verses that apparently express something so obvious, we merely read them quickly and then move on. But there's much more here than first meets the eye.

St. Augustine once wrote, "He who sings, prays twice." Sad to say, most of us Catholics don't seem to have taken that insight to heart. We tend to sing without exuberance in Mass, and many of us refrain from singing altogether.

Nevertheless, singing in worship is critically important. When we sing aloud our praises to God, either individually or in community, we engage far more of ourselves — our mind, our heart, our vocal cords, our breathing, our entire selves — than when we merely pray vocally or mentally. In song we can be far more focused and intent. And when singing with others, we unite our minds and hearts together in worship and surrender to our God.

This is what the psalmist is beckoning his hearers to do. Given the intensity of focus that sincere singing in worship requires, I think this verse refers to far more than the mere act of singing. We can see it as an invitation to the conversion that is symbolized by our singing. Our songs of worship and praise are empty unless they come from hearts turned toward God.

How does this continual conversion take place? First, we must recognize to what extent we are "singing" in the wrong direction — that is, focusing on the world, on the delights and enticements of the flesh, and on the Devil. To what extent do we focus our minds and hearts in directions other than those God wants for us?

Second, once we're aware of such distractions, we must repent of the sometimes mindless, sometimes intentional, ways we "sing" away from God, in the wrong direction. We must make this change intentionally, aided by grace, especially the graces we are given in the Sacraments for our help.

Third, we must turn our song, our focus, in His direction, away from all those other distractions in life, bad or good. In some situations we must even turn our "song" away from those people in our lives we most love, for we must not let our "songs" to them distract us from the one Source of all that we have.

Finally, we must make a focused, fervent effort to "sing to the Lord!" For many of us, this will mean we must "sing to the Lord a new song" (Ps 96:1). We'll have to give up old habits for new ones, because for too long we've joined in chorus with the songs of a culture absorbed in self-focus.

Our prayer, then, should be this: "Lord, help us sing to you." But what songs should we sing? What should we say? How can we know that what we're "singing" is true and trustworthy?

To answer these questions, we should recall that Christ made us members of the greatest "choir" in the world, the Church. The Church helps us to discern which "songs" we should sing.

No wonder, then, that our Lord calls every one of the choir's directors (bishops, priests, deacons, and religious) to begin their day with the same beckoning call: "O come, let us sing to the Lord."

CHAPTER 62

The Dark Side

Several years ago many around the world were celebrating the thirtieth anniversary of a movie that probably most Americans, young or old, have seen at least once: *Star Wars*. The names of the main characters have become household words. I can attest to the movie's influence, because my three sons have spent many hours using whatever props were handy to fight mock light-saber battles among themselves or with imaginary imperial storm troopers.

Admittedly the writers utilized a complicated mixture of philosophical, pseudo-religious, and New Age ideas to create their imaginary otherworldly universe. So I'm reticent to join the ranks of those anxious to paint glowing parallels with Christian ideals. Nevertheless, I want to point out one overarching idea that emerged in the first episode and continued to set the theme for the entire series. A moral imperative, it rings true to the conscience of any lifelong Christian: *Don't give in to the dark side.* Which of us has not heard from childhood the clear warning to resist the temptations "of the dark side" — temptations from the world, the flesh, and the Devil?

I'll venture to propose that, for the most part, most of us through the merciful assistance of grace have successfully resisted the more obvious, external temptations of the dark side. To most of our friends, family, and coworkers, we look and sound like good, faithful followers of God.

Yet one particularly difficult battle with the dark side — the battle that was most clearly depicted in the *Star Wars* movies — never ceases. What inner conflict is that? It's the temptation that emerges when someone hurts us, betrays us, lets us down, cuts in ... Instead of forgiving the person immediately, we find ourselves tempted to justify being critical, angry, or bitter in response, or even to rehearse scenes of retaliation in our minds.

Given the frequency with which such scenarios develop, for most of us it's probably rare that a day goes by when we aren't bombarded from within by the tempting voices of the dark side to give in. Outwardly, we may show no signs of this internal struggle, but inwardly we may actually have surrendered to the dark side.

On the other hand, sometimes this internal battle does ooze outward, resulting in negative attitudes and behavior: smug aloofness, pouting silence, grouchy self-centeredness. Tragically, the problem usually shows its ugly head with the persons we love the most.

In Galatians 5:22–23, St. Paul itemized nine attitudes that should characterize our lives: "love, joy, peace, patience, kindness, goodness, faithfulness, gentleness, self-control." The dark side would tempt us to practice the opposites: hatred, discontent, anxiety, impatience, anger, meanness, dishonesty, rashness, and reckless abandon.

In certain circumstances and with certain people, it's hard to resist the dark side. But we can be encouraged to know that St. Paul calls these nine godly virtues "fruit of the Spirit." This means that they aren't habits we can just make happen on our own. Rather, as Jesus teaches in John 15:1–17, they are the fruit or result of our remaining (abiding, continuing) in Him.

When the internal onslaught of the "voices" tempts us to turn from our Lord and give in to the attitudes of the dark side, we're essentially being tempted to abandon Christ and follow our ancient foe. Resisting the enemy, then, we must instead rely on the power of the grace of Christ to help us abide in Him.

But how do we receive these graces to abide? Jesus clearly explains in John 6:56: "He who eats my flesh and drinks my blood abides in me, and I in him." Jesus gave us His Body and Blood in the Eucharist to strengthen us for the battle and to unite us with Him and with each other. We cannot successfully fight the dark side alone!

Yet how do we fight the battle in those times between the sacraments, when we're alone and standing face to face with temptation? Jesus promised that whatever we ask in His name, He will grant (see Jn 16:23–27). So when you feel the dark side coming close, turn to Him and pray the prayer of countless Christians since ancient times: "Lord Jesus Christ, Son of God, have mercy on me, a sinner!"

CHAPTER 63

The Devil Made Me Do It?

Temptation comes at us incessantly, from every avenue and angle, in every imaginable voice, friendly as well as sinister. So how do we know when we're being tempted? How do we respond?

St. Francis de Sales, in his classic *Introduction to the Devout Life*, began several detailed and helpful chapters on recognizing and handling temptation with this summary:

> When Satan, the world, and the flesh see a soul espoused to the Son of God, they send temptations to it. By these temptations, (1) sin is proposed to the soul; (2) it is either pleased or displeased by this proposal; (3) finally, either it gives consent or it refuses. These are the three steps in the descent into iniquity: temptation, delight, and consent.

In the first step, when "sin is proposed to the soul," why don't we always recognize the temptation for what it is? Sometimes it's because we have so often succumbed to lesser, seemingly insignificant sins that our ability to discern correctly has become muddled. Often, however, the problem may be that these temptations can sound so logical, so reasonable.

Think of Jesus' temptation in the wilderness (see Mt 4:1– 11). The Devil actually quoted Scripture in His efforts to tempt our Lord. And what Satan proposed *seemed* so reasonable.

After all, someone might ask, what was so wrong with Jesus' using His power to change stones into bread? Wouldn't you be famished after forty days and nights without food or drink? Or what was so wrong with Jesus' performing an awe-inspiring public act to prove to the people and leaders of Jerusalem who He was?

A day in our lives — maybe even an hour — doesn't go by when we aren't tempted to do seemingly innocent, pleasing, logical, yet devastating, damaging, even damnable things. So how do we know when it's the Devil trying to trick us?

Consider St. Francis's three steps. First, we must recognize that there is such a thing as temptation. For many reasons, far too many people today are caught unawares by the voices of temptation. Like Eve, they are deceived and choose evil, self-destructive behavior: "This is the real me trying to break free from the constraints of puritanical guilt!" And the Devil laughs.

Once we recognize the reality of temptation, we must discern whether the voice speaking to us on a particular occasion is good or bad. If we're being led to do a good thing, it may well be the voice of God; if it's evil, we must recognize its source and turn away.

The problem is that far too many people today, though they may recognize the reality of the Devil and evil, have been poorly formed. Their consciences have been swayed and diluted by the opinions and pressures of the world. They confuse the voices, calling good evil, and evil good (see Is 5:20), and once again the Devil laughs. To avoid this problem, we must be willing to have our conscience formed by the Church.

If by God's grace we're able to discern that we're indeed being tempted, then we must firmly choose to resist that temptation and do what is right. Here is actually where most of us fail. We correctly recognize temptation, but we're weak and give in.

St. Paul, who had the same problem, gives us the solution. After lamenting that he often does what he knows to be wrong, he exclaims: "Wretched man that I am! Who will deliver me from this body of death? Thanks be to God through Jesus Christ our Lord!" (Rom 7:24–25).

By His grace, Jesus not only helps us discern the voices, but also gives us the strength to say yes or no when appropriate. We need only turn to Him in prayer in the moment of temptation.

As St. Paul promises (1 Cor 10:13): "No temptation has overtaken you that is not common to man. God is faithful, and He will not let you be tempted beyond your strength, but with the temptation will also provide the way of escape, that you may be able to endure it."

CHAPTER 64

What's in a Name?

Did you ever see that television ad for the CD entitled *Country Classics*? You know, the one with all those good old story songs such as "Big Bad John," "Old Rivers," "Wolverton Mountain," "Harper Valley PTA," and "The Battle of New Orleans"?

Well, when our boys were young, they were given the CD for Christmas and listened to it at least four bazillion times. (I've not decided yet whether the giver was trying to widen our boys' musical appreciation or merely to drive my wife and me batty.) All three boys, especially the youngest, learned the words of every tune, and a day didn't go by when we didn't hear about a gator getting his behind "powdered" before he "lost his mind." (Don't ask — just order the CD.)

The boys got a particular charge, though, from that infamous song by Johnny Cash, "A Boy Named Sue." You know it, of course. A "no-good" father abandons his family and leaves his son only an empty booze bottle and the name "Sue." That certainly didn't win the boy any popularity contests or the title of "most likely to succeed"; in fact, he was always in fights with other boys who mocked his name.

As the song draws to a close, the reunited father and son have beaten each other to a pulp, and the father has explained the altruistic motives behind his cruel gift of the name. (He knew the scraps his son would get into over his name would make him tough.) You think the son, with grateful tears, is about to promise to do the same thing someday for his boy.

But what does he say? "And if I ever have a son, I'm going to name him … Bill, or Joe, or Sam, *anything* but Sue!"

My sons got a kick out of this and waxed melodramatic whenever they recited it.

Now, granted, this *Country Classics* CD probably doesn't rank very high as a resource for instilling good Catholic culture. In fact, the only song with any Catholic leanings on the CD is the pseudo-Mexican song about "Maria's Cantina."

However, it struck me that each of us, as an American with the name "Catholic," may feel at times like the boy named "Sue."

We could certainly live our faith, practice its disciplines, and obey its standards more easily if most people in our society had the name "Catholic" (and, of course, took the name seriously). If no one in our neighborhoods, our families, or at work believed that a woman has the "right" to an abortion or contraception, or that an individual has the authority to decide for himself what the Bible means and what truth is, or especially that the pope is the antichrist and the Church the whore of Babylon — if no one around us believed these things, life would be much easier.

But this isn't the world in which our good heavenly Father has called us to live.

Instead, we stand apart, and God has given each Catholic a name that, to many people's ears, is "fighting words." The only reason we aren't publicly and brutally ridiculed the way Catholics once were in this country is that, sadly, indifferentism has won the day. We are surrounded by people who believe that it really doesn't matter which church you belong to, as long as you love Jesus, or live a good life, or just keep your nose out of other people's business.

This situation came to mind when I began researching my family name and ancestry after I entered the Church. I've learned that our name was originally "Grondin" and of French-Canadian lineage, but also that my immediate family members were Catholics up until my great-grandfather left the Church. All the way back before that time, at least into the seventeenth century, the Grondins had been Catholics. But for the last three generations, as far as I know, none of my family members have been Catholics.

As I looked back at my Catholic ancestry, I discovered many situations in which my ancestors must have faced ridicule, maybe even violent persecution, for bearing the name "Catholic." I wonder whether the Americanization of our name to "Grodi," when my ancestors immigrated to Michigan in the 1830s, had anything to do with appearing less French and less Catholic?

I've yet to discover all the reasons my grandfather left the Church. But I wonder whether the situation was anything like the one in "A Boy Named Sue." Was he tired of fighting the battles that come from having the name "Catholic"? And did he decide that his children would have any name but that?

Shakespeare once said, "What's in a name? That which we call a rose, by any other name, would smell as sweet."

This may be true in some regards, but I believe that our name "Catholic," handed down to us by millions of faithful men and women, connected as a great chain of witnesses back to the Apostles and to Jesus himself, is a name worth bearing

— no matter how much ridicule it might bring in this world of ignorance, prejudice, and indifference. Please pray for those still on the journey who are in the midst of facing the many ramifications of accepting this name.

CHAPTER 65

That Nagging Dust

Jesus told the Apostles before He sent them out, "And if any one will not receive you or listen to your words, shake off the dust from your feet as you leave that house or town" (Mt 10:14).

How many times have ministers tried to motivate you to evangelize (as you ought) by reminding you how, whenever you receive a wonderful gift or make a fantastic discovery, you just naturally want to tell everyone? Of course, some of you, like me, may have been on the preaching side of this process.

Our congregations had received the greatest gift in the world: salvation in Jesus Christ! Yet they were surrounded by dozens of friends, family members, neighbors, and business associates who had not received this free gift. As their pastors, we just wanted to prod them into pushing beyond their fear of rejection or ridicule to do their duty: "Go therefore and make disciples of all nations" (Mt 28:18).

Even so, their fears are well-founded. Each of us has experienced the rejection that comes with taking a stand for Jesus.

Such rejection may be subtle, or it may be overt. It may be a harsh word or a cold shoulder. It may be the settling in of an endless silence. Whatever form it takes, it can lead to discouragement and an understandable unwillingness to fulfill our calling to be His witnesses.

So what did Jesus mean when He told us: "Shake off the dust from your feet as you leave that house or town"? Sounds kind of harsh, especially when coupled with what He said next: "Truly, I say to you, it shall be more tolerable on the day of judgment for the land of Sodom and Gomorrah than for that town" (Mt 10:15).

The key to understanding this statement, of course, is that His words must never be interpreted apart from the rest of His teachings. How did Jesus tell us to treat those who reject us, who treat us like enemies? "You have heard that it was said, 'You shall love your neighbor and hate your enemy.' But I say to you, 'Love your enemies and pray for those who persecute you, so that you may be sons of your Father who is in heaven'" (Mt 5:43–45).

Shaking the dust of rejection off our feet must not be understood as a sign of judgment. We must consider the ultimate judgment of our rejecters to be something between them and Jesus; it's not our affair. Instead, I believe, "shaking the dust off" means setting aside any lingering emotional effects of being rejected.

Did you ever sink knee-deep in a muddy, mucky mire of clay and cow manure? Just try walking around the downhill side of our barn! Even once you're rescued, you'll still find it nearly impossible to walk with your boots encased in the residual smelly muck.

We face a similar situation when we allow the dust of rejection to accumulate in our hearts. It discourages us from telling others about the joy of knowing Jesus. Worse yet, the accumulated bitterness of being rejected makes it increasingly difficult to love and pray for our rejecters.

Of course, this problem is equally true for the rejection we receive when we tell others about our openness or even conversion to the Catholic faith. The ridicule, the suspicion, even the outright expressions of hatred can make for dust-covered, mucky feet.

I recall the disastrous, discouraging experience of one clergy convert I know. Not long after he entered the Church, he came home to find his wife packing to remove herself and their children from his influence. Her extremely anti-Catholic parents had convinced her that because her husband was thinking about seeking the priesthood, he must be a pervert and untrustworthy.

How should this clergy convert respond to the "dust" of this rejection by his wife and her family? From the same chapter of Matthew, we find Jesus' difficult words:

> Do not think that I have come to bring peace on earth; I have not come to bring peace, but a sword. For I have come to set a man against his father, and a daughter against her mother, and a daughter-in-law against her mother-in-law; and a man's foes will be those of his own household. He who loves father or mother more than me is not worthy of me; and he who loves son or daughter more than me is not worthy of me; and he who does not take his cross and follow me is not worthy of me. (Mt 10:34–38)

Jesus never said that conversion would be easy, but He did say He would never leave us or forsake us.

Converts often face one other layer of dust, however, that they must shake off before it accumulates into bitterness: the rejection by lifelong Catholics — priests and bishops, religious and other laity, who do not understand, appreciate, or even agree with our enthusiasm for Jesus and His Church. Sadly,

I know of many former clergy who have had painfully negative experiences once they were hired by a parish or diocese to teach adult education, or direct evangelization, or lead a particular ministry. For these highly trained and experienced men and women, it becomes increasingly difficult to shake the dust of bitterness off their feet once they have given up everything to become Catholic only to discover that no one seems interested in their skills.

Following Jesus is truly a dusty job, but also a rewarding one. As He said about radical discipleship earlier in the same chapter of Matthew: "Every one who acknowledges me before men, I also will acknowledge before my Father who is in heaven" (Mt 10:32).

Please remember to keep in your prayers all those on the journey, as well as those who have already come home. For a day rarely passes for many of us when the dust doesn't try to accumulate.

CHAPTER 66

So What Happened Next?

"And the shepherds returned, glorifying and praising God
for all they had heard and seen, as it had been told them"
(Lk 2:20)

Imagine for a moment that you're a shepherd — not a modern shepherd with air-conditioned barns, automatic feeding troughs, and electric shears, but a first-century-B.C. shepherd living out in the hills, sleeping on the ground, owning only one well-worn homespun robe and sharing everything with your sheep, including the mites. Day after day, week after week, the same old same old, and nary a thought about career advancement, health care benefits, stock options, or retirement.

Then one cold winter night, when your only thoughts are the same as on every other cold winter night — stay warm, keep the herd safe, get some sleep — you and your fellow herdsmen are startled off your nice, comfortable rocks by a stranger standing in your midst, glowing with a bright, unearthly light. As the 1840 version of the Douay-Rheims Bible translation puts it, you fear "with a great fear" (Lk 2:9). A more forceful translation of the Greek text here might say that you are scared spitless.

The stranger then speaks, proclaiming that the long-awaited Savior has come, born just a stone's throw down the hill in Bethlehem. Before you and your friends even have a chance to wonder, the sky is brimful with a heavenly choir singing praise to God. Then they're gone, and the night returns to normal.

You and your friends stand for a moment in awe, then sit back hard on your rocks. Finally, your fellow shepherd, Yachem, states the obvious: "Let's go and see this thing!"

Leaving the sheep to fend for themselves, you all bolt down the hill in twenty-foot strides and, sure enough, you find Mary, Joseph, and your Savior. With utter excitement, you tell everyone there about the message of the angels, and the Scripture says, "All who heard marveled" (Lk 2:18 Douay).

Then remembering your unguarded sheep, you plod back up the hills, "glorifying and praising God for all that you had heard and seen" (Lk 2:20).

So what happened next?

What happened to the witness of the shepherds?

Why weren't Bethlehem and the surrounding villages overwhelmed by the news? Why didn't the message of the birth of Jesus spread out like molten gold until the entire region knew that the Messiah had come?

How is it possible that these shepherds, whose otherwise normal, repetitive, maybe even hopeless lives had been shattered by heavenly angels and the birth of a Savior, let the message die? Did they begin to second-guess what they had seen and heard? Once things returned to normal, did their pride prevent them from admitting to one another their beliefs?

Or maybe no one believed them when they got home. Maybe their wives and neighbors belittled them, accusing them of drunkenness — the accusation that the first hearers of the first Christian preaching leveled against the Apostles after the Resurrection (see Acts 2:13). And maybe they stopped talking about it rather than face further ridicule.

Is it possible, perhaps, that no one believed them because the poor witness of their lives before this event made their new witness of "glory to God" hard to believe?

All this is speculation, of course. More important is this question: What has happened to *your* witness?

Haven't you experienced the new life and grace, the forgiveness and love of the Savior Jesus Christ? Haven't you reaped infinite blessings through the sacraments and teachings of His Church? Haven't you discovered that through Jesus you are, in fact, a child of God, among the "joint heirs with Christ" (Rom 8:17)?

If so, are you still hesitant to tell those you love about this great discovery, this infinite Gift of God's love and grace?

CHAPTER 67

Pray Without Ceasing

St. Paul tells us to "pray without ceasing" (1 Th 5:17). Quite a tall order! We already have more than enough good and holy things to fill our time — and on top of this, we must pray without ceasing?

When I became Catholic, I discovered plenty of fine methods, manuals, sacramentals, and prayer books to make this possible. At times it has even seemed that we've been given *more* than enough! In fact, to be honest, the addition of the Liturgy of the Hours, rosaries, novenas, traditional brief prayer, and sometimes weekday Masses to my long-established daily devotional routine made me feel at times farther from God and drier spiritually.

The writings of St. John of the Cross and others suggest that for some this dryness could be a sign of a transition from a lesser degree to a deeper, more passive contemplative degree of spiritual unity. I hardly think, however, that this is my situation. (Just ask my wife, Marilyn.)

For me, part of the problem involved my making the spiritual transition from my long-standing Protestant devotional habits to more traditional Catholic ones. At first, through the encouragement of my new Catholics friends and their books, I believed that I had to follow Paul's advice and make a clean break from my past: "Forgetting what lies behind ... I press on" (Phil 3:13–14). But then, again through their insight, I discovered that in some ways I was misapplying this biblical text.

During the twenty years after my adult reconversion to Christianity, I had developed and practiced a disciplined, daily "ritual" of prayer that involved settling down, reading, and reflecting on Scripture, journaling my reflections, and then talking intimately with Jesus. After becoming a Catholic, I left this practice behind and replaced it primarily with the Liturgy of the Hours, the rosary, and other devotions.

However, I eventually discovered that what I had always done as a Protestant was more than just legitimate. It was actually an ancient Christian custom traditionally known as *lectio divina*, "divine reading." With joy I returned to this form of morning devotion using my own Bible as my devotional source.

Nevertheless, I must admit that traditional prayers such as the rosary still continued to leave me cold. Now mind you, I've known all along that the problem wasn't in the prayers. The problem was truly and completely in me and in my hardness of heart. So I kept plodding along, praying for a breakthrough, and especially for help from the bazillion distractions that rob me of focus.

After eighteen years of this plodding, I have gathered a few insights that have helped me greatly. I would like to share these, especially with those of you who, like me, experienced a harsh disconnect between our past Protestant spiritualities and our new, wondrous, and deep wealth of Catholic spiritualities.

The Liturgy of the Hours, also known as the Divine Office, was the most difficult form of prayer for me, though it was the one that made the most sense. When I was a Protestant minister, especially when I was a Congregationalist, it only made sense that there ought to be a well-honed, centuries-old manual for pastors to follow for morning devotions; I just had never heard of one. The discovery of the Divine Office was a godsend!

But then after years of trying, I was beginning to wonder whether the Vatican II renewal of this official prayer book of the Church hadn't worked. I thought, with all the problems in the priesthood and religious life, what was the one thing that linked them all? The Divine Office even more than the Mass! The problem, of course, was not in the Office, and particularly in my case, the problem was me.

Even so, holy friends, priests, and books have helped by giving me these hints:

Seek out whenever possible a quiet place to pray with limited distractions, and the same place every day.

Use a candle and icon or other religious image to help in worship.

Remember that in praying the Divine Office we are not praying alone, but rather as part of the one, holy, Catholic, and apostolic Church. The Office involves praying through the Psalms, and sometimes a particular Psalm doesn't seem to fit our life personally. When that's the case, we should think of ourselves praying as the Church. Every Psalm applies to the Church somewhere in the world.

Since Jesus specifically commands us to love and pray for our enemies, what do we do with all those Psalms that ask God to deliver vengeance upon our enemies? Spiritual writers encourage us to pray these Psalms while recognizing that our most common enemies are the temptations and struggles we experience with the world, the flesh, and the Devil. So when we pray these psalms against these enemies, we are praying, as Jesus taught us to pray, that God will "deliver us from evil" (Mt 6:13).

Read and meditate on the descriptive sentences and Scripture quotes that precede each Psalm. These have been carefully selected to help explain the meaning of each Psalm and especially their connection and fulfillment in the New Testament.

Don't hurry. Make time for silent reflection often, and especially add your own personal prayer between the supplications and the Our Father in the Morning and Evening Offices. It has helped me to remember the old "ACTS" acronym that's popular in some Christian circles: Adoration, Confession, Thanksgiving, and Supplication. Even though these aspects of prayer are all covered at some point in the Divine Office, it still helps to personalize these at this particular place in the Office.

Finally: Keep doing it! The daily routine digs the trustworthy furrows of prayer habits in our souls!

The Jesus Prayer is the mainstay of Eastern Rite Catholics, though it also has a rich heritage in the Western Rite as well. I am particularly drawn to this prayer because of its scriptural emphasis on the name of Jesus. Consider only a sample of the hundreds of references in Scripture to His name:

> Whatever you ask in my name, I will do it, that the Father may be glorified in the Son; if you ask anything in my name, I will do it. (Jn 14:13–14)

> In that day you will ask nothing of me. Truly, truly, I say to you, if you ask anything of the Father, he will give it to you in my name. Until now you have asked nothing in my name; ask, and you will receive, that your joy may be full. (Jn 16:23–24)

And his name, by faith in his name, has made this man strong whom you see and know. (Acts 3:16)

Always and for everything giving thanks in the name of our Lord Jesus Christ to God the Father. (Eph 5:20)

And whatever you do, in word or deed, do everything in the name of the Lord Jesus, giving thanks to God the Father through him. (Col 3:17)

Yet if one suffers as a Christian, let him not be ashamed, but under that name let him glorify God. (1 Pt 4:16)

I have found the Jesus Prayer especially powerful to help pray without ceasing while walking (or even milking our cow) because it sets a rhythm for both work and prayer. I guarantee that you too will find this prayer a lifesaver in transforming what is sometimes drudgery into a peaceful, rhythmic, contemplative stillness with the Lord.

Making use of these and other Catholic devotional traditions, let's "pray without ceasing" for the Church, her leaders, and of course for each other, our families, and especially for those still on the journey home.

CHAPTER 68

Turning Toward God Through the Rosary

With the encouragement of many great Catholic spiritual writers, I've come to understand prayer as a positioning of myself directly before God, no matter where I happen to be.

In the traditional sense, conversion means turning willfully into God's direction in response to the gift of faith and aided by the power of grace. Sin, on the other hand, involves turning away from God. Distractions, even good ones, can turn our attention away from God, and this is why Jesus encouraged us to lock ourselves away from distractions: "When you pray, go into your room and shut the door and pray to your Father who is in secret" (Matthew 6:6).

Growing in perfection and union with Christ involves turning fully and perfectly in his direction. Like so many others, I've discovered that the rosary is a wonderful means to help us turn into God's direction through the intercession of Mary.

The Apostles' Creed. The Fathers of the Church taught that "as we pray, so we believe." They observed that our prayers spring forth from our beliefs. Prayer is a fruit and a sign of our faith.

It's no accident, then, that the rosary begins with a statement of faith. By professing the Creed, we turn ourselves firmly in the direction of Jesus and the fullness of His Church, and we turn away from the myriad competing beliefs that would contradict our faith. We face Our Lord's direction mentally, so that our prayers can freely be said within this rule of faith.

Having entered in the correct "door" of the Creed, we are ready to pray next the Our Father.

The Our Father. Other than in Sunday worship, funerals, and weddings, I rarely "recited" the Lord's Prayer as a Protestant. I even have evangelical friends who insist we should never pray this prayer because they believe that Jesus never intended it as anything but a model. "Repeating it," they claim, "would be failing to heed His accompanying warning of mindless repetition!" (See Matthew 6:7–8.)

Of course, this isn't true. Millions of Christians throughout Church history, both Catholic and non-Catholic, would testify that this prayer need not be mindlessly repeated, but instead can serve as a profound conversation with God when recited in faith. Nevertheless, it's possible to get so lost in our distractions that once we've refocused on the words of our prayer, we may not be certain that we've said all the phrases, let alone prayed them.

Books on the Our Father by such authors as Dr. Scott Hahn, Fr. Thomas Dubay, and Fr. Reginald Garrigou-LaGrange help greatly, especially when we have time to meditate fully on the multiple meanings of each phrase. But more often than not, I pray the Our Father with the congregation gathered at Mass, at least twice daily in the Liturgy of the Hours, or when I'm saying the rosary while driving or walking. Especially when I'm driving or walking, it's hard to focus on the underlying meaning of each phrase, let alone keep my mind from wandering off into all the other stresses of my day.

The following approach, though, has helped me.

The great spiritual writers have generally divided the Our Father into seven "stanzas," and they have offered many good reasons for doing so. Nevertheless, encouraged by St. Paul's personal confession of surrender — "I have been crucified with Christ; it is no longer I who live, but Christ who lives in me" (Gal 2:20) — I have found it helpful to think of the Our Father as divided into five stanzas, each one helping me in a particular way to surrender myself to the Lord at that unique moment.

It seems to me that this intimate family prayer is first and foremost a prayer of conversion and recommitment. Jesus gave it to us in the midst of His Sermon on the Mount (see Mt chapters 5–7), and this context emphasizes surrender and detachment:

"Blessed are the poor in spirit... be perfect as your heavenly Father is perfect... do not lay up for yourselves treasures on earth... you cannot serve God and mammon... do not be anxious about your life...about tomorrow... seek ye first the kingdom of God."

With that in mind, here's one way you can approach this prayer.

To start, in your mind's eye see yourself standing directly before Jesus, with five mental "locations" that represent five aspects of your life:

First, in front of you is the One to whom you are committed, God Himself.

Second, the spot where you stand is the "now" of your spiritual journey.

Third, to your left lies the past you are to leave behind.

Fourth, to your right is the future you must trust to God.

Fifth, behind you lie all those things on which you must turn your back.

Next consider how, if you divide the Our Father into five stanzas as noted below, they will correspond to these five "locations" in prayer.

Stanza One: "Our Father who art in heaven, hallowed be Thy name. Thy kingdom come, Thy will be done, on earth as it is in heaven."

This stanza calls you to adoration of the God who stands before you, with complete surrender to His will.

Stanza Two: "Give us this day our daily bread."

This stanza reminds you that where you are standing now, in the present, you must detach yourself from everything unnecessary and ask only for what you truly need from God's hand.

Stanza Three: "Forgive us our trespasses as we forgive those who trespass against us."

This stanza directs your attention to the past (your "left") to forget and forgive what has happened, wiping the record clean.

Stanza Four: "Lead us not into temptation, but deliver us from evil."

This stanza turns your attention to the future (your "right"), calling you to relinquish into God's hands all anxiety about what is to come.

Stanza Five: "Amen."

This final stanza refers to all those things on which you must turn your back, because they take you away from Jesus. When you say, "Amen," you are accepting all that God places before you, and you are saying to those things behind you, "I am done with you."

Thinking about these acts of commitment helps me grow closer to Jesus every time I pray the Our Father. And because my mind is always being led at least a little astray by distracting and sinful thoughts between each recitation of an Our Father, I can never recommit myself too often.

The Hail Mary and the Glory Be. As a convert to the Catholic faith after forty years of an active Protestant faith walk, I struggled with my prayers to Mary and other saints, primarily because I had become centrally loyal to praying to Jesus. Other than in worship or public religious ceremonies, I rarely prayed to the Father or the Holy Spirit. My prayers were formally "to the Father through Jesus by the power of the Holy Spirit." But in private, it was always Jesus and me.

Praying to Mary and other saints seemed disloyal — at least that's what that nagging, accusatory inner voice kept saying. I learned, of course, that asking Mary and the saints for intercessory help is valid and extremely efficacious. But this didn't prevent me from becoming at times hopelessly distracted while repeating decades of the Hail Mary.

In time, however, I learned to pray the Hail Mary with a mental focus similar to the one I had developed in praying the Our Father. This approach helps me grow spiritually as I pray the Hail Mary, even when it's repeated over and over during the recitation of the rosary. I think of the Hail Mary as divided into three parts: one of veneration, one of petition, and one of adoration.

Part One is the veneration of Jesus' mother, who is also my mother by adoption: "Hail Mary, full of grace, the Lord is with thee; blessed art thou among women, and blessed is the fruit of thy womb, Jesus; Holy Mary, Mother of God ..."

Having positioned myself directly before God in the Lord's Prayer — with the past, present, and future surrendered into His care — in my mind's eye I first envision Mary standing affectionately beside Jesus, pointing to Him. The first part of the Hail Mary has three "stanzas," and as I'm praying them, I recognize that each one draws my attention to Jesus with a key word: *Lord* ("the Lord is with thee"); *Jesus* ("the fruit of thy womb, Jesus"); and *God* ("Mother of God").

Part Two is my humble petition for her intercession with her Son: "Pray for us sinners, now and at the hour of our death. Amen." Continuing a longstanding tradition, I strike my breast as a sign of my sinfulness and need for God's grace, which flows mightily through her.

Part Three is a traditional prayer of adoration, the Glory Be (also known as the *Gloria Patri*). This Trinitarian prayer ties our veneration and petition all together, leading us to re-confess in praise our love for God. Following an ancient tradition, I like to cross myself and bow slightly every time I address each person of the Trinity: Father, Son, and Holy Spirit.

I hope these hints from a prayer novice are at least a little helpful as you seek to turn fully and perfectly in God's direction.

CHAPTER 69

Lessons From Litanies

As a convert to the Catholic Church, I must admit that I've experienced some frustration in learning Catholic forms of prayer.

When I was an enthusiastic evangelical Protestant, I understood true prayer to be the free, spontaneous expression of heartfelt adoration, confession, thanksgiving, and supplication to God, whether "delivered" vocally or silently.

Admittedly, I often felt that it was a one-way street. But I knew I was in conversation with my loving and merciful Creator, and I patiently and silently listened for His still, small voice. For many Christians like me, to read or recite a formal prayer — that is, one with a given form, composed by someone else — was anathema.

Upon becoming Catholic, I was introduced to written or memorized formal prayers: the Our Father, the Hail Mary, the Glory Be, the Divine Office, the prayers of the Mass, and many more. Though all Catholic spiritual writers emphasized the importance in the spiritual journey of spontaneous prayer as well, I found myself slowly becoming awkward, self-conscious, even paralyzed when I prayed unless I followed some official form.

For fifteen years, on a daily basis, I struggled with this problem. I would pray the written prayers of the Church yet feel adrift — where once I had felt so free — whenever I tried to pray spontaneously to my loving Lord. And often, after I'd prayed the Liturgy of the Hours or the rosary, I'd wonder: Had I merely recited words? Or had I in fact done what I most truly needed to do, as a son to a Father: listen and learn and then follow His most intimate instructions?

I asked several spiritual confidants, "How should I pray?" One loving, insightful, humble friend answered, "Listen to the Church."

At first this advice didn't really help. I thought I was already doing precisely that. Then one day, by the grace of our Father's intimate love, I was able to "listen to the Church."

I was sitting at Mass, admittedly distracted by a crying baby, an uncomfortable pew, and a once-beautiful sanctuary that had been wrecked in the name of "renovation." I was repeating with those around me the Prayer of the Faithful.

The deacon was progressing through his list of requests, which we obediently punctuated with "Lord, hear our prayer," when I experienced a new and liberating insight: How do we pray every time we recite the Psalm in Mass or join in the prayers? How do we pray at the closing of every aspect of the Liturgy of the Hours? What is the model for prayer we learn from the Psalms themselves?

We pray in litanies — a form of prayer that brings great power and freedom.

I suspect that many of us view the litanies of the Church as just another written devotion for us to "offer up" as we kneel painfully through line after line of praise, earning us some

307

level of meritorious indulgence. But in truth, I think, litanies can train us to pray.

Generally, litanies consist of a series of petitions or praises followed by a repeated phrase or antiphon, such as "Hear us, O Lord" or "Have mercy on us, Lord Jesus." Usually the assembly repeats a brief antiphon while a priest or other leader reads more extensive lines.

For this reason, some may think that the repeated words are less important. But on the contrary, it's here that we discover a great aid to spontaneous prayer. The continuing, even ascending, focus of a litany is in the repeated line of praise, petition, or thanksgiving, being progressively informed by the content of the various interspersed petitions.

If you struggle with spontaneous prayer, consider this approach. Recollect yourself in a peaceful, quiet place. Choose a phrase of praise, petition, or thanksgiving, such as, "Praise to You, Father, Son, and Holy Spirit."

Repeat this phrase slowly, silently, several times, as you focus your attention. Then begin inserting between your repeated antiphon spontaneous words of adoration, confession, thanksgiving, and praise. As you pray, be sure to thank God for the graces He has already given that initiated your desire to grow closer to Him in prayer.

CHAPTER 70

A Convert's Carol

Most of us see the Christmas season as the most joyful season of the year. Some merchants have taken financial advantage of this perception, trying to convince us that the real source of such joy is buying, giving, and receiving. They have even turned a great saint into nothing more than a fat, jolly toy-producer!

Of course, we really can't point fingers. My three boys, my wife, and I have had our own fair share of joy-producing gifts on Christmas morning. And at least half of those gifts came from "Santa."

Nevertheless, I recall one Christmas when the joy just wasn't there for me. Not because we had missed the point of Christmas; we had made a number of efforts as a family to make sure we kept before us the true meaning of "Christ-Mass." But I couldn't shake a lingering sense of depression, an aching, empty feeling. It seemed to invade my soul like a creeping cloud of dread.

And then I had a dream, in some ways like the dream of Ebenezer Scrooge in Charles Dickens' *Christmas Carol.*

An Angel of Christmas Past woke me and put before my eyes Christmases of the past, and I remembered. I remembered the long and frenzied days of planning and preparing for the highly pressured Christmas Eve services during my years as a Protestant pastor — those services in which half of my congregation would make one of their twice-a-year appearances. The pressure was on to produce, inspire, and impress.

The sermon had to be the best. The music had to be truly inspirational. The candle-lit environs had to be life-changing. And then the long lines of cheek-aching smiles and the creative fumbling through long forgotten names.

This pattern was repeated for several services each Christmas. When it was all over and the lights had been darkened and the doors closed, I would return home with a sense of joy that God had been so gracious.

But then the Angel helped me to remember that on the next morning, after the presents had been opened, the breakfasts had been prepared with some new kitchen utensil, and I had begun driving the family on their annual Christmas pilgrimage to grandparents, a similar depression would enter my soul.

It was partially the result of being physically, emotionally, even spiritually drained. Preaching had always drained me — that's why God gave us Sunday afternoon NFL ("Now Feel Lazy"). But the Angel also helped me to admit that I had tried to be the people's "savior." I had tried so hard to make everything so right, so perfect, so that their lives would be changed.

I was working to make sure that when it was all done, they would return home different people, exclaiming, "Wasn't that the best Christmas Eve service ever? And that sermon!" But I would feel depressed because I would wonder whether through all the pageantry, preaching, and self-promotion, they had ever found Jesus.

Later, another Angel came. This Angel of Christmas Present let me stand back and reexamine the Christmas I had just completed: no longer shouldering all the responsibility, no longer pontificating from the pulpit, no longer greeting long lines of well-wishers, but sitting with my family in the pew, a member of the congregation. I looked at myself and saw my depression. It had affected my expression, infected my attitude, embittered my love; it had even shortened my fuse.

As I looked, I saw that I missed being the "savior." I missed the preparation, the planning, the frenzy, the aching cheeks. I missed the attention. And I wondered whether through all this, I had seen Jesus at all. I also wondered whether my self-centered depression had prevented my family from seeing Him.

Then, of course, a third Angel came: the Angel of Christmas Yet to Come. But what the Angel placed before me was not a gloomy graveyard scene with a looming tombstone carrying my epitaph, as in the Dickens tale. Nor was it a surrealistic future Christmas Eve service with my growing Catholic family overflowing a pew and cowering about me, a depressed, self-centered, angry old Scrooge.

Rather, the Angel merely took me for a quiet walk. And as we walked my attention was drawn to a distant pillar of salt, a reminder of someone whose yearnings for the past had blinded her to the blessings of the present (see Gn 19:26).

Finally, the Angel pointed to a distant mass of people, the ancient Israelites wandering in a desert wasteland, who had so thanklessly yearned for the past that their present was an aimless confusion (see Nm 14). Then I saw a plowman (see Lk 9:62). The tires and blades of his tractor were buried deep in the muddy middle of a partially plowed field, whose furrows were anything but straight; they were twisted and crossed.

While the air was pierced with the deafening noise of the repeating back-up alarm, I saw him sitting there, grasping the steering wheel with one white-knuckled hand, looking hopelessly behind him. And as I looked I saw his face. It was me!

Immediately I awoke and found myself sprawled headlong over my computer keyboard, with the cursor signal bleating in my ear. A joy filled my heart, lifting me ecstatically out of my cushy office chair, for I knew the state of my future Christmases was not coldly predestined! I could change!

I didn't have to be enslaved by my yearnings for past pulpits! I could be free to enjoy the present opportunities God had given me! With trusting submission I could enjoy Mass sitting contentedly beside my wife and children.

I could relinquish the unresolved, irrational resentment that I harbored against God and His Church for not letting me continue in pastoral ministry. I could let go of my past and with joy trust Him with my present and future. What a joy it is to find myself safe in the hands of a loving Father!

"God bless us, every one!"

CHAPTER 71

Three Steps Closer

One of the greatest reasons for being a Catholic — safely and actively ensconced in the bosom of the Church established by Jesus Christ in His apostles — is the reception of the graces of the sacraments. Jesus strongly warned His disciples that apart from Him we can do nothing (see Jn 15:6), and it is in and through the sacraments that we most intimately receive and remain in Him.

The reception of these sacramental graces — which is essentially the reception of His divine life and, therefore, akin to the indwelling of the Holy Spirit — empowers us to change. These graces make it possible, as St. Paul wrote in Ephesians, "to lead a life worthy of the calling to which you have been called, with all lowliness and meekness, with patience, forbearing one another in love, eager to maintain the unity of the Spirit in the bond of peace" (Eph 4:1-3).

All this is so that we can "put off [our] old nature which belongs to [our] former manner of life and is corrupt through deceitful lusts, and be renewed in the spirit of [our] minds, and put on the new nature, created after the likeness of God in true righteousness and holiness" (Eph 4:22–24).

My guess is that I may just be preaching to the choir. We all know these truths. In fact, I bet many of you have even preached on this subject, in either Protestant or Catholic settings. We know all this stuff. So why can't we do what St. Paul is talking about?

Am I the only one with this problem? I've been receiving Catholic sacramental graces for more than seventeen years now, yet I'm not yet leading "a life worthy of the calling," nor have I successfully eradicated myself of my "old nature" and "put on the new."

Actually, I know I'm not the only one with this problem, because Church history is riddled with sacramental Christians who have failed to live up to their calling. In fact, the worst scandals, schisms, and heresies in the Church's history were caused by those who had received the most sacraments!

Unless something is wrong with the sacraments (a notion I reject by faith), something must be wrong with me. What's wrong, of course, is sin. St. Paul clearly presented it when he described his own struggle in Romans 7. It's that constant battle with the world, the flesh, and the Devil that the Catholic tradition knows as concupiscence.

What can we do to utilize and not squander those graces we receive every time we encounter Jesus in the sacraments? Perhaps it ultimately comes down to three steps that I must take to get closer to Him. These steps are reflected in the writings of St. John of the Cross, St. Teresa of Avila, and other Catholic spiritual writers. We can sum them up as *outward*, then *inward*, then *outward* again.

Doing what St. Paul exhorted us to do begins with cleaning up our outside — how our actions and attitudes affect the lives of others. Our sinful actions don't just break one of the laws of

God or His Church; they affect the lives and hearts of others. So the first step is to eradicate from our lives lying, stealing, cheating, gossip, vengeance, and so on — all those external expressions of our less-than-perfect state, and the graces of the sacraments are there to help us.

My guess is that any of us who have lived Christian lives for any length of time have become quite successful at this first step. In fact, most of us look like pretty dang good Christians — some of us might even be mistaken for saints! But having cleaned up the externals, we could still be, to use Jesus' terminology, nothing more than "whitewashed tombs" (see Mt 23:27).

The next necessary step is harder and even more important: cleaning up the inside. God sees the inside in a way we can't. And He's just as interested in what's going on inside our minds and hearts as He is in our outward actions.

St. Paul quoted a psalm when he warned the Ephesians, "Be angry but do not sin; do not let the sun go down on your anger" (Eph 4:26). Now anger is something we can't always prevent. It rises up within us as an emotional response to all kinds of things that happen in our lives.

The essential question, of course, is this: What do we do with our anger? In managing our outsides, we might have progressed rather far in making sure that the rising feeling within doesn't express itself in words or actions towards others. But have we allowed this anger to fester, spoil, rot, and contaminate our very being from within?

We may have been successful in controlling ourselves so that we can finally say the sun sets each day without our lashing out in wrath. But has the mental rehearsing of "how could that person have been so shallow/mean/inconsiderate/selfish" poisoned us from within, for days into the future? Maybe the most important reason for the gift of the Sacrament of Reconciliation is to allow us to confess this internal pollution that ruins our lives from the inside out.

The final step, however, is probably the most difficult. We may have successfully cleaned up our external lives so that no one can find fault with us, and maybe by grace we have come to grips with our internal struggles, at least to the extent that no one (other than God) knows we are having them. But as a result, on the outside it's possible to come across to others as cold, heartless, detached, even self-focused.

We may not be acting out our internal turmoil, but we're also not acting in love. Love — which is the other name for the third step — involves actively expressing, through words, actions, and even body language (such as a smile) not necessarily what's going on inside, but how Christ wants us to seek the best for the other person.

Aided by grace, we clean up the outside, we work on the inside, and we show Christ on the outside — not just as a lifelong process of stages, though in many ways this is required — but every instant of every day.

And when we fail? Ask for St. Paul's intercession, for he knew well of this struggle! Many years after his conversion to Christ he wrote: "I do not understand my own actions. For I do not do what I want, but I do the very thing I hate. ... Wretched man that I am! Who will deliver me from this body of death? Thanks be to God through Jesus Christ our Lord" (Rom 7:15, 24, 25).

To the Philippians he wrote:

> Not that I have already obtained this or am already perfect;
> but I press on to make it my own, because Christ Jesus has
> made me his own. Brethren, I do not consider that I have
> made it my own; but one thing I do, forgetting what lies
> behind and straining forward to what lies ahead, I press on
> toward the goal for the prize of the upward call of God in

Christ Jesus. Let those of us who are mature be thus minded; and if in anything you are otherwise minded, God will
reveal that also to you. Only let us hold true to what we have
attained. Brethren, join in imitating me, and mark those
who so live as you have an example in us. (Phil 3:12-17)

We are not alone in the struggle for holiness. Thanks be to
God that the Church not only provides the graces of the sacraments to help us, but also has surrounded us with "a cloud
of witnesses," the saints (see Heb 12:1), to give us examples to
live by.

CHAPTER 72

"Choose This Day"

The Lord is not slow about His promise as some count slowness, but is forbearing toward you, not wishing that any should perish, but that all should reach repentance.

But the day of the Lord will come like a thief, and then the heavens will pass away with a loud noise, and the elements will be dissolved with fire, and the earth and the works that are upon it will be burned up.

Since all these things are thus to be dissolved, what sort of persons ought you to be in lives of holiness and godliness, waiting for and hastening the coming of the day of God, because of which the heavens will be kindled and dissolved, and the elements will melt with fire! But according to His promise we wait for new heavens and a new earth in which righteousness dwells.

Therefore, beloved, since you wait for these, be zealous to be found by Him without spot or blemish, and at peace. And count the forbearance of our Lord as salvation (2 Pt 3:9–15).

Some years ago my father, Daniel, made his final journey home. His departure was truly a source of joy as well as grief, because on his last day he told us clearly that he was ready to die and go home to Jesus. This blessed admission was a long-awaited confession; as is the case with so many, he had rarely talked openly about his spiritual life.

For nearly twenty years he struggled under the increasing debilitation of emphysema, the last two of which he spent enslaved to oxygen cylinders twenty-four hours a day, seven days a week. During those last years, his world consisted of his bedroom, the hallway, the bathroom, and the kitchen. Yet his world became greatly expanded and enriched by his email community of friends.

Five years before his death, he was told that he had six months to live, but by the miracle of modern technology and God's mercy, he just kept holding on. In fact, even on his last day we weren't sure how close he was to the end. His last words to me, which he uttered just before he fell into a sleep from which he never awoke, were these: "Marc, I love you, and I'll see you in the morning."

Two hours later I sat next to him, holding his hand, as he left this world for the next. I didn't realize until a week later, though, that his words were literally true, for he certainly was there with us all week long during our "mourning."

There is so much I could say — I still miss him dearly — but what I need to say is this: Never take anyone in your life for granted. Never put off saying you're sorry and asking for forgiveness, or saying how much you love them. And never be too busy for your wife and children.

What keeps me going is that I know my father is not dead, but very much alive. I have a firm hope that he belongs to the communion of saints, and it's very possible that he is closer to us now, healed and whole, than he has been for a long time.

Where we still see in a glass dimly, I trust that he can now see face-to-face. Where we still know only in part, I have hope that he now knows fully, as he has always been known by his loving Lord.

The words cited from St. Peter's epistle above remind us all that we must never take today for granted. Yesterday is gone, and in this world of shadows, tomorrow is but a fleeting possibility in God's mysterious plan. How many of us continue to procrastinate on decisions — especially spiritual decisions — that for the sake of our souls and the souls of our families should be taken care of immediately?

Let us never put off what we know in our hearts must be done, for as Joshua declared: "Choose this day whom you will serve" (Jos 25:15).

PART FOUR

The Coming Home Network International

Chapter 73

A History of the CHNetwork

The Coming Home Network International didn't appear overnight like a surprise winter snow. Nor did it emerge as a finished product from the bantering calculations of a carefully selected committee of highly trained spiritual guides. It began solely as a response to specific needs and cries for help.

We never intended for it to become an organization. It began simply as a fellowship of Protestant clergy who had two things in common: They loved Jesus Christ enough to go wherever He called them, and they had discovered that He was calling them home to the Catholic Church.

Here's the first description of the formation and work of the fledgling "Network," as presented in our first newsletter, June 1993. It begins with the text of a letter I had recently received:

> "I am a Protestant minister with a family of five. However, after many years of searching, study, prayer, and at times painful disagreement, my wife and I now know that I must resign from my pastorate so that our family can come home

to the Catholic Church. We are not scared. We have been completely broken down and now have nothing to do but trust Him. We are certain of His call to become Catholics. We just need support.

"This cry for support and encouragement from a Protestant pastor is one of many I have been receiving over the last few months. Ever since we let the word out that we were starting a fellowship for clergy converts and their families, the floodgates have been overflowing. We thought there might be just a few, but the Holy Spirit has overwhelmed us by the work He is doing in the hearts of our separated brethren.

"The idea for this type of fellowship came about as the result of my own struggles along the faith journey from ordained Protestant ministry to the Catholic Church. I felt as though I were making my way along a scarcely walked path, only to be pleasantly surprised to discover the great number of others also being called by God to make similar journeys. It is like driving a long distance to a meeting only to find upon arrival that dozens of others from your same town had also made the same journey, each driving alone, oblivious to the others. We could have car-pooled! We could have chartered a bus and fellowshipped along the way!

"The purpose of the Network is to help those who, though once called to ministry in the Protestant faith, are now on the road to the Catholic Church or have already become members and who want to continue serving Christ in ministry in the Church. This desire brings up many questions concerning vocation, protocol, finances, educational needs, opportunities, and more, in an ecclesial structure and system that is strange and foreign to many. We hope that the Network will serve as the charter bus, or at least the carpool, so that no one has to face these challenges alone."

Within a short time, numerous Protestant pastors and laymen on their journey toward the Catholic Church were contacting us through letters, faxes, e-mails, and phone calls, with new contacts every week. Some came from as far away as Canada, England, Australia, Israel, Africa, Guatemala, and the Philippines. Articles about the Network, especially two that appeared in the *New Oxford Review* and *Sursum Corda* magazines, were increasing our visibility.

Because of the great needs and concerns we encountered, in 1996 we established the Network as a non-profit organization with a Board of Advisors consisting of both clergy and laity. We gave the Network a new name that more clearly reflected its mission of helping non-Catholic clergy come home to the Church: The Coming Home Network International (or CHNetwork).

In June of that year, I resigned my position as executive director of Christian outreach at the Franciscan University of Steubenville to establish and run the CHNetwork fulltime. Interestingly, the day I resigned, I injured my back enough to need back surgery. So I spent the first month of fulltime employment leading the CHNetwork on my back.

In the beginning, all our CHNetwork contacts were done by mail or over the phone. But very quickly it became obvious how important e-mail and the Internet would become to our work. The same year we became a non-profit, we loaded up our first simple website, which now has grown to offer many informative pages, archives, links, a bookstore, and especially a very active forum.

We also chose a new logo to represent our work: a hand sketch of St. Peter's Basilica at the Vatican. What better way to symbolize coming home to the Catholic Church than with the Church building that best represents our Catholic home, the See of Peter?

We asked for the intercession of Mary and Joseph, along with the patron saints of our work: Sts. Barnabas, Francis de Sales, Edmund Campion, and Isaac Jogues. St. Barnabas, you may recall, sought after the man named Saul, a clergy convert, to bring him back into service after his ten years in Tarsus. St. Francis de Sales committed his life to bringing back those who had been enticed away from the Church by Calvinism. St. Edmund Campion, an Anglican convert priest, died a martyr proclaiming the Catholic faith in Elizabethan England. And St. Isaac Jogues died a martyr as he sought to bring the gospel to the Huron Indians of North America.

Because of the different needs and concerns brought about by the journey home, we came to establish three types of membership in the CHNetwork:

Primary Membership is for former ministers, missionaries, seminarians, academics, and others and their families who are somewhere along the journey into the Catholic Church. The needs of this group are particularly acute, involving for many the loss of job, family, friends, and vocation. As those whose transition often requires the most sacrifice, their testimonies are particularly encouraging to Catholics who have always had the faith, but may have taken it for granted.

Secondary Membership is for laity of other traditions and their families, who also are somewhere along the journey. Though this group generally does not suffer the same sacrifices as clergy converts, they too may suffer the loss of friends and family, as well as the stress and confusion that comes from adopting new traditions and practices.

Tertiary, or Associate Membership, is for Catholic laity, clergy, and religious who support the CHNetwork with their prayers and generous contributions. The success of the CHNetwork depends upon the encouragement and support of this group.

Drawn from these three groups are the *Helpers*, a network of volunteer Catholics who have indicated that they are willing to take an active part in standing beside inquirers either by phone, letter, or e-mail. As we are contacted, we forward these contacts on to volunteers who feel comfortable discussing and counseling inquirers with regard to the issues their questions raise.

A month after I began directing the CHNetwork fulltime, I was invited to appear on an EWTN program to discuss the conversion of Protestant clergy and the formation of the CHNetwork. Scott Hahn, Jeff Cavins, and Kenneth Howell appeared with me. During the taping of this program, the producer of Mother Angelica's program overheard our discussions and invited me to appear on it with her. (Mother Angelica is the founder of EWTN — more about her amazing story in a later chapter.) Dr. Howell and I did this in December of 1996.

Mother was so moved by the stories she heard of clergy on the journey that she invited me to come back. I thought she was inviting me to appear on another evening of *Mother Angelica Live*. But what she actually wanted was a new series, which became the weekly live program called *The Journey Home*. This program started in September 1997, and since that time, God has continually provided a steady flow of strong, intelligent, inspiring converts and reverts as guests.

During my years with EWTN, they invited me to host several radio programs as well: *Abiding in Christ, EWTN Radio Live*, and then CHNetwork's own program, *Deep in Scripture*, which we have been broadcasting since 2004.

Back in October 1997, as I was preparing a CHNewsletter article about the seasonal celebrations of Reformation Day, All Saints' Day, and All Souls' Day, it struck me that we were exactly twenty years away from the five-hundredth anniversary of the start of the Protestant Reformation. On October

31, 1517, Martin Luther posted his "Ninety-Five Theses" on the door of the church in Wittenberg, Germany, the spark that started the Protestant revolt. I realized that when this anniversary would occur, the Protestant world would probably celebrate with conferences, television programs, publications, and more.

We had twenty years to prepare for this event by helping Catholics understand their faith and history, and introducing non-Catholics to the Faith. So to accomplish this purpose, in 2002 we began to sponsor our annual "Deep in History" conferences, which we will continue to hold, God willing, until the five-hundredth anniversary in 2017. The name of the conference comes from Blessed John Henry Cardinal Newman, the famous nineteenth-century English convert, who once famously said: "To be deep in history is to cease to be a Protestant."

The conference motto is "Deep in Scripture, Deep in History, Deep in Christ," and its accompanying logo includes pictures of historic Church figures. The idea for them came to me on one of my trips to EWTN in the late nineties. As I travelled, I wanted an evangelistic discussion starter — a motto and logo — that could appear on coffee mugs, bookmarks, hats, T-shirts, and more.

When people saw only our CHNetwork name and logo, they would usually ask, "Excuse me, but what is the CHNetwork?" Once I explained that we help Protestant clergy become Catholic, the conversation usually ceased. But the conference logo and motto allow the discussion to focus on how becoming deeper in Scripture and history draws one deeper in Jesus Christ. Now this motto and logo (some aspects of the logo change each year to reflect the theme of that year's conference) has become a part of all our outreach efforts: conferences, retreats, regional gatherings, and media.

In the beginning we had never intended to publish our own books or to build and operate our own television and radio studio. However, as the CHNetwork grew, both of these expansions seemed to make sense. CHResources was established to produce evangelistic materials, aimed at reaching out to our separated brethren. They are intended specifically for our membership to give away to their friends and families to encourage them to come home to the Church.

As our involvement with EWTN increased, especially as we began broadcasting our *Deep in Scripture* radio programs live from our offices, it became obvious that God was calling us to expand our media capabilities. Now we are able to produce both the radio program and EWTN's *Journey Home* program in our own studio.

Over time we have also developed a fellowship especially for assisting the teenagers of Primary members, called *Quo Vadis*, and a support group for the spouses of Primary members. Our newest development is a confraternity specifically for clergy converts, established to encourage and enable clergy converts to continue using their gifts for ministry after they have "come home" to the Church. We have found that task to be an increasingly important part of our mission.

In all these ways, then, the CHNetwork labors to take part in the Church's task of evangelization and reconciliation.

CHAPTER 74

The Ongoing Mission of the CHNetwork

When we established the CHNetwork as a non-profit corporation, its official goal and purpose statement was quite specific:

GOAL: To assist the Catholic Church in fulfilling its mission of evangelization and its call for Christian unity, as most recently proclaimed by Pope John Paul II in his encyclical *Ut Unum Sint.*

PURPOSE: In cooperation with the Catholic bishops, to help inquiring clergy and laity of other traditions return home and then be at home in the Catholic Church, by providing:

    1. *Resources* that give clear expressions of Catholic Truth in ways that our separated brethren will hear and understand,

2. *Contacts, assistance, and fellowship* for those who are considering coming into full communion with the Catholic Church,

3. *Continued fellowship and encouragement* for those who have entered the Church,

4. *Vocational guidance, training, and assistance* for clergy and academic converts until they have been integrated into the Catholic community, and

5. *Opportunities* for these new Catholics to share with the Catholic Church ideas for renewal and evangelization which the Holy Spirit blessed in their previous experiences.

As we seek to fulfill this goal and purpose, we try to keep in mind Acts 6:2, which records a crossroads event in the history of the Church: "And the Twelve summoned the body of the disciples and said, 'It is not right that we should give up preaching the word of God to serve tables.'"

If taken out of the context of what the New Testament teaches about the actual and necessary virtues of an apostle, it might sound as if those arrogant apostles presumed that their unique calling of preaching the gospel was naturally superior to all other work done by lesser beings in the Church. Serving tables was beneath them!

Yet this was not at all the case. In fact, this event recorded in Acts has always been considered the birth of the office of deacon. The Apostles were recognizing, as St. Paul tells us, that "there are varieties of gifts, but the same Spirit ... varieties of service, but the same Lord ... varieties of working, but it is the same God who inspires them all in every one" (1 Cor 12:4–6). Later in the same chapter he presents a long list of roles and tasks that members perform in the one Body of the Church, a Body to which we all equally belong by baptism.

Granted, at certain times in history (sadly, far too many) members of the Church — clergy as well as laity — have lifted themselves up above others, as their unfettered egos were tempted by pride, power, prestige, and prosperity. It's even safe to say that if this kind of one-upmanship had not happened, most of the Church schisms throughout history might never have occurred, and the Catholic gospel would be far more pervasive in our world. Yet the Church has always emphasized that in the work of spreading the gospel, there's always more than enough work to go around, and everyone's calling is equally essential and important in the eyes of God.

This reality is also true in the work of a Catholic lay apostolate such as ours. Some of us may have more visible roles and tasks. But we're in this together, and it's critically important that every one of us does our part if we're to accomplish the goals God has given us.

What specifically are these goals with regard to the CHNetwork? Simply and yet very specifically, we are here to stand beside any of our separated brethren, clergy or laity, who are being drawn home to the Catholic Church. The primary thrust of our work is with clergy, because their conversions require drastic vocational and occupational sacrifices. But from the beginning God has called us to help laity as well.

We emphasize "stand beside" because we don't believe that God is calling the professional staff of the CHNetwork either to go out and directly evangelize non-Catholics or to "push, pull, or prod" them along their journeys home.

Maybe I ought to clarify this position, because it's very central to how we understand our work. Back in 1991 and '92, my wife, Marilyn, and I were Presbyterians on the journey home. I had already resigned from my pastorate, and many lifelong as well as convert Catholics helped us along this journey by praying, sharing literature and resources, and especially by making time to answer our questions. Most of these now-dear friends were patient and caring. They certainly wanted us to "cross the Tiber," but they were willing to let us follow the Spirit's leading and timetable.

One particular Catholic friend, however, departed from this model. His daily efforts to "push, pull, and prod" Marilyn and me into the Church, barely leaving me time to ponder all the new information he was forcing us to read, nearly turned us permanently away. I also know of two Presbyterian pastors who once were considering the Church but eventually turned away and now are closed to any discussion, primarily because this Catholic friend not only pushed too hard but also did not protect their anonymity.

I'm writing this not to castigate my friend, but to identify why we are so careful about how we carry out our work. In the years since the CHNetwork began, we have never intentionally or knowingly made a first contact with a non-Catholic. They must come to us.

When they do, we promise to protect all their information. We have never intentionally or knowingly revealed the name of someone on the journey. We give them whatever information and resources we have that might help them on their way, and we list their needs (while protecting their identities) in the newsletters for prayer. We give them the names of our Helpers if they want one, and we always try to be available whenever they have questions or needs. We're here to stand beside them.

We recognize that we aren't perfect and may not always have been here for those who needed us. But our intent has always been to stand alongside them. This role doesn't end after someone enters the Church. We want to continue to stand beside converts to help them continue using their gifts in the Church and, when necessary, help them navigate around the barriers sometimes erected. Our conversions never end with our entrance into the Church; we are always on the journey toward holiness and the Beatific Vision.

Yet this role is not the only or even the most important work of the CHNetwork. This is what the staff and I do, but others — our members, supporters, donors, prayer partners, volunteer helpers, as well as those still on the journey — have an even more important task to offer in our work. While we have a "constraint order" that limits our outreach, they do not. We depend on them, not only to tell their friends and family about the CHNetwork, but also to serve as the frontline witnesses for the Church. Our main purpose for establishing CHResources, our publishing outreach, is to provide carefully selected books, literature, tapes, DVDs, and other materials that they can distribute to those they know outside the Church.

If you have a friend — especially a clergyman — who you think might be open to the Catholic Church, don't ask us to contact him. First talk to him yourself about the Church, and then encourage him to call us. I'm not saying that our work as a staff is so uniquely important that "we can't serve tables." Quite the contrary. As the Scriptures teach, "How beautiful are the feet of those who preach good news" (Rom 10:15). We're just encouraging you to use those beautiful feet of yours to go next door and help your neighbor discover the fullness of the Faith!

CHAPTER 75

The CHNetwork and the Eternal Word Television Network

In many ways, the history of the CHNetwork is closely associated with the history of another network that's known all around the globe: the Eternal Word Television Network (EWTN). As we noted in an earlier chapter, our apostolate's first introduction to a wide international audience came through invitations to appear on EWTN broadcasts. Once Mother Angelica invited me to host a live weekly program, the CHNetwork was in a position to expand its outreach significantly.

Over the years, countless non-Catholic viewers who are taking a serious look at the Catholic Church have had the opportunity to hear, on *The Journey Home*, the compelling stories of converts to the Faith, many of them former Protestant clergy. Hundreds have followed up by contacting the CHNetwork and asking us for help to make their journey home. In addition, through the same TV program, millions of Catholics have been edified and encouraged to learn what God is doing to bring these converts into the Church. That audience has been multiplied considerably through our ETWN radio programs as well.

Having sketched the story of the CHNetwork's birth and development in an earlier chapter, it seems only fitting, then, to provide as well a brief history of the EWTN Global Catholic Network. That remarkable story begins with the life of the amazing woman who founded the network.

When Mother M. Angelica, a cloistered nun, fulfilled a promise to our Lord in the early 1960s by founding Our Lady of Angels Monastery in Irondale, Alabama, she had no idea she would one day found the largest religious media network in the world. Who could have imagined that a cloistered nun would found a global television network? Who could have predicted that a network funded entirely by donations from people in the pews instead of advertising would become the largest religious media network in the world? Yet that's the story behind EWTN.

The future Mother Angelica was born on April 20, 1923, in southeast Canton, Ohio, to Mae Gianfrancesco Rizzo and John Rizzo. The couple named their daughter Rita Antoinette Rizzo. She would come to face considerable challenges in her early years.

Rita's parents were not devout. In fact, when Rita was only seven, her mother divorced her abusive father. It was a time when broken families were stigmatized, so we can only imagine what Rita had to endure.

To make matters worse, Rita was so poor and her mother so mentally fragile that the child eventually had to run her mother's dry cleaning business while trying to keep up with her studies in school. As a result, she learned to be distrustful of outsiders, she never made friends, and she never dated.

Nevertheless, Rita experienced two miracles in her pre-convent days that changed her life. The first occurred in 1934. One day the eleven-year-old went running for a bus — and missed seeing an oncoming car. When she finally saw the car, she froze.

As she recalls, however, "two hands" picked her up and placed her on the median. The bus driver would later say he had never seen anyone jump so high.

Her second miracle occurred in 1942. For years, the teenager had suffered from a stomach ailment that made her hands shake, her left arm go numb, and her stomach spasm. She had difficulty eating and sleeping.

One day Rita visited the Catholic mystic Rhoda Wise, and afterward she experienced a miraculous healing. This healing made Rita realize that God loved her personally — and she began to love Him back. Her love became such that on August 15, 1944, she entered a Cleveland convent and became Sister Mary Angelica of the Annunciation, a Franciscan nun of the Most Blessed Sacrament. The order would later change its name to the Poor Clares of Perpetual Adoration.

Sister's brash personality and poor health — she was troubled with pneumonia, tonsillitis, and water on the knees — made it unlikely, many thought, that she would remain a nun. But an overnight healing of her knees convinced the women of the order that the young woman did indeed have a vocation. Sister Angelica made her final vows on January 2, 1953.

Making vows didn't cure Sister of all ailments. She fell and injured her back while washing the floor. Nothing, including a body cast, a back brace, and leg and neck traction, was able to heal the injury.

But just before undergoing a risky operation on her back, Sister made God a life-changing promise. She told Him she would start a monastery in the Southern U.S. (which was still largely mission territory for the Catholic Church) if He would allow her to walk again. The surgery was a medical failure. But Sister found, nevertheless, that she could indeed walk.

To make good on her promise, Sister wrote a letter to Archbishop Thomas J. Toolen of the Diocese of Mobile-Birmingham, Alabama, in January, 1975. She asked him to allow her to build a cloistered community in his diocese. Archbishop Toolen said yes, and the seeds of a new apostolate were planted.

Of course, Our Lady of the Angels Monastery in Irondale, Alabama, from which EWTN would eventually spring, had its share of start-up problems. Despite Archbishop Toolen's yes, Sister Angelica had to obtain approval from her bishop in Ohio, as well as waivers from Rome: According to the Church's norms, at thirty-seven she was too young to become abbess of a new monastery.

It was five long years before Rome granted Mother Angelica permission to establish an Alabama foundation. She obtained the waiver and the title "Mother." As she and a handful of nuns drove south to Birmingham in February, 1961, they stopped in a roadside motel for the night. There, Mother saw a television set for the first time.

Once in Birmingham, a former mayor showed Mother the site on which EWTN would be built: fifteen beautiful acres of mountainside in the city of Irondale. Archbishop Toolen broke ground for the monastery on July 24, 1961. Neither he nor the nuns expected any trouble. But trouble there was.

In those days, only two percent of the local population was Catholic, and not everyone was happy about the new monastery. The nuns were shot at. The monastery site was vandalized every Saturday. The project was plagued with costly overruns. But the publicity brought the monastery and its nuns to the attention of the general population, who eventually embraced it.

The new monastery was dedicated on May 20, 1962, and Mother immediately began giving speeches in its parlor. She even did a television interview in September, 1967, to explain how the Second Vatican Council was changing things in the monastery. Meanwhile, the sisters sold fishing lures and roasted peanuts to support themselves, all the while imploring God to send them work that would reveal more clearly their part in the mission of the Church.

In 1969, Rome gave Mother permission to continue her parlor talks as a missionary activity. The talks were taped and sold. By 1971, Bishop Joseph Vath, the first bishop of the newly formed Diocese of Birmingham, was encouraging Mother to accept invitations to speak to Catholic groups outside the cloister.

In the ensuing decade, Mother would record a radio program and publish small books on the Faith. These books would eventually be printed on her own printing press and, along with her tapes, distributed throughout the country by a group of dedicated lay people.

Even so, it wasn't until Mother visited a Baptist-run broadcast operation atop a Chicago skyscraper in March, 1978, that she turned her attention to a new medium: television. It was then that she famously declared: "Lord, I gotta have one of these."

Never one to do things by halves, Mother's first foray into television was a sixty-part series for the Christian Broadcast Network, filmed from May to August 1978. Then, while she was filming her second series in November, 1978, Mother discovered that the local station where she was filming planned to air a blasphemous movie. She threatened to pull out.

The station manager told her that her television work would end without his facilities. Mother told him she'd build her own studio. The station manager said she couldn't do it. Mother said: "You just watch me!"

Armed with only two hundred dollars and twelve cloistered nuns with no television experience, Mother proceeded to turn the monastery garage into a television studio. EWTN received its FCC license on January 27, 1981, making it the first Catholic satellite television station in the United States. A few months later, on August 15, 1981, EWTN began broadcasting four hours a day to sixty thousand homes.

The network was funded (and continues to be funded) solely by viewer contributions. EWTN accepts no advertising. So Mother had to go millions of dollars into debt to build the network.

Few would have been willing to risk so much. But Mother says that when you want to do something for the Lord, then just do it.

"Whatever you feel needs to be done," she counsels, "even though you're shaking in your boots, you're scared to death — take the first step forward. The grace comes with that one step, and you get the grace as you step. Being afraid is not a problem; it's doing nothing when you're afraid."

Mother was no stranger to fear. But she kept moving and, through the grace of God, the network grew, and the debt was paid.

Meanwhile, EWTN has continued to grow: from the original four hours of broadcasting a day to twenty-four hours a day; from pre-taped programs only to live programs in the U.S. and around the world; from one feed in English to eight feeds in English, Spanish, German and French; from television to radio, shortwave, and the Internet; from sixty thousand homes to more than 150 million homes.

And all because one cloistered nun said yes to Jesus.

CHAPTER 76

Final Thoughts on the Journey

In one sense, the CHNetwork exists to help undo the deleterious effects of the Church's schisms throughout her history. I realize that this statement may seem a bit audacious and even presumptuous. But having spent the first forty years of my life fanning the flames of separation from the Church, I would like to spend the latter forty, God willing, bringing healing.

The Catholic Church in every age has surely been in need of renewal. But the methods of renewal initiated by those who condemned and abandoned her and her authority, starting new churches and denominations of their own creation, have caused great and continuing disunity and confusion. Millions of men, women, and children have been led out of the Church, away from the sacramental graces and the guidance of magisterial authority.

The Devil thought he was destroying the Church by leading millions away. But "we know that in everything God works for good with those who love him, who are called according to his purpose" (Rom 8:28). Many of those who left the Church

continued to follow Christ with sincere hearts. They built ecclesial structures and established standards of faith designed
to lead their followers toward holiness and salvation.

Here's how the *Catechism of the Catholic Church* (817–820)
describes the situation, quoting the Second Vatican "Decree
on Ecumenism" (*Unitatis redintegratio*) and the "Dogmatic
Constitution on the Church" (*Lumen gentium*):

> The ruptures that wound the unity of Christ's Body — here
> we must distinguish heresy, apostasy, and schism — do not
> occur without human sin. ... "However, one cannot charge
> with the sin of the separation those who at present are born
> into these communities [that resulted from such separa-
> tion] and in them are brought up in the faith of Christ,
> and the Catholic Church accepts them with respect and
> affection as brothers. ... All who have been justified by faith
> in Baptism are incorporated into Christ; they therefore
> have a right to be called Christians, and with good reason
> are accepted as brothers in the Lord by the children of the
> Catholic Church" (*Unitatis redintegratio*, 3 § 1).

> "Furthermore, many elements of sanctification and of
> truth" (*Lumen gentium* 8 § 2) are found outside the visible
> confines of the Catholic Church: "the written Word of God;
> the life of grace; faith, hope, and charity, with the other
> interior gifts of the Holy Spirit, as well as visible elements"
> (*Unitatis redintegratio* 3 § 2; cf. *Lumen gentium* 15). Christ's
> Spirit uses these Churches and ecclesial communities as
> means of salvation, whose power derives from the fullness
> of grace and truth that Christ has entrusted to the Catholic
> Church. All these blessings come from Christ and lead to
> him (cf. *Unitatis redintegratio* 3), and are in themselves calls
> to "Catholic unity."

> "Christ bestowed unity on his Church from the beginning.
> This unity, we believe, subsists in the Catholic Church as
> something she can never lose, and we hope that it will con-

tinue to increase until the end of time" (*Unitatis redintegratio* 4 § 3). Christ always gives his Church the gift of unity, but the Church must always pray and work to maintain, reinforce, and perfect the unity that Christ wills for her. This is why Jesus himself prayed at the hour of his Passion, and does not cease praying to his Father, for the unity of his disciples: "That they may all be one. As you, Father, are in me and I am in you, may they also be one in us, … so that the world may know that you have sent me" (Jn 17:21; cf. Heb 7:25). The desire to recover the unity of all Christians is a gift of Christ and a call of the Holy Spirit (cf. *Unitatis redintegratio* 1).

We in the CHNetwork see these words as our charge. We recognize that the work of unity is primarily a work of Jesus Christ, for as He said, "apart from me, you can do nothing" (Jn 15:5). The CHNetwork desires only to be a channel of His grace, responding to those the Holy Spirit is calling to listen to the Catholic Church and come home to the "one, holy, Catholic, and apostolic Church."

For many, conversion requires great sacrifice, even repentance for active promotion of schism and heresy. Ultimately, though, this decision requires of all who come the willingness to accept the same requirements Christ gave to the rich young man: "Go, sell what you have, and give to the poor, and you will have treasure in heaven; and come, follow me" (Mk 10:21).

Though the transition from separation into full communion can take literally only moments, the full transition mentally and emotionally can take years and may involve many "dark nights of the soul." So we strongly encourage members to gather in local groups for prayer and fellowship, for small group studies of Scripture and Church tradition, and for reaching out with the truth of the Catholic faith to friends and relatives outside the Church.

We believe this work of ours, undertaken together, is a grand and blessed work. We serve in the light of these words from Pope John Paul II in his encyclical *Ut Unum Sint* (literally, "That They Might Be One"; see Jn 17:11):

> The unity of all divided humanity is the will of God. For this reason he sent his Son, so that by dying and rising for us he might bestow on us the Spirit of love. On the eve of his sacrifice on the Cross, Jesus himself prayed to the Father for his disciples and for all those who believe in him, that they *might be one*, a living communion. This is the basis not only of the duty, but also of the responsibility before God and his plan, which falls to those who through Baptism become members of the Body of Christ, a Body in which the fullness of reconciliation and communion must be made present. How is it possible to remain divided, if we have been "buried" through Baptism in the Lord's death, in the very act by which God, through the death of his Son, has broken down the walls of division? Division "openly contradicts the will of Christ, provides a stumbling block to the world, and inflicts damage on the most holy cause of proclaiming the Good News to every creature" (*Unitatis redintegratio* 1).

> "The Lord of the Ages wisely and patiently follows out the plan of his grace on behalf of us sinners. In recent times he has begun to bestow more generously upon divided Christians remorse over their divisions and a longing for unity. Everywhere, large numbers have felt the impulse of this grace, and among our separated brethren also *there increases from day to day a movement* fostered by the grace of the Holy Spirit *for the restoration of unity among all Christians*" (*Unitatis redintegratio* 1). ... This unity bestowed by the Holy Spirit does not merely consist in the gathering of people as a collection of individuals. It is a unity constituted by the bonds of the profession of faith, the sacraments and hierarchical communion (see *Lumen gentium* 14). ...

> For the Catholic Church, then, the *communion* of Christians is none other than the manifestation in them of the grace by which God makes them sharers in his own *communion*, which is his eternal life. ... To believe in Christ means to desire unity; to desire unity means to desire the Church; to desire the Church means to desire the communion of grace which corresponds to the Father's plan from all eternity. Such is the meaning of Christ's prayer: "*Ut Unum Sint.*"(6–9, emphasis in the original)

To this end, under the maternal intercession of Mary, Mother of the Redeemer, and the paternal care of St. Joseph, we in the Coming Home Network International dedicate our lives.

CHResources has more to offer.

Check out these titles in your local Catholic bookstore,
visit us online at **www.chresources.com**, or call **1.800.664.1150**

**How Firm a
Foundation**
by Marcus Grodi
(fiction)

Journeys Home
*edited by Marcus
Grodi* (conversion)

**Christ in His
Fullness**
by Bruce Sullivan
(apologetics)

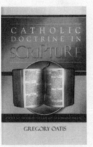

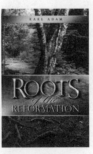

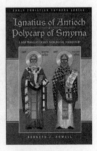

**My Journey to
the Land of
More** *by Leona
Choy* (conversion)

**Catholic Doctrine
in Scripture**
by Gregory Oatis
(apologetics)

**Roots of the
Reformation**
by Karl Adams
(historical)

**St. Ignatius &
St. Polycarp**
*by Dr. Kenneth
Howell* (historical)

INTRODUCING

"With great joy we publish this truly inspiring account of Leona Choy's journey to the Church. She covers all the bases, presenting in a concise yet fully readable apologetic format all the major issues that discourage Jesus-loving, Bible-believing Christians from considering the Catholic Church. Please, read this book prayerfully. If you love Jesus Christ and are willing to follow Him anywhere, you may find yourself on a journey you never dreamed of."

— *Marcus C. Grodi*

My JOURNEY to the LAND of MORE
Evangelical to Catholic

LEONA CHOY

My JOURNEY to the LAND of MORE   LEONA CHOY

Published by *CHResources* — Order by calling 1-800-664-5110 — www.chresources.com

NOTES

NOTES

NOTES

NOTES

NOTES

NOTES

NOTES

NOTES

NOTES

NOTES